TRAVELLING IN A BOX

Mike Wood

Thanks to Sarah, Kevin and Amanda for agreeing to have their ups, downs and everything else in between, held up to public scrutiny.

Thanks to Janie at Lector's Books for her meticulous care and sterling patience in guiding me through the editorial process.

Thanks to Madeleine K at 99Designs.com for a truly awesome cover design.

Thank you to Sprite caravans for building a box on wheels that, after thirty-five years of loyal service to several owners, managed the two-thousand-mile journey across Europe and back without so much as a squeak.

Thank you, also, to Jeremy Clarkson for being the archetypal caravan hater. Also, I should apologise for being mean, because it is wrong to mock the unemployed.

To Sarah

Good times

Prologue: The Year 2000

"What's that? Up ahead, in the road?" I said.

"Hmm?" Sarah looked up from her book.

"Looks like..."

"Is it a ladder?"

"Couldn't be. Not in the middle of the motorway. It's..."

...a ladder. An aluminium triple-extension ladder. Even more incredible, it was balanced on its side. Thinking distance was over. We were there. Sixty mph and a ton of caravan in tow. I flicked right. I clipped the ladder. Plink! A gentle kiss. Not enough to even shave any Turtle-Wax off the nearside front wing. The caravan missed it altogether.

The kids, Kevin and Amanda, loved it.

"Oh, cool. Did you see that?"

I saw them twisting and jostling for position to get some kind of view in the extension mirrors, since the white bulk of the caravan hid most of the rearward action.

"Look at them slide," said Kevin.

"He's going to hit... ooh!" said Amanda.

But their teenaged hunger for mayhem would not be satisfied this day. There was plenty of stunt-driving and blue tyre smoke, but nothing exciting as far as they could see. No barrel rolls, flapping doors or flying, bouncing wheels. I didn't look. I stared straight ahead with boggling eyes and a white-fisted death grip on the steering wheel.

Twelve miles. We'd driven just twelve miles from our home. We live on the Wirral, a sleepy peninsula tucked up in the northwest of England. The Wirral is a long way from Dover, let alone our ultimate destination. We had a thousand miles ahead of us. Was this just a taster?

It had been a close one, but we had survived. The Force had been with us.

The Force stayed with us for another twenty miles or so, then, on the M6 just north of Stoke-on-Trent, The Force packed his bags, gave an apologetic little shoulder-shrug and went off to rejoin Luke and Obi-Wan in a galaxy far, far away, leaving us to face the The Dark Side alone.

The Dark Side. The Unholy Trinity. M6, M1... and M25.

"We have a decision to make," I said, raising my voice to include Kevin and Amanda in the democratic process. "We can go cross-country on the A50, or we can stay put on the M6. Option one is farther, but guaranteed traffic-free. Staying with the M6 is shorter, but there are always traffic problems through Birmingham; might take longer. What do you think?"

We discussed and we dithered for half a mile.

"Come on, decision. Junction's coming up."

"Don't know. You choose."

I chose the "guaranteed-congestion-free" option. I made the turn.

We coasted into the traffic jam four hundred yards later. I shifted down through the gears.

Half an hour on, and our Mondeo hadn't moved more than a yard. Our car was blue –deep blue; a colour that does not reflect any heat but instead, calls out to the sun with an offer of hospitality. Inside the car I could smell the engine – that rusty, warm-water smell that forewarns of imminent distress amongst the mechanicals.

"This is ridiculous!" I shouted. "What does a person have to do to make a simple journey in this country?" I slapped down on the steering wheel. I roared and waved impotent fists of lard.

"Dad, you're giving me a headache. You're always moaning." Amanda's voice was raised above mine. She's a teenager, so I must accept some rebellion.

"If I'm always moaning it's because I have something to moan about," I said.

"So, instead of moaning, do something about it."

"It's not moaning. I'm expressing a grievance."

"Who to? Nothing any of us can do. Write to someone. Ring your MP. Go into politics. Just don't moan. You're doing my head in."

"She's right, you know," Sarah said, in the calm, irritating voice of reason. They were all ganging up on me now. Kevin was the only one not saying anything. He was doing the other teenaged thing and hiding between headphones, slumped so low in his seat I could only see the top of his bobbing head in the mirror.

"So, what do you think?" I said. "Amanda, you think I should go into politics? Do you think I'd be good as a politician?"

"No, you'd be useless. I think you should just shut up moaning."

I fumed in silence for a few minutes.

"Amanda is right," I announced after a while. "I will do something about it."

They all looked at me with round, scared eyes.

"I will write down all my complaints. A compilation. I'll publish them. The Chronicles of—"

"Chronicles is the wrong word," said Sarah. "They're moans. Call them your Moanicles."

"Okay, I like that. The Moanicles of Michael."

Sarah nodded and went back to her book. She is able to do this: to ignore the fact of society crumbling around us, of everything and everyone going to the dogs. Sarah has a natural calm that stems from a passion for yoga. She has been interested in yoga for some years, still is, and her hour-a-day devotions have left her lean, agile and mentally attuned to the cosmos. She is unmoved to fight against nature or against the natural ageing process. She allows the occasional appearance of grey to gradually highlight her brown hair. She acknowledged this, then, as she does now, with dignity and passive acceptance. What will be will be.

The traffic edged forward a foot or two then stopped again.

"This is stupid! Why didn't they tell us about this on the radio?"

These were pre-smartphone days. Pre-mobile-internet. Pre-Satnav. Technology was fresh and exciting and not yet ubiquitous. We hauled out the brick-like mobile. We rang the AA and RAC hotlines.

"Bog-all of a mention. I hate this." Passive acceptance doesn't come quite so easily to me.

"Is this chapter one of the Moanicle or just the prologue?" Sarah asked. "Keep this up and I'm getting out and walking."

"Could be the best option. You'd probably get to Dover before the rest of us. We're going to miss the ferry."

"We'll make it," said Sarah.

"No we won't. Do the maths. Two hundred and sixty miles divided by two-and-a-half miles per hour."

"Tell me," said Sarah

"Er... can't do it in my head."

"You're an accountant. You used to be a bus scheduler. You know, times? Numbers?"

"I need a calculator. Look, try it this way: we're moving at slower than walking pace. We have thirteen hours. Could you walk from Stoke-on-Trent to Dover in thirteen hours?"

I was worried.

On paper, six hours was comfortable. I'd been extra-cautious and built in a generous BRBF (British Roads Buggeration Factor). I'd allowed fourteen hours. We'd used up one of the spare ones already.

Perhaps the roads would clear.

I was bored. I fiddled with the sun visor, first up then down. I noticed a smear of grease on the rear-view mirror so, with some contortions, I pulled out a tatty and decaying tissue from my pocket and started to rub at the spot. The smear got worse; the tissue turned into a cloud of dust that irritated my nasal passages and launched me into an odyssey of ear-popping sneezes.

We waited.

Sometimes we moved. Mostly we didn't.

"Should we abandon this and turn back to the M6?" Sarah asked.

"No," I said. "We've been delayed too long. If we go back to the M6 now we'll hit Birmingham at rush hour, and that would be really bad news."

I drummed my fingers on the dashboard and hoped that the traffic would clear.

It did begin to clear. I shifted into second gear, then even managed the odd mile in third, and then... Sally Traffic's cheerful banter came onto Radio 2. "A lorry has shed its load on the M1 near Derby. The M1 is closed, southbound!"

None of your namby-pamby slow-moving traffic today. Oh no. Today the M1 is closed.

Traffic jams are like the annoying adverts you get right in the middle of the cliff-hanger film on the telly. But this wasn't adverts, this was: the film will continue after the News at Ten... an extended News at Ten... then live, over to snooker, and you have an early morning meeting the next day, so you just have to go to bed, but it's already late so you're going to be knackered and ineffective throughout tomorrow anyway.

We turned around, back towards Stoke and the M6 and back into the traffic mayhem that we'd just started to leave behind. Down to second gear, then first, then stopped. Another hour, gone.

We reached Birmingham at rush hour – I had been correct about this.

The traffic was bad – in this, too, I had been correct. It would have been a comfort to have been able to say to someone, 'There, I told you so,' but I couldn't; no one had given me any argument. We'd been here before. We had all known exactly what was coming.

The hour of standing traffic in Birmingham did, however, give us time to consider a new and forthcoming problem. Sally, the trucker's friend, had just given us another juicy morsel of news. An accident on the M25 had closed that motorway clockwise; everything east of the M1 intersection was gridlocked. The police were unable to predict when it might all clear; certainly not for many hours; perhaps not even in my lifetime.

Our route to Dover was closed. So, now we needed to take the M40 then the M25 the other way, west and south of London.

Near Heathrow we stopped. A million people sat in their cars, fuming and watching the jumbo jets flying overhead; flying so low you felt you might reach a hand up through the sunroof and spin their wheels as they passed; something to kill a little time.

We watched the sun as it dipped toward the horizon, casting its warm, rusty colours onto the shiny paintwork of a thousand parked cars. Beautiful. Nearby, an overhead gantry, that had, for the past hour, shown a maximum speed limit of forty mph, reduced this limit to thirty. I laughed at the mockery.

"Ha!"

It was a strange laugh, barking and unhinged.

Time defied Einstein's laws and began to pass at two distinct but simultaneous speeds. We had the Forever-Time of boredom and the Insane-Galloping-Ahead-Time of the impending appointment with destiny: a paid-for-in-advance car-ferry.

Ten yards, stop. Fifteen yards, stop. Five yards, stop. You think it's frustrating in a car? Try it on a gradient with a ton of caravan hooked onto the back, and with a clutch that has started to smell like an arson attack at the Dunlop factory; a clutch that is heavy, feeling as though it has been fitted with a spring borrowed from a McAlpine gravel truck. Your knee begins to throb. You begin to wimp out of important gear shifts, then you cringe at the shuddering and rattling – the sound of falling cups from inside the caravan behind – in protest against a hill-start in third, and so with gritted teeth you accept that your wrecked left leg is going to have to reach through the pain barrier one more time.

We crept around London.

We crept around London in silence, having said everything that needed saying.

We crept around London... and, in time, the traffic began to ease.

I saw a service area and darted in for a pit stop. Just petrol and "comfort" – no time, now, for food or rest. We pushed on. Midnight came and went, but at last we were moving, devouring the miles. We dared to hope. Hope turned to optimism. We were going to be okay.

We arrived in the outskirts of Dover at about half past

midnight; we swept down the hill from the top of the white cliffs... and joined a queue.

A bored young police officer was controlling traffic. Controlling is probably the wrong word. He was watching the traffic. The police were probably posted more as a deterrent. Their job was to stop the fights that erupt between motorists when the strain and tension of going nowhere in a car becomes just too much to bear.

"Excuse me, officer," I asked, out of the car window. "Is there a problem? An accident?"

He looked at me as if I'd just asked: 'What colour traffic light means go?'

"It's the third week of July," he said in reply. *You moron*, his tone of voice added.

"Of course," I said. I wound the window back up.

The residents of Dover must love this. Nobody goes to Dover in July. They just creep through, at one in the morning, in a haze of exhaust fumes, in cars, motor-homes and grumbling sixteen-wheelers. Nobody smiles. No happy, excited holiday makers here, just a bunch of miserable sods who've been on the road for hours without a break – hungry people, tired people... bloody angry people.

We'd travelled three hundred miles. I felt as if I'd driven from Beijing.

"What are you thinking? You seem miles away."

I looked at Sarah, standing beside me at the ship's rail, and I shook my head.

"Just thinking about that ladder... and the other stuff. We made it. We won." I put my arm around her waist. "You know, if you look back, it's like everything we've done together – even before we were married or even knew each other –

14

everything that's happened has been coming together, towards this. Do you know what I mean?"

"Hmm... I think I do."

I let go of Sarah's waist. I tousled Kevin's hair, then Amanda's.

"It's as if lots of separate, unconnected events – inconsequential events – ups and downs from the past thirty years, are coming together here, now, today. They're like strands in the plotting of an epic novel, or... I don't know, a military campaign maybe. This moment, now, it's a big deal, and I was thinking, I want to be able to remember it. We need to relish this; every single part of it."

My moment – our moment; the four of us, at the rail of the P&O Car Ferry at two o'clock in the morning. The sodium-orange townscape of Dover, shimmering under exhaust fumes and made all the more eerie and surreal by the hallucinogenic effects of journey-induced exhaustion, began to recede as we sailed. England slipped away behind us, with its ladders and its funereal motorways... its Dark Side. Ahead lay Europe, seven hundred miles of it – and a thirty-year-old caravan, a night on an autoroute, a flying visit to Paris, a stopover in the Marne valley, then Switzerland... and the Alps.

Our journey proper was about to begin; a journey that had been a lifelong ambition, both for me and for Sarah, and it felt to me that perhaps this was a journey that had really started, not fourteen hours earlier, but twenty, maybe thirty years earlier.

I reached out for Sarah's hand and gave it a squeeze.

We were nervous.

We had never been abroad.

HOTELS: 1979

"Hard shoulder closed for 2 miles." That's what the sign says. Then the cones start. Familiar, yeah? No work being done. No holes in the road. No workmen. Just cones. Why?

Can anyone put their hand on their heart and tell me that, given a blow-out at this point, they would respect those cones and continue on for two miles, running on the rim, sparks flying past the windows? Or worse, an engine failure; the car begins to slow. Are you going to roll to a halt, park on the motorway, leap out of the door and scramble up the embankment to watch what happens next to your car?

No? No, I don't suppose I would, either.

Might you, instead, be more inclined to slam through those cones, sending them every which way, and getting you, your car and your passengers the hell off that motorway?

So I ask again, why two miles of cones?

—No. 51 from the Moanicles of Michael.

"You are rather late." The hotel manager nodded towards the clock on the wall and tutted.

It was May 1979. Fawlty Towers was not yet legendary, not quite, but the show had become prominent in the public consciousness. This manager was the very image of Basil Fawlty.

"We had some car trouble. Sorry."

I had apologised. Why on earth should I apologise? So, we were a bit late. Surely that was our problem.

16

"We have finished serving dinner now," he said.

"We couldn't have a sandwich or...?"

"The kitchens are closed." *So is this subject*, said his tone.

"If you would like to follow me, I'll show you to your room."

He led us up narrow, winding stairs that opened onto a dark landing, then down a couple of steps, through an arch, and up another, steeper staircase. Sarah and I toiled behind him with all our bags. We climbed up, up and up. We were shown into a tiny attic room with claustrophobic, inward-sloping walls. The room was yellow – not a warm and cheerful yellow; sunflowers and daffodils, but a shade of yellow that might have been bequeathed by emphysemic Woodbine smokers. There was one tiny window, painted closed, through which could be seen the slates of the adjoining gable roof. There was an en-suite bathroom with walls that also sloped, so steeply that it would be impossible to stand upright in the shower. This was to be our home for the next week.

I should have said something. We were paying a standard rate, not some bargain deal to reflect our having to sleep in the loft. This was probably the worst room in the hotel; quite possibly the worst room in Bournemouth, but we were very young and very shy, and we were on our honeymoon. We didn't want to draw attention to ourselves.

My parents had offered us plenty of practical advice when we were booking the hotel.

"Be sure to make it clear in your letter that it's your honeymoon," Mum said. "You'll get special treatment: flowers, basket of fruit, the best room."

This was not advice based on much practical experience; my family were campers. I was a camper. As a boy, I loved being in a tent. I loved having the excuse not to wash; to be able to wear the same clothes for a week. I loved to lie awake at night listening to the owls hooting in the trees a few feet above my head; and to hear the sounds of a campsite coming to life early in the morning. I especially loved hearing the weather on the canvas and feeling warm and snug and secure in my sleeping bag.

We once went to a hotel in Llandudno. I must have been eight or nine years old. I hated it. We ate meals at a table. I was expected to be clean and to wear stiff clothes. We never repeated the experience, instead my parents bought a bigger tent and I was rescued from enforced civilisation for the rest of my formative holidaying years.

The girl that I fell in love with, and married, was a caravanner. Sarah had only known caravans. She would go away for the entire school holidays to North Wales, with her mum and her brother and sisters. Six weeks. Her father worked in his own business during the weekdays but visited each weekend, bringing them food parcels and dry clothes.

We had, thus, both been brought up to appreciate long holidays in remote fields, with rain and mud and stinging nettles.

So, why on earth would we turn our backs on these idyllic childhood memories, and opt for a hotel honeymoon? Maybe peer pressure; maybe we had been lured by the promise of a little luxury. Or maybe we'd just been watching too much television; too many idealistic holiday shows.

Whatever the reason, here we were, at the Perona Hotel in Bournemouth. I put down the cases, and our Basil Fawlty look-alike manager retreated, but only for a second. He put his head around the door again.

"Thursday night," he said. "Please don't make arrangements for Thursday night. Thursday night is dance night."

He disappeared again, this time closing the door. I flopped down onto the bed and gave a heartfelt sigh. Sarah went straight over to the window and tried the curtains.

"How are they? The curtains?" I asked.

She gave me a thumbs-up. "They're fine. We'll be okay here."

"We're high up, anyway," I said.

"Yes, I know but... it's left a scar, mentally, I mean," she said.

I stared up at the ceiling and rubbed my eyes. "I for one will never again feel the same about soft furnishings," I said.

We were referring to our previous night at the Stagecoach Motel near Bath; our wedding night. We had been married in the morning, at St Barnabas Church, on the Wirral. We had left the wedding reception at around three in the afternoon and had driven to Bath. Apart from the car trouble we had a good journey (see how easily I can dismiss the car trouble? The mystery vibration; the double vision; the billowing steam? There has always been car trouble) and we found the motel easily enough. The motel would have been difficult to miss, mind you – buildings that ugly are hard to hide. The motel was a long way outside Bath, but I doubt it was distant enough for the peace of mind of the residents of that elegant Georgian city. The Stagecoach Motel would have been far more at home in the American mid-west, on a dusty and desolate stretch of Route 66. Constructed entirely from corrugated plastic, plywood and dry-rot, and all held together with a coating of brown paint, thinner than motorway-services tea, it nestled in a wilderness of gravel and solitary sickly-grey shrubs. It even had the obligatory tacky neon, defective and flickering.

Why did we choose the Stagecoach? Remember, this was in the days when the internet was just a bunch of news groups and chat rooms. Even posh hotels didn't have websites. We researched the old way. We sent for leaflets and compared photos and prices. The Stagecoach Motel was cheap. There was no photograph on the leaflet (this should have set the alarm bells ringing), instead there was an imaginative artist's impression, the kind with sweeping perspective and happy holiday smiles on all the faces.

The worst thing about the Stagecoach Motel, though, was the curtains. They were smaller than the windows. No matter what we tried there was always a two-foot opening somewhere. Our ground floor room was adjacent to the car park, and every few minutes a pair of goggling eyes would appear, moth-like, at our window, drawn by the lights within. It wasn't as if there was anything warped about these people. Try walking down a residential road in the early evening, before the neighbours have got around to drawing the curtains. Try to stop yourself from looking in; from having a good old nosey round; checking out the décor and the size of the TV screen. It's impossible. You can't help yourself. So it's not like we were sharing the motel with a perverts convention or anything (although, god knows, it would be difficult to imagine a more uniquely suited venue).

Our immediate priority, then, was to construct a makeshift screen from the available materials (bed linen, towels, clothing, etc.) and for me to perform a Billy Smart's balancing act atop piles of rickety chairs and coffee tables in order to hang the improvised drapes from the curtain rail. The ceiling was high. The windows were tall. I fell several times and I didn't do it quietly. My antics began to draw more than casual glances from the car park, and in no time at all we had a fan club.

You will understand why, then, here in Bournemouth, we were willing to overlook the sloping, cancerous walls; the room-without-a-view; the bed as soft as a butcher's block; because here, at the Perona, we had curtains.

We saved the unpacking until later, and headed into Bournemouth to find food. It was Sunday night. There was no food. A packet of cheese and onion crisps each was the best we could manage to sustain us until breakfast. We took it all rather well, considering. This was our honeymoon. Nothing was going to spoil it for us.

We awoke the next morning feeling like LS Lowry's stick people. We made an early start because we wanted to get our little Riley Elf booked into a garage round the corner. The vibration that first set in just outside Bath had not gone away, so rather than risk losing any more fillings we decided to get a mechanic on the job.

"Can't promise anything," he said, after sucking copious quantities of air through his clenched teeth, "but I'll try to have a look at it later today."

As it turned out, that was the last we would see of our little car for the best part of the week.

We ran back to the hotel salivating for breakfast. The manager and his wife were waiting for us outside the dining room.

"Whatever you do, you must be sure to be here on Thursday evening."

Hadn't Thursdays been mentioned to us before? What was it with Thursdays?

The manager's wife was about five foot two in every direction, and all tweed and brogues. She was the sort who gets in too close; the sort who touches. She laid a hand on my forearm and brought her face right in, so that I couldn't breathe for lavender. I was too close to simply look vaguely in her direction. I had to choose a facial feature on which to focus. It was difficult. Should I select an eye? Do I examine a nostril, with its intricate network of nasal hair? I did the natural thing; I backed away. But then the manager was right behind me and I was walking all over his feet. I felt beads of perspiration breaking out on my face. I was in a panic.

"Thursday night is dance night," said the manager, an inch from my left ear.

I started, and moved my face forward and I was back inside the personal space of the manageress and all her lavender. I tried to move left but the banister blocked this manoeuvre. Sarah was to my right. She couldn't move because the manageress had a hand on her shoulder. We were like pilchards in a net.

"We have a live band," said the manageress. "It's a terrific night. Will you be there? You must be there."

"Why did you say yes?" I whispered to Sarah, when we'd escaped to our breakfast table.

"I don't know. I just... I had to get away. Anyhow, it might be fun."

"You think? Do you see the other hotel guests?"

I made a gesture round the room with my eyes.

"Okay, so they're getting on a bit. What makes you think we won't enjoy it, though?"

"I play these kind of gigs, remember. Trust me. It's not our scene."

I play sax in a big band. It's a hobby. The concerts are good, people sit and listen and appreciate, and the audiences are a mixed range of ages, but from time to time we do dances. I get to see old age. The shuffling. The constant battle against fatigue, and legs that are as supple as drinking straws. It comes to us all, it's coming to me, now, but at twenty-three I didn't need reminders, I needed to keep the blinkers on.

Bournemouth, I suppose, was a strange choice for a honeymoon. There was an ageing population in the late nineteen-seventies, and it was not really a destination for the young, but I have to say we liked it. It had a special charm and a great many endearing features. We loved the walk down Durley Chine, beneath the dripping trees, to the promenade, then the stroll towards town with the sea on our right and the orange cliffs rising high on our left. There was often a bracing wind that cut you off at the knees, but this was the seaside and that is how it should be; with the smell of salt and seaweed and the angry squeal of gulls overhead. Sometimes we walked into town along the top of the cliffs, and we'd try to spot the pier, lost in the swirling rain and mist.

There was plenty to do in Bournemouth. One of the bigger attractions for me was the Bournemouth Symphony Orchestra, at the time one of the best provincial orchestras in the country. There were two theatres, one in town and one at the end of the pier, and there was the usual seaside stuff, like crazy golf (which we played in a torrential downpour one afternoon, and this added an extra competitive dimension, especially when having to putt against the tide). There were bands in the park and lots of walks through the gardens and chines.

We explored Bournemouth, and with no car on hand we had to use public transport to get around. It's kind of liberating. You get to see stuff. We went to Christchurch on one of the yellow open-top buses. We sat upstairs and were blasted by the wind and rain. On an open-top bus you don't sit downstairs, in the warmth, on dry seats – not if you're British.

At Christchurch we hobbled (the way you do while thawing out) around a model village. It was quite a new model village and might have become spectacular had the passage of a little time allowed it to mature. I'm not sure if it ever did mature, though, it was gone by the time we returned to the area some years later.

As the days passed, the ever-present spectre of Thursday night – Dance Night – loomed with a grim inevitability. We'd failed to make it back to the hotel for meals on a number of days – we just couldn't reconcile holidays with strict meal-times; these are mutually exclusive concepts, particularly to campers, but on Thursday we skipped our evening meal on purpose. At breakfast on Thursday we'd been reminded about dance night again, and I have to admit, we were chicken.

"Yes, we will be back in time for the dancing. We are so looking forward to it. Yes, we love to dance."

We took our ever-growing, two-foot noses into town and went in search of eateries. We ate late. We ate slow. We pushed our spaghetti Bolognese around our plates until it went cold. We had no other plan. There was nothing left to do. Earlier in the week we'd done the theatres, we'd done the orchestral concerts, we'd done the cinema. We'd exhausted the entertainment opportunities of Bournemouth and, after succumbing to the temptation of expensive Italian food, we'd also exhausted all of our money. We couldn't even afford to go to the pub. And it was raining. And it was cold. The one thing we could not do, though, was go back to our hotel. At the Perona we'd have to go dancing with the old and the infirm.

So we walked around Bournemouth.

In the rain.

In the dark.

We passed by the cheery lights of pubs and hotels, gazing in at the warm, dry, happy folk inside. We trudged. We did the full length of the prom with a bracing sea breeze at our backs. Then we turned and fought our way back, right into the teeth of a salt-eyed gale.

We returned to the hotel at around ten-thirty. Were we late enough? Our eyes were drawn to the illuminated hotel window. Inside, all was warmth and camaraderie. The muffled dum-chuck-chuck of the waltzing organ and drums combo. The residents, some lining the room, upright in relentless wooden chairs, others dancing; zimmering and shuffling around the room in sequinned carpet-slippers and cardigans. They had stamina. Ten-thirty. Why weren't they all in bed? Why weren't *we* in bed?

We couldn't go in. We'd be spotted. We'd be interrogated... humiliated. Where have you been? You said you'd be here on time. What time do you call this?

We turned our backs on the tableau of gyrating geriatrics and ventured back into the darkness for another SAS tour of Bournemouth.

"So, how much do we owe you?" I'd dreaded asking the question. Our car had been holidaying in the back lot of Perona Motors for the best part of a week, and by all accounts it had been something of a conversation piece for every mechanic in Bournemouth. Spot someone in town with oil underneath their fingernails and chances are you'd hear them talking about our Riley Elf.

"Well, Mr Wood, I'm not going to charge you."

This was a surprise.

"The thing is this: I haven't got a clue what the problem is. I've test driven it. There is no doubt something is wrong. I've had her up on the ramps, we've had the wheels off... I dunno."

"Well, is it safe to drive home?"

Mr Perona (that wasn't his name, really – I never asked him his name) pushed his cap up onto the back of his head, rubbed his neck with an oily hand and did the sucking thing through his teeth again.

"She *should* be okay. Just... well don't do more than twenty in her, yeah? Stay off the motorway. Take it easy. Oh, and Mr Wood, if... er, *when* you get her home, have someone take a look at her, okay?"

It took us nineteen hours to drive home. Twenty miles per hour. Three hundred miles of minor roads. For most of those nineteen hours we led a cavalcade of irate, horn-happy motorists. We were like the opposite of the circus coming to town.

What was the mystery defect? I resolved it the very next morning when I had to change a front tyre that had gone flat. The tread had come loose all the way round. Ten quid for a new remould – and bingo, smooth as a Swiss watch.

We enjoyed Bournemouth. It's gone now. Not Bournemouth, of course, but the Bournemouth of 1979. Sarah and I returned recently. The Perona Hotel has been pulled down and replaced by a modern old folks' home, all featureless red brick and PVC window frames. It was sad to see. The Perona Hotel was a small but important part of our lives. We wanted to see it again, go inside and look around, disturb some dormant memories and laugh about them.

THE LITTLE YELLOW TENT: 1979

What do UK roads appear to have more of than any other roads in Europe? Road signs. We love our road signs, even though most of them are irrelevant or just plain stupid. My personal favourites:

Arrows in the Mersey Tunnel that suggest you drive straight on. In a tunnel. What alternative is there?

Warning signs for deer on the M6 just north of Birmingham. When did you last encounter a deer on the M6 near Birmingham? Ok, benefit of the doubt, assume there is some substance to the warning. What are we supposed to do about it? Do we pull on tweed hats and reach for our shotguns?

Low flying aircraft on the M40. Okay, I'm vigilant. I'll keep an eye open. How do I avoid an aircraft, though, should the need arise? If they're coming down to the motorway to get me, then I figure there's not going to be a whole heap of options open to me and my little car.

—No. 82 from the Moanicles of Michael.

By July of 1979 we were thinking about real holidays. Our flirtation with hotels was over. As newly-weds we were poor. We had a house. We sometimes had a car. We had a black-and-white second-hand telly which stood on four coffee table legs that I had reclaimed from a skip in the next road, and which were fixed too closely together, so that whenever you made a sudden move to change channels or draw the curtains, the telly would fall crashing face down onto the rug. (It has to be said, that was one robust TV; we got years out of it.) And we had a green chair, and a deckchair. We rotated, taking turns on the green chair or deckchair on alternate nights, unless we had guests – then we both used the floor.

So, any holiday we took would, by necessity, be a budget affair – and by budget we are not talking in terms of the BBC Holiday programme's idea of budget, where you make do with half-board in Bermuda, we were looking at budget in terms of it being cheaper to go away than to stay at home.

We made an investment. We bought a tent. A yellow tent. It cost fifteen pounds. It was a two-man ridge tent with a sewn-in groundsheet. This was class! When I camped with my parents we had a loose scrap of navy-surplus sailcloth, and I had to endure parades of insects marching across my face during the long nights.

We began to collect equipment. Sleeping bags we owned already, a legacy from our respective family camping or caravanning holidays, but some new things had to be bought – a single burner Calor gas stove, a double airbed (an indulgence – saw it in the shop – couldn't resist) and a chemical toilet. The toilet was a necessity. We would be staying at inexpensive and rudimentary campsites. Sites where the list of available facilities was short:

Drinking Water
Grass

Chemical toilets have come a long way. Ours was from the days when such things were in their infancy, and it consisted of a large bucket with a snap-on lid, and a thin plastic toilet seat attached to the rim. Hmm.

So, we had a tent, we had equipment. We could not wait to try it.

Friday night we each rushed home from work, threw

everything into the back of our little brown Riley Elf and headed off, on our first camping weekend, to a small site close beside Bala Lake. The sky was darkening when we arrived, but we had practiced in the garden and our tent erection skills were slick and militaristic. Our little camp was in order before the last of the evening light left the sky, and we sat outside the tent admiring the lights of Bala (the town), on the opposite side of the lake, twinkling on the mirror-like surface of the water.

"This is the life," I said.

"Mmm, yes," said Sarah. "Shall we try making a cup of tea?"

Another milestone. There's something special about the first cup of tea on any camping holiday. This was our first cup of tea on our first camping holiday. It was special. The single-burner gas stove was wobbly. The kettle barely managed to boil. The tea had the colour, texture and flavour of a horse. It was a fine cup of tea. I had a second cup. I was at peace with the world.

"I think we should set up the toilet," said Sarah after a while, just to spoil the mood. "Your job, that one."

The chemical toilet. The Elsan. We hadn't paid much attention to this area of our camping accoutrements – and why should we? Shopping for camping gear is a pleasurable experience, despite the eventual capital outlay. There is so much cool stuff in camping shops; tools that perform a thousand tasks yet fold into a corner of your pocket; outdoor gear that will keep you seriously alive even in the event of meteorological apocalypse; and there's torches and webbing and waterproof matches and... and maps! I love maps! And then – oh, yeah, we need a toilet. Here's one.

The toilet bucket lay on the back seat of the car, still wrapped in pristine cellophane, awaiting my attention. I reached it out, took off the lid, and put about an inch of water in the bottom together with a measure of blue chemical liquid, all the time referring to the instructions.

"Okay," I said.

"So," Sarah said.

I stood, shuffling, transferring weight from one foot to the other. Sarah nodded to herself, over and over. Words were unnecessary.

We didn't have a toilet tent.

We had not thought this through.

"I suppose we'll just have to pull it inside the tent when we want to use it," I said.

Sarah gave me a look.

"It'll be okay, see." I lifted the bucket through the tent doorway.

"Ahh."

Picture this. The toilet bucket stands about eighteen inches from the ground. The tent, at its apex, is about twenty-six inches. I have a mental image, now, of one of those contortionist performers who are able to fold themselves into a two-foot-square box. I am less pliable. I have problems reaching my shoelaces. Sarah does yoga, not circus.

We crouched outside the tent looking in. Maybe we could use it, but we were going to have to choose our moments, when nobody was around.

"You know what?" I said. "That brew? I shouldn't have had two cups."

I was appointed chief test pilot.

I eased into the tent. My head pushed into the roof, lifting it. The rubber peg-bands stretched and sang with the urgency of banjo strings. The canvas, now damp from the chill night air, clung to my body like a second skin. It was full dark, and I needed the torch. It was like potholing. Sarah swore that from outside I could pass for a ghost; all glowing orange and moaning in the dark. It wasn't the best place to go to read the newspaper.

As the weekend progressed the problem got worse, because the bucket got heavier... and it sloshed. Heaving it in and out of the tent doorway became ever more perilous. Then late at night you'd lie there thinking, *I don't need to go, I don't need to go*, but in the end you did, and it was awful. You had to come fully awake, climb out of the sleeping bag and go outside. I'd go in the bushes, but Sarah...

"Mike?"

"Mmm."

"Mike, are you awake?"

"Mmm. What's wrong?"

"I've been putting it off for hours, but... you know."

"Can't you just go out—"

"Don't even think it."

I would suppress a sigh. Then the operation would begin. The air bed had to be moved, sleeping bags – everything. Then, carefully, the slopping bucket had to be lifted inside, and I would be sent out into the cold to hop and to wait. A proper toilet tent rocketed to the top of our shopping list.

The site itself was wonderful. It's located on the quieter side of the lake near the village of Llangower, and is on a spit of land that juts right out into the lake. It is the perfect location for a quiet weekend away, and we returned to it a number of times over the following years. There were boats, mainly catamarans, pulled up onto the pebbly shore, and I loved the nightlong sounds of ropes rattling against aluminium masts – it was restful, like nautical wind chimes.

We had our tent pitched close to the edge where the grass ended in a short drop down onto the narrow shingle beach. We were five or six paces from the lapping water. This was a place where one could simply sit and watch and never get bored.

The best watching was the catamaran club, whose members arrived on Saturday morning. We loved trying to spot the equipment freaks; the sailors who made the biggest show of assembling their gear, changing into wetsuits worn only up to the waist, then striding up and down amongst everyone else's vessels making suggestions, discussing sheets and cleats and wind-direction and drinking tea – but never, ever going near the water. If you find a few spare hours, locate a sailing club and go and watch. Look out for the equipment freaks. They are the ones with the biggest, shiniest, most expensive boats, but they never sail. Every hobby has its equipment freaks, but the nautical variety are far and away the most entertaining.

At some point during the weekend our toilet bucket became unfashionably full. The site, as I said, was rudimentary, and there was no provision for toilet emptying. I had planned to dig a hole – but I was struck by the thought that we were camped only a few inches higher than the water level of the lake, and so anything we put into the ground would eventually migrate to the water. Bala flows into the river Dee. The Dee winds its lazy way through Wales, into England and on towards the city of Chester, where there is a pumping station. This is where the Wirral sources much of its drinking water. As long-standing Wirral residents and water consumers, we were unenthusiastic about hole-digging. So I put the toilet bucket into the boot of the car and we drove, carefully, to some public toilets in a car park further up the lake.

A sign warned against the emptying of chemical toilets. I'm not a wanton law-breaker (honest, m'lud!) but what else was I to do? I sure as hell didn't plan on driving home with the stuff all slopping and slurping around in the boot. The car park was busy so we waited. Whenever a suitable moment presented itself I'd put a foot outside the car door, but then a coach would arrive, or the little lakeside steam train would puff into the adjacent station and disgorge a thousand onlookers.

We lurked for what seemed like hours, until the right moment arrived. Now. The car park was ours. I pulled up my collar and with shifty sideways glances I sidled into the gents with my bucket and locked myself in one of the cubicles.

I poured. The toilet filled and splashed and gurgled. It became obvious that I'd been a little overenthusiastic to be rid of my cargo. The toilet blocked. Now, I don't know what possessed me to do this, but it seemed to me that the logical thing now was to flush. I had this idea that a sudden onrush of clean water would have a purging effect, pushing the blockage on through the plumbing.

I watched with growing agitation as the water level rose. It climbed the last few centimetres and then began to overflow. I pumped away at the flush handle in a desperate and foolish attempt to halt the deluge, but I was as powerless as Canute. I goggled as a whirling tide of fluorescent blue liquid surged over the toilet rim, swept down onto the terracotta tiles, then on and out under the toilet door. I hastened from the cubicle and out into the squinting sunshine. The car park was now full of people, their attention drawn by my cries of distress. They watched as I stumbled to the car, red-faced, pursued by a blue tsunami of disintegrating toilet tissue and rolling turds.

So yes, there were setbacks, but despite these it had been a successful weekend. The sun had shone; we had walked; we had rested. Returning to work, the following Monday, seemed strange. I felt compelled to ask everybody what had been happening while I had been away, for it felt, to me, as though I had been missing for weeks and that the world of Public

Transport and Bus Scheduling had been moving along without me. This was the first time that we had been away for just a weekend, and we had learned one of life's most valuable lessons. We had learned how to cheat time.

August came, and we were ready for a full holiday. We had used the tent on two or three further weekends and we had bought a toilet tent. The time had come for the real thing. We packed for a week-long holiday.

We decided to stay at a farm site that Sarah had stayed at many times as a child. On the Welsh coast between Harlech and Barmouth there is a small village called Llanbedr, pronounced klanbedder, with a lot of phlegm on the kla. More Welsh pronunciation lessons will follow, because we have spent a lot of time in Wales, absorbing none of the language but a lot of the rain water.

So, if you leave the coast road and drive inland for a few miles, following a babbling stream, the Afon Artro, a narrow lane brings you to a group of secluded valleys that have escaped tourism. This really is a delightful area. The farm at which we stayed lies a little way beyond the juncture of Cwm Bychan (w is pronounced oo, so koom bikkan. Later there will be a brace of double ds, pronounced th. I bring this up now so as not to keep chipping in with annoying educational matter) and Cwm Nantcol. It is peaceful. Traffic is minimal, leaving the air filled with the restful sounds of bleating sheep, leaf-rustling breezes and trickling water. The mountain scenery is splendid, with clumps of yellow gorse and the reds and browns of rowan trees set against pale, outcropping limestone; and there is boundless scope for walking.

I know all this because we have returned there a great many times. I did not learn it from that first week of camping in the valley. We arrived in the dark and in the rain. Not ordinary rain, you understand – Welsh rain. Welsh rain is special. It strikes the body from the side and cuts you down like rifle bullets. It is colder than ice and yet remains liquid enough to penetrate down to the bone. Welsh rain has the ability to soak one's clothing faster and more thoroughly than a total immersion at sea.

This was our first wet pitch.

One of the features of secluded country locations is that at night it goes dark. This may seem an obvious thing to say, but a townie might not fully comprehend the overwhelming impact of the phenomenon. In towns and cities, night is less light than day. Bright sunlight is replaced by a dimmer, orangier illumination from the glow of sodium street lighting. There are shadows, certainly, places where a mugger might lurk; but in the country – the real country – it goes dark. A clear sky and moon will provide light, but on a night when the cloud ceiling is several hundred metres beneath your feet – it goes really dark.

We arrived, and in the feeble and ever-dimming light from our car's headlamps, we pitched. The wind howled. The rain lashed. We struggled and we fought and we got very, very wet. But we were well drilled by now, and the tent was soon erected, and we were beginning to feel quite smug about our tent-building abilities.

Then we tackled the new toilet tent. We hadn't practiced in advance, and whilst a ridge tent is low and aerodynamic, hugging the ground like a friend – a toilet tent isn't. A toilet tent is square and tall and aerodynamically absurd. A toilet tent embraces the wind and desires to run free with it. In a north wind a toilet tent yearns to go south.

"Hold it!" I shouted.

"I've got it. I... I've lost it again."

"Pull it off my head – argh, you've got my hair!"

"I'm sorry, but why's your head inside anyway?"

"Look," I said, trying to be patient, "just get the damn thing flat on the ground again. That's it. Now, carefully, there's a lull in the wind, onto the frame."

"That's it!" Sarah was triumphant. "Now, peg it down, fast."

"Where are the pegs?"

"You've got them."

"You took them out of the car."

Sarah gave me a look. "You've left them in the boot, haven't you?"

"Look, let's not fight. I'll hold it. You go and get the pegs."

Sarah ran to the car. She was less than ten seconds.

"I've got them, they... where's…?"

"Gone. It just went. A sudden gust. Couldn't hold it." My voice was sheepish. I shrugged. We crawled into the ridge tent to regroup; to rub our hair dry; to accuse.

Ten minutes later we were back outside. We collected the toilet tent from the gate at the bottom of the field and dug deeply into our reserves. Whenever thoughts of submission entered our heads we reminded each other of the consequences of failure; of midnight bare-bottomed excursions into this hydrological evil.

In the end, yes, we won through. Our toilet tent stood proud and defiant in regal colours of burgundy and grey; a monolith, resisting the elements; a place of refuge. It is not, however, a fun place. Anti-Tardis-like, it is a tall box that is smaller on the inside than it looks from the outside. It is home to spiders the size of cow pats and countless other night-horrors of entomology. It is not a place to linger, but it is a vast improvement on the alternative.

I charged the toilet bucket with the blue liquid then rejoined Sarah in the safe haven of the mothership.

A tent can be a cosy and pleasant place in adverse weather, huddled in your sleeping bag, warm and secure, while the wind howls and moans, but it is better if you start dry. When you start wet, a tent is purgatory. Our sleeping bags were damp; most of our spare "dry" clothes were damp. We had no safe means of cooking inside the tent, so our food was cold and, of course, damp. Still, we thought, if we could just get through the night, things would look better in the morning.

In the morning things did not look better. The rain was relentless. A quick peek out of the tent doorway showed that we were inside a cloud, a cloud the size of Wales. There was nothing to see except grey mist. We ate soggy cornflakes and lay in our sleeping bags reading. We had jam sandwiches for lunch. In the afternoon we stayed in our sleeping bags and read some more.

Sarah, at this time, was just starting out on a career as a starving artist. She worked mainly in watercolour but was still seeking a style, trying different subjects. In years to come she would discover botanical art, but with a difference. Sarah's botanical art is painted in the rain. She captures the light and beauty in the raindrops. Perhaps she owes her style to these early holidays.

She tried to do some painting in the tent. She found it difficult inside, in the monochrome yellow light that was our universe. Colours were guesswork, but as she said at the time, she was learning, and who knew what strange and surreal creations might result from the exercise. She might inspire a whole new school of colour-deprived, wet-on-damp tent-scapes.

There was spillage. She watercoloured her sleeping bag, the

wet-on-wet technique. We tackled the flood with the last thing of mine that was still dry – tomorrow's boxer shorts. Sarah packed away her paints and the world was denied a modern abstract masterpiece. Raindrop realism, though? Perhaps, that day, a seed was sown.

"We have to eat something warm for tea," Sarah said. "We need real food or we will die."

"We'll go out somewhere," I said.

It was strange going out. For twelve hours we had been reading and failing to paint in that filtered ambience of pure yellow light, and when we clambered outside everything was purple. Our eyes were wrecked. All of the overused yellow colour receptors had closed down and the only colour we were left with was purple. The whole world was an Andy Warhol poster, and it took hours to clear.

We found a purple chippy in Barmouth. There were about a million purple campers queued up outside. We didn't mind waiting; there was nothing else to do. We ate our chips from soggy purple newspaper then squelched around Barmouth. We noted and admired the way this little seaside town was able to adapt, chameleon-like, to the conditions. Gone, now, from outside the shops were the plastic buckets and spades, the flip-flops tied together with hairy string, the inflatable swimming rings and dolphins. Instead there were wellies, umbrellas and plastic macs.

We expressed our wonder and horror at the number of shops that brazenly displayed for sale air rifles and vicious knives and other instruments dedicated to the pursuit of death or injury. Why? Is this what people are driven to after a week of Wales in the rain? Might this be the holidaymaker's only means of seeking some kind of retribution against the bastard who convinced him that Barmouth might be a good place to go in August?

We bought books from a charity shop and magazines from WH Smiths and we went back to the tent.

Sunday was the same. Rain. Cornflakes. Reading. Jam butties.

At teatime we decided that we just had to cook something. We had to be moving – to be doing. Another of our recent acquisitions was a windbreak; something to make cooking on our single-burner gas stove easier. We hadn't tried it yet, but after a struggle I managed to convert it into a kind of extended flysheet over the end of the tent. It wasn't waterproof, but it delayed the rain. It slowed it down just enough to enable us to cook. I have a treasured photograph of Sarah, squatting over the stove in our makeshift awning. She is in a soaking-wet anorak, worn beneath an entirely non-waterproof yellow cagoule. The cagoule has become transparent. The whole ensemble is so wet that each raindrop is producing ripples. She is wearing a red and blue flowery summer bush hat hanging limply around her ears, and from which there is a steady stream of water decanting into the pan of tomato soup that she is stirring. It is the only summer holiday photograph we have from that year.

The soup was lovely.

We lasted until Tuesday. Four days. We revisited Barmouth, and we also spent a déjà vu afternoon in Harlech, examining *their* knife shops. We had read all of our books and all of our magazines. Car Mechanics is a fascinating magazine, but there is a limit to the amount of entertainment that can be drawn from accounts of clutch changes and camshaft modifications. We'd had enough.

We broke camp and walked down to the farmhouse to settle

up. Mrs Evans, the farmer's wife, was lovely. She would not accept any payment.

"I couldn't take it from you," she said. "You've had a terrible time."

"Are summers always like this?" I asked, with a smile.

She thought for a moment.

"Yes," she said.

I didn't give her an argument about having a terrible time, but really, despite the weather and the problems and the prolonged confinement, we'd had a good time. You will have to trust me on this one, but nearly forty years later, both Sarah and I still remember that holiday with fondness. Wales had thrown its worst at us and we had come out of it smiling. We were never tempted to abandon camping, on the contrary, we couldn't wait for the next outing. We had created a little home from home for ourselves out of canvas and a few square yards of meadow. At first there had just been the tent, but now we had our tent, our toilet tent, and of course the car – our refuge of last resort. We were expanding, village-like. We had a base camp, just like on Everest, and it was portable. We had escaped the material world for a few days, and if we could get so much fun out of this kind of holiday, what might it be like if the sun were ever to shine?

And as holidays go it had been cheap. The entire adventure had cost us the price of three-quarters of a tank of petrol (still fairly inexpensive back in the seventies), some second-hand paperbacks, a handful of magazines and two bags of chips.

CAMPING IN STYLE

Why are food and drink so expensive on motorway services? There are coffee chains, for example, that are identical to their high street counterparts in every way, and yet they charge a hefty premium for all their products. On the high street these shops have to compete for custom. Not so at motorway service stations, where the customers are delivered into their care by the car, bus and lorry load. On the motorway there are no alternatives. There is no competition. Custom is guaranteed, no matter how bad the weather or how miserable the service. The supply chain could not be simpler. No pedestrianised zones to negotiate. These are on a motorway for heaven's sake!

So why the extra cost? Could it be, I don't know, corporate greed?

—*No. 78 from the Moanicles of Michael.*

The telephone rang.

"Hello?"

"Hi, Mike." It was my mum. "There's a tent advertised in the local paper, second-hand."

"We have a tent."

"Yes, but it's tiny. This one's a frame tent. Bigger. We worry about Sarah... and what about when you start a family? You have to think about these things."

"Okay, but we can't afford a frame tent."

"I've spoken to your dad. We'll help you out with the cost. It'll be worth it to know you're dry and comfortable."

"But I like our little tent."

"Just think about it – and tell Sarah."

So, with substantial financial assistance, we bought a bigger tent. A palatial tent. A tent with rooms. We picked up some more equipment, also second-hand, from ads in the local paper, and we spent the winter getting very excited about our next season.

Easter. Our first outing with the big new Barnum & Bailey tent. We headed for Snowdonia, to a site within reach of the mountains. Real mountains – pointy and wild. This was very exciting for me. I was looking forward to having a go at Snowdon before the crowds of flip-flop hikers started to swarm.

The site we chose was small. It was an open meadow with no trees and surrounded by low dry-stone walls – nothing to obscure the view of the mountains. There were a couple of green and mildewed static caravans at the low end, and a handful of small tents – squat little ridge jobs, low and rugged like our old one — that clung tenaciously to the top end of the sloping field like lichen on rock.

I switched off the car engine and we sat for a moment admiring the view. It was difficult not to stare at the people in the static caravan, opposite, because they were staring at us.

"What are they looking at?" Sarah said. "They've been staring at us since we arrived."

"They've even moved the telly out of the window so they can see us better," I said.

"Well they're freaking me out."

"Ignore them. Don't let them catch your eye."

They stared. I stared back. I couldn't help myself. Maybe it had been our arrival – our little Riley Elf, pop-pop-popping up the field on one cylinder, with the vast blimp of a tent-bag strapped to the roof. Maybe, to them, this was a portent of future entertainment that would be better than the telly.

"Anyway," I said, "it's a lovely day. The sun is shining. What are they doing cooped up in there with the TV? They should be outside."

I opened the car door, climbed out, and the wind blew me over. It wasn't just a strong wind, either. It was cold, bitterly cold. My Ethel Austin jumper was as wind-proof as a dolphin-friendly tuna net.

I scrambled back into the car and rubbed my hands together.

"Bit breezy out there? We'll be needing our bobble-hats, I think," said Sarah, with a grin.

"Still watching us," I nodded towards the static.

"Maybe we can find another spot, more sheltered, less on view," said Sarah.

"Don't worry about them," I said. "They'll get bored soon enough."

Other than the wind it was a lovely Good Friday morning. The sky was crystal clear and, against it, the mountains were sharp and defined. I love the mountains. I love Snowdonia. I hadn't been here for a while, and more than ever they just kept on drawing my gaze. I cannot look at a mountain without a part of my brain searching for routes to the top. Don't get me wrong, I'm no rock climber, or even a proper mountaineer. I'm not sporty in any way, in fact. Some people are born sportsmen, they can kick or throw a ball, or hit one with force and accuracy with any kind of stick or racket. These people can run like the wind and they have the agility of a cat. They can compute angles of deflection and vectors on the fly, whilst at the same time imparting killer spin on any projectile.

I don't fall into this bracket and I usually try to avoid all exposure to the inevitable humiliation that accompanies any attempt at sporty stuff. I once bought five wooden balls at a fair; balls that were meant to be thrown at plates with the object of breaking them. Just before my turn came around, a sturdy little guy with a shaven head, polished ebony skin and a tight vest-top that showed all of his rippling muscles, stepped up and began to throw. He was impressive. He was the embodiment of explosive power. Plates didn't just break, they were annihilated. He threw those balls so hard they went straight through the plates and then through the hardboard wall that they were leaning against. He drew an appreciative audience and he worked them, throwing harder and harder. He was given another five balls and he threw them like artillery shells, and everyone was clapping and cheering.

And then it was my turn.

The audience, now whipped up into a froth of anticipation, wanted to see more destruction. They had a blood lust for dead crockery. I felt the weight of expectation on my shoulders. I wound up for the first throw. I concentrated and focussed all of my will on those plates. I hated those plates. Those plates were toast. I drew my arm back and let fly.

I missed the marquee. The ball went sailing over the top. There were howls of mirth and derision. The back of my neck began to glow like a three-bar electric fire. I tried again. Again I missed the marquee. The crowd was growing, people wandering over from other stalls to see what all the whooping and laughing was about.

I adjusted my aim and tried to get the ball lower. It hit the ground in front of the plates and rolled harmlessly a few inches short of the plate rack. I tried again, but this time I was wide and I hit the stall-holder in the knee. It didn't hurt him at all, there was simply no power, but the audience loved it. One ball left. I had to make this one count. I went for accuracy instead of futile limp-lettuce power. I bit my lip and let loose the final ball. It flew in a gentle arcing trajectory and hit a plate. The plate wobbled, steadied, then fell off the shelf and landed harmlessly on the grass below without breaking. The crowd roared and whooped with mock approval. Those behind me slapped me on the shoulders in an exuberant display of appreciation. But I ignored their mockery – I was triumphant. I had dislodged a plate. I was a sporting legend.

Now, what was I talking about? Oh yes. I don't do rock climbing. If at any time in my life I'd have ever attempted the sport, you wouldn't be reading this. I'd be dead. Mountains are for walking in, and I prefer nice safe routes to those where a trip or stumble might take me sailing over an edge, because if there's an opportunity for this to happen you can be sure I'd take it. So I surveyed those mountains for good, safe routes. I could see many, and I was relishing a full weekend up there with the wind and the views.

For the moment, though, we had quite enough wind to contend with in the valley, and after a quick tour of the field it was soon apparent that our first choice of pitch was by far the most sheltered.

We began to unpack.

On a calm day the tent would have been easy to erect. It is two tents in one, really. The outer goes right over the square frame, and then there's an inner tent that hangs from hooks and elastic bands, so avoiding the need for any apertures for poles and pegs, places that the bugs might crawl through. The inner tent is a secure and cosy haven, safe from the mandible-clacking, blood-sucking unpleasantries of nature. We'd worked through all the build issues at home, in the garden, where we'd soon run up against one of the problems in buying second-hand. The poles were meant to be held together in sets, by spring-ties, and all but two of these were corroded and broken. Anticipation and Preparation. My watch-words. I had done my homework; Sarah and I had figured it all out before setting off. We had colour coded the poles ourselves, using multi-coloured insulating tape wound around each pole end. (I'd bought a bumper bag from the 50p shop.)

I emptied the pole bag out onto the grass.

What I got was a clanking heap of poles and some curly bits of non-stick coloured tape that leapt into the wind and were gone. I swore for a bit, and then we started trying to sort the poles as best we could remember. It took us nearly half an hour of fumbling with frozen fish fingers before we had a frame that seemed similar in outline to the canvas that was still waiting patiently in its bin liner on the roof of the car.

The static people, opposite, were having lunch. They were sitting in their shirt-sleeve environment tucking into a roast. They weren't entirely without their problems, though. The steam from their hot dinner was fogging up the windows and spoiling their view of the show, which, round about now, was reaching something of a climax.

I untied the bag from the roof and we unrolled the tent.

The wind roared. The Beaufort scale had taken its socks off and was counting toes. We got the frame on its knees, half-height. We hoisted the canvas, Sarah on one side, me on the other. It filled with a snap and was away. It came out of Sarah's hands instantly. I was stronger; I held it; I ran with it. I tacked across the field taking great seven-league strides, tugging, heaving, swearing, wrestling, trying to bring it under control. A reef of fence posts and barbed wire loomed, but my flight was arrested by a stunted, wind-withered rowan tree. Sarah caught up and together we began to disentangle the fabric.

The static people had moved to a side window, six of them

fighting each other for a better view, their treacle sponge puddings left steaming and forgotten on the dinner table.

It took an age to free the tent then haul it back up the hill, fighting all the way into the teeth of the gale. No round-the-world yachtsman was ever so cold, so miserable, and so in need of cocoa with a dash of rum.

This time we pegged the leading edge first, with the canvas still flat on the ground. Still no easy task; the grass seemed to be growing out of solid rock; the pegs just jumped around and gave off sparks. It was like pegging into pavement. I searched for cracks and managed to get a couple of pegs in, and, working backwards away from the wind, we did what we could to create some sort of tent-like shelter. We could worry about the niceties later – like setting the poles straight and getting the canvas pulled evenly. All we wanted for the moment was somewhere to rest our throbbing ears from the wind; somewhere we could boil a kettle.

I pulled the car in as close to the tent as possible so that it might offer some protection. We began to unload. In a few short minutes we had a home, and, sheltered from the wind, it was cosy and warm. This must have come as a huge setback for the static people as it seemed to signal an end to the theatricals. We could have entertained them with the toilet tent but we wisely chose to leave this in the boot for the moment.

The tent building had taken most of the afternoon. It was getting dark. I lit the storm lantern and we tucked into our roast chicken dinner. We made a point of making sure the static people could see this. We too could eat civilised food. Not a bad meal from a portable gas stove, you might say. We were acquiring nifty camping skills. Sarah had cooked the chicken at home, in the morning, before setting off, and she'd wrapped it in layers of foil. It is surprising how long this will stay warm, and it easily stretches to two good meals.

We were now warm and well fed. Our weekend was becoming pleasurable again. We were determined to have fun despite the howling wind and the flapping canvas. We got the cards out. The pack was still soggy from previous weekends and the cards were beginning to delaminate into a one-hundred-and-four-card set. It was time to start the weekend's rummy contest. Every weekend away was marked by a new contest lasting for two or three evenings. We gave these contests silly alliterative names like "The Conway Cup" or "The Tryfan Trophy". This weekend would see a fierce battle for "The Snowdonia Silver Salver".

Rummy is meant to be a game of chance but Sarah tells me she has two secrets – demon strategies that she will never reveal. She tells me this each time we play. I always lose. To this day, years later, I always lose.

On this occasion I didn't just lose. I was thrashed without mercy. I sulked and suggested we have an early night. There would be no lengthy preparation involved, because no way were the two jumpers, the anoraks or the woolly hats coming off that night. I topped up the air in the inflatable mattress and we climbed into our sleeping bags. It was about nine o'clock. My watch had stopped, having been dropped into the washing-up bowl, and was now just a useless trinket filled with mist and water droplets, but I knew the time because I could clearly make out the music for the nine o'clock news coming from the telly in the static, carried over to us on the wind.

There is a nice cosy feeling about being in the grip of a storm at night in a tent, even though it is difficult to sleep. I lay for hours with my nose peeping out of my sleeping bag and I felt warm and happy, listening to the sounds of battering canvas and creaking poles... and munching.

"Can you hear something?" Sarah asked from out of the darkness.

"Yeah. What is it?"

"I don't know. It's like... chewing. I think you'd better look."

"But I'm warm," I said. "I'm comfortable. I'm happy."

Sarah has always known how to use silence as a tool for argument. We lay there listening with growing curiosity to the munching sound until at last I caved.

"Okay, I'll look. Where are my glasses? Have you got the torch?"

I crawled up to where I could reach the zip of the inner tent. I stuck my head out through twelve inches of opening and flicked on the torch. Not more than two feet away, squatting in a nest of shredded tin foil was a beautiful red fox. It stopped eating our chicken and looked at me, its eyes glittering green in the torchlight; then, without rush or panic, it picked up the remains of the carcass and casually walked out into the night.

I leaned across to the tent door and zipped it closed, then crawled back into bed.

"What was it?" Sarah asked.

"Fox," I replied. "Dinner's gone."

"Oh."

I went back to sleep.

Sarah was first to wake in the morning.

"There's something on me," she said.

"Uh?"

"I'm all damp. And there's something cold and clammy on my face."

I was fully awake now. Something cold and damp and not very nice was on *my* face. It was the tent. I found the zip, which now lay across my shoulder, and opened it. There was the sky. The outer tent lay flat and soggy from the morning dew. Our pitch resembled the site of a light aeroplane crash. Things were scattered across the field for as far as I could see. Crows and other carrion birds picked through the wreckage looking for interesting titbits amongst our food.

The heavier stuff – poles, twisted and mangled; canned food; footwear – were still quite local, but the lighter things, our clothes mainly – were in bushes, up trees, or displayed across the barbed wire fence at the end of the field.

The static people seemed pleased to see us emerge from our wreckage. Had they woken up especially early so as not to miss this? They were already eating their cornflakes and munching toast. Our cornflakes were probably somewhere over Machynlleth.

We rubbed the sleep from our eyes and began to rebuild. I straightened the poles. Sarah harvested knickers and socks from the trees. The wind had dropped so now we could tackle the job in a more relaxed and methodical manner. This time we double-pegged.

In the final analysis we only lost a few socks, a couple of magazines and a packet of cornflakes... Oh, and the chicken. It wasn't a disaster. The weekend was saved. Snowdon awaited.

I'd been up Snowdon twice before; the first time was when I was at school and we took the easy path from Llanberis, and then a few years later via the tougher, but far superior, Rhyd-Ddu path, starting near the Beddgelert Forest.

This time we drove to Pen-y-Pass with our sights set on the Miner's Track. The advantage with this route is that the car park is over a thousand feet up, so there's not so much climbing to be done. The walk out from the car park is easy; it's level and it takes you across a scenic walkway over the lake, Llyn Llydaw, right in the shadow of Snowdon. Snowdon appears very high. It looms. Everything looms – Snowdon itself, ahead; Crib Goch to the right. The climbing isn't rationed out, it all gets saved up for one monster slog up a route that is all boulders and scree. It's a terrific route. The only view is up, because you are surrounded on all sides. You climb up out of a hole, a crater. There's nothing green. Right from the car park it is all desolation. The sky is filled by Snowdon. You know that you are amongst real mountains.

"Where's the path?" Sarah asked. She was sure I'd brought us the wrong way.

"See ahead? The boulders?"

"No way!"

But this is the good thing about the Miner's Track. It looks steep and scary and impossible from below. You can't see the path, just the multicoloured ant-like train of hikers that zigzag up the side. You follow them. You climb. It's difficult, yes. It's hard work, but not threatening. You gain height quickly and you feel a real sense of achievement. You head for a fingerpost on the ridge above your head. You grind and you toil, and, when it looks to be getting harder, it actually begins to get easier. The path begins to twist and turn and this makes the going a little less strenuous.

We stopped to eat amongst the boulders. We had wanted to save lunch for the top but our legs were demanding food. We should have been eating chicken sandwiches but since the local fauna had been round for supper, it was jam instead. They were the best jam butties, though.

Llyn Llydaw – we had crossed it an hour or so earlier – was now a sparkling blue puddle far below us. We were amazed at our altitude gain, and we knew that we could not give up now.

We pressed on and soon reached the ridge. This is where a number of paths merge: Snowdon Ranger, Crib-Goch, Miner's Track, Pyg Track and the traffic jam of ill-shod walkers who have tripped and stumbled their way up from Llanberis. This is where Snowdon gets busier than Regent Street in the New Year Sales. I get infuriated by the flip-flop brigade – not so much because they risk their lives, and the lives of others, embarking on so ill-prepared an adventure, but because so many of them seem to find it so sodding easy! I'm up there in my heavy, Swiss-made, Raichle boots (I didn't buy them – they were my brother's cast-offs), and the waterproofs and the windproofs all stuffed into a rucksack the size and weight of a skip (because today it's sunny) and I'm gasping and wheezing and woefully unfit, *but prepared!* And there they go skipping up Snowdon with nothing, and they survive. Why? Because they've been lucky with the weather, and they'll never even realise just how lucky.

Sorry, I'm off on one again. But it bugs me.

So, we reached the ridge, and the rest is a breeze. It's a gentle slope that follows the railway to the summit. It's sometimes hard to see the summit cairn on Snowdon. It looks more like a squirming, writhing mass of bodies, because during peak times it has a larger population than Caernarfon.

We ignored the ruck on the summit. We found a relatively quiet spot that took in the wonderful south-western view over Y Lliwedd, the craggy lower summit that loops round and down, back towards the lake, Llyn Llydaw. The weather was clear. This was my third time on Snowdon but it was the first time I'd seen anything but the inner workings of clouds, and I could see why people – so many people – come here. Every direction; every turn of the head... The view! You cannot get enough of it. This is why they built a railway up here. The view from Snowdon is one of life's must-sees.

Sarah made a stew when we got back. It was exquisite. It had a certain something extra. Could it be the effects of the mountain air? Was it the exhaustion and the need for protein? After tea we walked up the slope of the field to a small lake from where the site's drinking water was taken, and here we found the certain something extra. The lake was full of tadpoles. When we checked, we found that our water carrier was also full of tadpoles. We had used the water in abundance in the preparation of the stew. Mmm... can you get them in Tesco's?

The May bank holidays were wet, so we didn't go away for either of them. We tried a couple of moderately successful weekends through June and July, just to see if the hand-straightened tent poles were still up to the job of supporting the canvas. Then came August.

Our proper holiday.

Two full weeks.

We didn't book anywhere; we just went. We liked the idea of just heading off, free spirits, no ties. Once more we were drawn to North Wales. We came to the Mawddach Estuary, and, searching through our only campsite book (ex-library stock for 20p), we found a small farm site that looked promising.

We began to have our doubts, though, when we turned onto the farm road. It was no wider than a footpath and was soon so steep we could only see sky through the windscreen. The "farm" was of an architectural style best described as post-apocalyptic. Derelict machinery, assorted scrap iron and burnt-out cars lined the lane as we approached. We passed a pair of sullen, sunken-eyed waifs who stared at us with unsettling malevolence. We pulled into the farmyard and a handful of malnourished chickens half-heartedly slouched out of our way. There was no-one to be seen. For this we were grateful. It was like a scene from 'Deliverance'. I wanted to turn around fast before we heard the banjos (or perhaps here they played 'Duelling Welsh Harps' instead). We were on the seventh leg of our rapid three-point turn when a woman of thirtyish, going on ninetyish, came out of the farmhouse, a half-naked wailing baby held casually under one arm. She looked at us without interest. We waved goodbye. On the way back down the hill we passed the sullen waifs. We waved at them also. They watched us (and our hub caps) as we passed, no doubt measuring the missed opportunity.

We reached the road and turned south. Throughout the whole encounter we had barely spoken. I felt sad and depressed. In Liverpool, just five miles from our home on the Wirral, Toxteth still burned after a week of rioting. It was on the news and I'd seen it with my own eyes; I passed through Toxteth each day on my way to work. Society was unravelling, but out here we were supposed to be on holiday. Idyllic hill farms in the picturesque Welsh countryside should not be slipping into a pre-industrial stone age, but again I'd witnessed it; something we thought only existed on Oxfam commercials, and we had the audacity to imagine we were poor?

We drove on in gloomy silence feeling pampered and spoilt and guilty.

We continued south. We stopped at a tea shop. Tea always helps. I had an idea. As a child I had once stayed in Tenby, in Pembrokeshire. I seemed to remember it being quite agreeable.

"Let's go to Tenby," I said.

"What's in Tenby?" Sarah asked.

"Don't know. The sea. I stayed there once. I think it was quite nice."

It took us a gruelling five or six hours, but my recollection had been correct. Tenby was quite nice. A great many other people seemed to think so, too, but, unlike us, the other people had booked in advance. We turned into the first campsite we found. It was on a bit of a slope but had a fabulous view out to sea. It was within easy reach of the town. It had toilets and showers. It seemed to have everything. What it didn't have was vacant pitches.

We didn't begin to lose heart until after we had been turned away from the fourth or fifth campsite. Our search area began to get wider. The sky started to get dark. We had been in the car since breakfast and we were getting desperate. All the car parks had signs in them warning of the penalties for overnight parking. We needed rest. We needed food, and we needed toilets.

Sometime after eleven, in total darkness, we came upon a gate along a lane with a badly hand-painted tent symbol nailed beside it. As we drove through the gate and into the field we were greeted by a surly old man in an overcoat and a woolly hat, who said that it was very late to be arriving and that we'd better be quiet pitching. There was room near the bottom near the path to the beach.

"You mean we can stay?" I asked. "You have room for us?"

"It's a quiet site," he said, "and my regulars don't like a lot of noise."

I could have kissed him. We could stay. A "quiet" site. A beach. In a few short minutes we would be pitched and asleep. We didn't know where this was, but it was wonderful.

We could see from the headlamps that we were in a large field with no more than a dozen tents pitched around the edges. We headed down to the "To the Beach" sign and found an empty corner with a tall hedge. We unloaded the car, erected the tent, wriggled into our sleeping bags and slept.

Morning. A bugle call. Tat-te-rat-te-rat-te Rat-te-rat-te-rat-te-ree.

Loud. Piercing. Early.

Then, the crunch crunch crunch of marching feet. Big diesel engines barking into life, and revving; harsh and raw.

Shouted orders.

An army was mobilising.

I scooped up my glasses, wriggled out of my warm sleeping bag and darted out of the tent wearing nothing but my boxer shorts. Outside, our field was deserted. Just us, and a dozen or so assorted tents, sealed up and snoozing peacefully in the early hours, and yet, from the other side of the hedge came the sounds of war and Armageddon. The very ground was shaking.

I squeezed through the hedge to our left. There were soldiers in full battle dress, some marching, some doubling, across a vast drill square. Massive olive-drab trucks trundled about, hauling huge pieces of military hardware, their engines shattering the still, early morning air, almost drowning out the barked orders of angry drill sergeants.

I crawled back through the hedge and returned to the arms of my wife, who was anxiously awaiting news from the front.

"It's an army camp," I said. "It's right next door. Soldiers. Hundreds of them."

"Let's have some breakfast," Sarah said.

Breakfast was interesting. The weather was fine. We ate our cornflakes outside the tent, sitting in the sun. The sounds from the army camp had diminished slightly, replaced by the thrum of traffic from the road on the other side of the hedge. The all-day traffic jam began to take shape, filling the air with carbon-monoxide and dusting the daisies with lead.

"What's that?" Sarah asked, pointing up at the sky. A plane

was going over. It had a long wire trailing behind, to which another, smaller, plane was attached. As we watched, fascinated, silent flowers of blue-grey smoke blossomed in the sky around the second plane. Then the sounds reached us. As a child I had once walked in a Sunday parade at my mother's church in Bolton. I had been directly in front of a very enthusiastic bass drummer. I always remembered the way each terrible beat of that drum was felt, rather than heard, deep in my chest, in my very soul.

This was much worse. Boom! Boom! Boom! The ground shook. The leaves fell from the trees. Birds took to the sky and headed south.

They were rotten shots, and they missed the drogue plane by miles. There was a slight lull as the tow plane turned for another pass, then all hell broke loose once more. Again and again the pair crossed the sky. There was so much smoke up there now that it blotted out all light from the sun, and the morning grew colder.

"Hit the bloody thing," I shouted. "Then we can have a bit of peace." But they never did, and eventually the two planes flew off in disgust.

We decided to take our chances on the road once more. We settled up with the site warden, who seemed surprised that we were leaving so early.

"You get used to the army, you know. It's a nice spot, this. The beach is nice, too, and it's only a couple of hundred yards down the path there; over the sand dunes."

My ears pricked up at this. Perhaps we were being a little hasty.

"Mind you," he said. "You can't use the path until Wednesday. It crosses the firing range. We're allowed to use it two days each week, when the red flags aren't flying. They're flying today, see?"

As if to emphasise the point, the crackling sound of gunfire started up from across the dunes.

I smiled at the warden.

"I'm sure it's great, but we have somewhere else booked for tonight," I lied.

We broke camp and were on the road within twenty minutes. A record.

We headed west. We passed through Pembroke and turned north towards Haverfordwest. We didn't have a clue where we were going, we just wanted to put the war behind us. In Haverfordwest we decided to head for Fishguard, for no other reason than the vague notion that a town with "fish" in its name might be near the sea; but we took a wrong turn. We seemed to be on a road to nowhere; boring and characterless. Our holiday was another write-off. We were depressed. We would probably drive from place to place until we ended up back home, where we would unpack the car and spend the rest of the fortnight visiting DIY stores or watching old films on the telly. We passed through bland countryside with sagging spirits.

Then, without warning, we came to a place where, after cresting a slight rise, the road fell steeply away before us. Opening out ahead was the most beautiful stretch of coastline I had ever seen.

There was a lay-by on the left. I pulled into it. We both stared, in awe, without exchanging a word. We were looking down onto a straight, golden beach. A perfect beach. A beach that ended at the foot of soaring cliffs that rose straight up from the sand and the sea. Beyond lay miles and miles of heart-stopping, dramatic coastline. Sea that glittered silver in the sun, cliff-tops, sweeping green hills, islands, coves and inlets. We were looking out across St Bride's Bay and the Pembrokeshire Coast National Park. We had never heard of it, but we were looking at paradise.

I glanced across at Sarah and realised that we were both grinning and laughing like idiots.

I put the car back into gear and we headed down towards the sea. At the foot of the hill was a campsite, right by the sea. It was obvious even from here that there was plenty of room. A sign told us that this was Newgale. We were sorely tempted to stop, but resisted. We had seen miles of splendid coastline from the top of the hill; if there was nowhere else to stay, further ahead, we would come back.

We climbed a daunting, steep and twisting road out of Newgale, then followed a short stretch of road along the clifftop and down again to a fishing village called Solva. The road was narrow, too narrow to stop and take it all in, but from what we saw during that brief passage, Solva appeared to be the sort of place were artists might choose to sleep on the streets rather than move on elsewhere. We said things like, 'Whoa!!!' as we drove through. It was just wonderful.

Up and onto the clifftop again, another slight dip, and there was a sign beside the road: "Nine Wells. Tents/Caravans". This time we had no hesitation. I turned into the lane. A love affair had begun.

The tent was erected. We made the necessary arrangements with the farmer's wife who looked after the site. We had a brew (sitting on our new camp chairs) looking out to sea. From our tent doorway we could see the whole glorious arc of St Bride's Bay.

I have to admit, I was a little dubious. We had had a bad start to the holiday and it seemed unreal that we could have just stumbled across such a place. It just wasn't us. And why were there so few tourists here? We hadn't been able to get within ten miles of Tenby without an advance booking, so where was the bad news? Perhaps there was an aged and leaking nuclear power plant just beyond the trees, or perhaps the Kerrang Heavy-Metal-Rock-Fest was about to get under way in the next field.

It was time to explore. From the camping field we found a path that led down a gently-sloping green valley. It seemed to be heading for the sea, but then twisted and turned in an indecisive manner that left our ultimate destination in some doubt until at last the valley opened out into a secluded rocky cove. We were alone. Waves crashed and boomed onto the rocks, sending up curtains of pure white foam. Gulls dived and screeched. This was all ours. Just a ten-minute walk from the tent.

Cliffs towered above us on both sides, and a footpath could be seen coming down from one clifftop then winding up the other. According to a signpost, it was part of the Pembrokeshire Coast Path. It was a path we would explore many times in the coming years.

We followed the path up onto the cliffs and walked; the sea to our right. The views changed every few yards, each vista more dramatic than the last. Waves crashed beneath us. Seabirds hovered in the updraft from the cliffs. The water was green and blue and Daz white.

After perhaps a mile or so the path turned sharply inland into a narrow estuary and began to gradually descend. Ahead of us, nestling in the corner of the inlet, was the village of Solva. It was even more beautiful seen from here than it had been from the road. Fishing boats bobbed up and down on turquoise water, which sparkled in the sun. A rough harbour wall ran alongside the water's edge beneath us. We could see at least three artists sitting at easels, hard at work, starry-eyed, orgasmic.

Sarah was mumbling incoherent phrases and pulling her sketch book out from her pocket in a frantic and absent-minded manner that involved the scattering of pencils and used tissues and other assorted pocket detritus. I wasn't at all surprised. Solva seemed just too magical to simply look at and admire. You had to do more; paint it; photograph it; write music or poetry about it – while always haunted by the realisation that you will never properly capture it. It was hidden, and we had found it. We felt ownership; party to a very well-kept secret.

Just five miles further up the coast is St David's. It's now a city, but that was still fifteen years in the future when we found it. City status was not conferred until 1995. St David's is more like a village in size, anyway, but it bustles with life and interest. We parked on the edge of town and walked in. There is a village hall – called City Hall — a few shops and many galleries. Walking down the high street you can see the sea sparkling in the distance with its rocky islands to remind you that this is a coastal town, because the usual coastal trappings, the rock shops and tacky souvenir shops, are absent. There's a small, attractive square, filled with flowers, and an ancient stone cross in the centre. We walked a little farther and seemed to have reached the end of town.

There's an impressive stone archway, so we just had to walk through that, and on the other side? A cathedral. We stopped dead and gasped. St David's Cathedral is huge, it's magnificent, and they've hidden it. It nestles in a hollow. There are sweeping grass banks, beautifully mown and manicured, that run down to it. I couldn't help thinking that the cathedral was, in a way, like all of the jewels of Pembrokeshire, so wonderful they have to be secreted away from jealous eyes.

We wandered around the grounds reading all the plaques and information boards. We had to know more.

The building work for the cathedral was started in 1181 (although the original monastery, above which the cathedral now stands, was conceived by St David way back in 589), and its various sections were built, knocked down, then rebuilt again over a period of time right up to the early 1900s. It has suffered from wars and earthquakes (yes, in 1247), but the present day result, the cathedral itself, the bishop's palace and the grounds in which they stand are a joy.

We went inside and found that there is a penalty for stealth. Whilst the outside is geometric and perfect, inside, the nave slopes upwards at a ridiculous tilt towards the altar. The columns and buttresses splay out under the weight of the roof, and you wonder how it all stays up. But it does stay up, and it has done for a long time. I'm no history buff, but I know "old" when I see it.

St David's Cathedral is probably at its best late on a summer's evening when the sun is low and big and red in the west, casting a coal-warm glow over the tower and buildings. Wonderful. It truly is wonderful.

We went to the beach. Whitesands Bay. It is an exquisite beach. Serious cliffs on each side; sand that is genuinely white, and islands – Ramsey Island being the biggest and only a short distance out to sea.

I have a dislike for wasting a holiday by sitting on a beach all day. If I wanted to sit on a beach and see nothing new, it seems to me more logical to do it closer to home and save the petrol.

If you have to waste a day anywhere, though, I find it hard to think of a more fulfilling place to do it than Whitesands Bay in Pembrokeshire, during a hot August fortnight.

And here's the thing: it *was* hot. Remember, we are talking about Wales here. We didn't have just the odd fair day interspersed with lashing rain, gales and an afternoon of drying out in a tea shop; we had sun, day-in, day-out. It was glorious. We swam. We lay on the beach. In the evenings, when temperatures became a little cooler, and colours became rich and saturated, we section-walked the coastal path. There are miles of it, and no two miles are the same. St Bride's Bay in general and St David's in particular have become special to Sarah and I. We discovered it. We didn't read about it in a guide book. It is ours. In St David's we had a real holiday.

Our last day was Sunday. We had to leave the site by noon. We packed slowly, then, with everything in the car, we drove to the beach. We stayed until sunset to eke out every last minute of a magical holiday. Then we drove home in the dark.

THE CAR-FREE YEARS: 1982-1985

I am a big supporter of off-road cycle routes. A few years ago I was put into hospital for a week after being knocked off my bike just half a mile from home, so I am somewhat biased when it comes to segregating cyclists from motor vehicles. There are all kinds of initiatives for cycle routes in Britain, and this should be a cause for celebration, so how come we are so crap at it?

Well, for a start, we build our cycle routes with paint. We take the busiest, deadliest roads we can find, we slap down a bit of pink Dulux and we call it a cycle lane. Paint! Paint will not protect our fragile bodies from the hurtling missiles of iron and steel with which we are supposed to share this safe haven. Am I missing something here? Call me a wimp, but I rather like the idea of segregation. I want to be on a track like the Tissington trail in Derbyshire, where, if a car wants to come and get me, it has to cross a boggy field first. It seems that in Britain, flush with excitement after building a handful of truly excellent off-road routes, we've gone galloping off with the idea of cycle routes and forgotten why they became so popular in the first place.

A little blue sign with a drawing of a bike on it, a tin of paint, and golly, we're on the National Cycle Network; and the politicians can all give themselves a pat on the back for several million quid well spent.

I say bollocks! I have scars. Do it properly or don't do it at all.

—No. 64 from the Moanicles of Michael.

Two major events occurred in the early 1980s and they were to have a considerable impact on our camping aspirations. Firstly, we had a baby, our son, Kevin; and then, a few months later, we lost the car.

Kevin was born on Christmas Eve. It is hard to comprehend the shattering change that a first child brings to one's life. It is a wonderful thing; an amazing thing; but it is also butt-clench white-knuckle terrifying. Suddenly you are responsible for a life – an actual person – who has to depend upon you for all things. You, however, are no longer a child. You've been yanked out of your comfort-blanket adolescence into the world of the "responsible adult", and you are not ready. You never will be ready. The change is total. Everything is different. And it is forever. The toil never stops. The nappy-boiling cycle is a treadmill of misery. A good night's sleep, once taken for granted, is a mocking, intangible daydream.

I had been told that normal babies settle down after a few weeks or months, and an approximation of the old sleep patterns might be resumed. Kevin did not allow us a decent night's sleep for *three years!* This is no idle exaggeration.

So when I say that we were brave to even contemplate a camping trip for the three of us in June, Kevin's sixth month, I'm not overstating this claim. We were brave!

The Riley Elf was gone. It had dumped its brake fluid and dashed itself against a dry-stone wall during a weekend in Llanbedr. The front end had crumbled to red dust. We now had an old Mk 1 Ford Escort. When it had been driven from the factory, several decades earlier, it had been light blue, but now it had so many rusty patches, painted over with red oxide primer, that I painted a sign on the back – "Red Oxide Owner's Club". This did not go down well with Sarah, who didn't really see the funny side of it. She claimed it was embarrassing parking the car outside the Kwik Save where her friends might see it. She complained for months until I felt pressured into picking up a couple of tins of Dulux from the local DIY shop and giving her a once-over in a tasteful Buckingham Green.

Painting a car in the front street is not ideal. It tends to attract foreign bodies such as leaves, insects and the neighbours' children, who are apt to take colour samples home with them. On the whole though, while we never got the car to actually shine, the colour scheme was moderately uniform, and to Sarah's delight the dreaded Red Oxide sign was gone forever.

We decided to try a week in Bala. An easy run; we knew the site; we could pitch a long way from anybody else – with due regard to the noise Kevin would be making throughout the night. It would be perfect. We began to pack the green car.

It soon became apparent that taking a baby on a camping holiday involves more packing than emigration. Sarah fetched everything from out of the house and left it for me on the pavement. I packed. The stuff just kept on coming, and I just continued to slot it all into the car. It was like a giant tetra-mania game. Often the car would reach capacity, with more stuff waiting on the pavement. Unperturbed, I would take things out and then put them back, but with more cunning. The skill was in the detail. The space inside the wellies was wasted first time, so the tent pegs went into the wellies. The spare wheel, in the boot, could be repositioned with the dish shape upwards – plastic plates would then go into the dish-shaped recess along with the kettle, which, in turn, had the guy ropes stuffed into it. The rolled-up sleeping bags would no way fit anywhere, but unrolled and draped over the car seats they went in easily, and gave the added benefit of improved seat cushioning for the journey (we had a few springs sticking up so I reckoned this might become a permanent feature), and on and on.

At last it was done. The poor little car sat there in the road, all green and creaking; but we were ready for the off. I strapped the carry cot into a little space between bin bags full of clothing and nappies, and Kevin was lowered into its womb-like embrace. Sarah wriggled into the space left on the passenger side, slipping her legs into the narrow gap I'd left in the foot-well between the bag of towels and the rolled-up groundsheet. I locked the house, opened the driver's door and gently eased into the driver's seat. It was a tight fit; I felt like Yuri Gagarin.

Kerchang!!!!!

For a long moment we said nothing. We just sat in silence staring at the curly protuberance that had just appeared from under the bonnet. The car now leaned. It most definitely felt nearer to the road on my side than on Sarah's.

"Hmm," I said. "That looks like a suspension strut."

We started to unpack the car.

Back in those days the council was very good about removing derelict cars. They would come and load a car onto a trailer and take it away for you for nothing. I knew the phone number by heart.

They came for the green car two days later.

For a number of years we faced life as pedestrians. I worked for a public transport company – still do – and this gives me unlimited free bus travel. Back then I was a clerk in the schedules department, where I concocted the bus schedules and duty rotas and answered the complaints, so as a public transport champion there has always been a strong cost disincentive to owning a car. There was also the other job-related disincentive: we didn't have any money.

We began to holiday in a static caravan – well, it was actually a tourer that Sarah's parents would tow out to Llanbedr (you may recall, we'd been there before – between Harlech and Barmouth on the west coast of Wales? The place with all the knife shops?). Sarah's parents would holiday for a couple of weeks, then drive home leaving the 'van behind for us to use for a further week or two. We were very grateful. We had to dig deep and hire a car for the week but this was the only way we were ever going to see the countryside.

It was my first taste of caravanning, of living in a box, and at first I rebelled. This was not proper camping. Caravans were for softies. I began to notice a few things, though. I didn't need to wear my anorak in the evenings. I didn't need to inflate the bed. And note this, the caravan had a little room, *with a toilet!*

I got to know the area around Llanbedr well. For Sarah, Llanbedr was almost a second home, having spent most of her summer holidays there as a child. The whole Artro river valley seemed to have been missed by the regular tourist trade. It was like stepping back into a past where it was still possible to strike out across the fields and mountains without encountering too many barbed wire fences and "Private" signs.

A favourite walk of ours started from the car park at the head of the valley, Cym Bychan, then snaked up above the treeline towards the Roman Steps – a cleft in the mountainside where a well-maintained staircase ascends to a saddle between that valley and the next. (The route's existence actually owes more to the National Park volunteers than it does to the Romans – in fact I don't think the Romans knew anything about it at all, but the name's a nice touch.) The steps go up and up, quite an achievement really; they climb to Bwlch Tyddiad, beneath the severe crags of Rhinog Fawr, from where, if you wish, you can descend into the next valley to Coed Maesgwm, beside a river, the Arfon Eden.

It's not a tough mountain walk by any means but it is impressive. Children can do it, it's hard to fall off, and the scenery is wonderful.

One of the nearest towns to our field (I won't call it a campsite because it wasn't, it was a field) is Harlech. Harlech is small but it has one of the most impressive castles in Wales. Seen from the coastal strip it is an imposing sight, perched atop vertical, brooding cliffs. I've never been a big fan of castles. They often cost a lot to go inside, and from within they are invariably far less impressive than when viewed from the outside. Harlech, though, is worth the entrance price, because the views from the walls and turrets are fabulous. On a clear day you can see right up the coast to the peaks of Snowdonia in the distance, and out to sea, the full sweep of the Llyn Peninsula.

There's a lot of Welsh spoken in this part of the country. I used to have mixed feelings about the Welsh language. I always thought, like many others, that Welsh was used solely for making the tourists feel uncomfortable while waiting in shop queues – that as soon as I entered a shop they'd all start talking about me. This is a myth born of paranoia; just as many English people talk about me in derogatory terms when I go into English shops.

I've come to envy the Welsh for their language. I was born Manx, not English, but I moved from the Isle of Man at the age of five, long before the current revival of the Manx language took hold, and so I never learned to speak a word of my native Celtic tongue. I admit to jealousy when I hear the ease with which true Welsh speakers can converse, for it is a beautiful and musical language. I'd love to have the guts to walk into a shop in Wales and say good day in Welsh, '*bora da*', or into a cafe in Douglas and say hello in Manx, '*dy bannee diu*', but I'm terrified they'd say something back to me and then I'd have to look stupid and admit that I'd used up the only words I know.

Welsh, like all the Gaelic tongues, is a strange language; a slippery language. It goes into English ears and then slips straight out again having had little in the way of neurological interaction during its brief visit.

Consider this: I have lived, for most of my life, on the Wirral; a green and pleasant peninsula of land squashed between the rivers Mersey and Dee. On the opposite bank of the River Dee lies Wales. I can look out from the windows of my house and I can see the Clwydian range and its tallest summit, Moel Ffamau. Moel Ffamau is one of those strange and mystical hills on which has been built, for no apparent reason, a folly – the Jubilee Tower – and like all such constructions it exerts a magnetic attraction. We all feel compelled to drive to one of the many car parks around its base, usually on moderately dry Sunday afternoons, and then walk to the top. I can drive to Moel Famau in a little less than thirty minutes and I can then walk to the top in less than an hour. And from the top I can see (with the aid of binoculars) my house.

In short, I live close to Wales.

If I felt so inclined I could actually walk to Wales. If, say, I were Dutch and I lived within walking distance of Germany, I would speak German. If I were German and I lived this close to France, then I would probably speak French, fluently. In fact, thirty years ago, at school, I stumbled through a French CSE (not GCSE, just plain CSE). I didn't listen at school, at all. I didn't learn, at all. I achieved a grade 4. For me this was miraculous, but in terms of academic achievement, well, you got grade 4 for turning up. Yet, against all the odds, I know some words of French. So do you, I'm sure. If a Frenchman says '*bonjour monsieur*' or '*merci beaucoup*', you know what he's getting at. I know some German, too. So do you. I know *ja* and *nein*. If I try very hard I can also think of *ein, zwei, drei*, and *sprechen sie deutsche* (though I had to go away and look up the spellings). That's several words of each language without really trying. I live 350 miles from France and perhaps 550 miles from Germany. I can walk to Wales and yet I know nothing of Welsh. I had to look up *bora da*, for this chapter, on the internet. (Oh, wait though; DIM PARCIO. You see that one everywhere, and there's always a "No Parking" translation next to it, just to be on the safe side.)

Take the word "yes". A useful word – so much so that you cannot but know it in several languages: *oui, ja, si, da*... So what is "yes" in Welsh? Dammed if I know. You see what I mean? It's a tricksy, slippery old language is Welsh. You're not going to master it; you're not going to even get a foothold in it. Learn *bora da*, good day, and try it out. Take satisfaction from any small successes.

FOUR IN A BED: 1986 – 1993

Traffic lights! Surely we can do better. I have a phone that knows, when I'm typing, what word I'm thinking of – even before I do! It knows where I am and where I want to go – even before I do. Using my phone I can control the central heating in my home, from Frankfurt. I can look out to sea and spot the mast of a ship over the horizon, and my phone will tell me the name of the ship, the cargo it is carrying and its origin and destination. My phone fits snugly in my pocket and weighs just a couple of ounces.

So, why oh why, in this age of electronic magic, can't we construct a simple set of traffic lights that can make easy choices based on traffic conditions? Why can't they stay on green when, at three a.m. I am the only car on the road for five miles in any direction? Instead they build lights that think, 'Hmm, I've not changed for a while. I'll change now.' Why are we still building traffic lights with brains that have lumbered out of Jurassic Park? Why do we have to sit, patiently, looking at a red light; cars behind, cars in front, cars all around, but nobody moving! We're all agitated and late for work – but the only light that's ever green is the one pointing up the only bit of road where there are no bloody cars!

So where's all this technology? Come on, guys. If my phone can do magical stuff, why are we going wrong in the roadside fixtures and fittings department?

—No. 45 from the Moanicles of Michael.

We swapped cars like shirts for a few years, never spending more than £50 on a new one. This kind of clipped our wings a little as far as camping went, because these cars were none too solid around the suspension points and we didn't want to see the springs coming through the bonnet again. But in 1986 our second child was on the way, and we felt it was time we had something better; for reliability, for strength and for size. We wanted a car that would seat four and take a tent.

We splashed out. We went way up-market. We spent £300 on a Mk III Cortina. This was a fine car. It was big and it was powerful; it had water that stayed in the radiator most of the time, and it had a tow bar. So we bought an old trailer, painted it up, and now there would be no stopping us. In July, Amanda was born.

A second baby was nothing like the culture shock of the first. We had all the stuff (except the baby clothes we'd kept were blue and we now needed pink), and we felt that this time we knew what we were doing a little better.

So in late August we returned to Sarah's parents' caravan in Llanbedr. There was no problem taking a two-month-old baby, we knew babies and we knew Llanbedr. It worked. Amanda started to do something strange, though, something that Kevin still hadn't really demonstrated in three and a half years; she slept at night.

"See your sister," we would say. "She's asleep. So is the rest of Europe. You should try it sometime."

The following summer, in fact the following two or three summers, we were in the comfortable position of being able to pack the tent and explore the entire country for weeks on end. Where did we go? We went to Llanbedr, again and again, in Sarah's parents' caravan.

Where was the adventure? What had happened to the frontier spirit?

It occurred to both of us that we should try something new.

We were getting stale. We'd done Wales. The Lakes were tempting but they still felt distant and remote.

But there was another national park, not too far away, and to us it was unexplored wild country. What about the Peak District?

It was only a weekend but we were very excited, and now that we had a trailer, we had lots of space to store lots of things, so we took lots of things.

The site we found was at a place called Wetton, near the Manifold Valley. The site looked great, close to a village that boasted little else than a church and a pub. Lovely.

We began to explore, and, by chance, came upon a rock feature called Thor's Cave. It is a huge hole halfway up the side of a cliff that towers above the Manifold Valley, and it's just accessible enough to reach on foot with a little scrambling. Once you're up there it's very exposed, very high and very scary. Not a comfortable place to take children. The view is terrific. There's nothing in the cave, but it's one of those curious features; it's not that easy to reach, so you have to get up to it just because it's there. We made a cursory exploration of the cave. The children were all over it, scrambling and slithering while we shouted and threatened. You try to take hold of a child's hand that doesn't want to be held and it has the ability to turn into wet soap. Children can make their bodies limp and unmanageable, then once free of your grip they're off again.

"Kevin, not near the edge!"

"Amanda, come back here, right now!"

"Not another inch, either of you! Come here!"

We couldn't wait to retreat down into the safety of the valley. The only one to fall was me, making a lunge to grab a handful of Kevin's jacket. The nettle patch saved me.

The Manifold Valley is strange. There is a substantial river in one part, a dry riverbed in another, and somewhere in between, within about a hundred yards, the water simply disappears. It's weird. We walked up and down several times, but the interesting bit is beyond a field that is protected and screened by a fence, so we weren't able to see exactly what happens. Is there a gaping pit into which the millions of gallons of river water cascade without a trace? What a sight that would be.

We walked up the valley a short way until we came to Wetton Mill. Here there was a café that seemed to thrive on the cycle and pedestrian trade. We stopped for a drink and I asked the helpful young waitress about the river.

"Oh, it just soaks into the ground. Does it most summers. I think the water reappears at the 'boil holes' near Ilam Hall, someone told me that once."

"Is it sudden? Does it just disappear?"

"Not really. If you follow the river the water level just starts to get lower and lower, then it turns into puddles, then... nothing, dry. It's just a summer thing. If you came back in, say, October, it flows normally. You wouldn't know there was anything strange happening."

I didn't know rivers could routinely do this kind of thing. It was fascinating.

We took our time over our tea then set off back down the valley. It was like one of those artist's impressions, you know, those they do for new shopping centres? Everyone smiling and happy; the sun warm but not too hot; everything, even the air, was clean and bright. We adored the Manifold Valley.

The fun didn't last, though. We settled in the tent for the evening. With young children who need their sleep, and with temperatures rapidly falling there is little else to do but retire for an early night.

At ten-thirty the pub in the village emptied, and everyone came back to the site. They sang, they laughed, they roared. I didn't mind – they'd be quiet soon. (Actually I lie – I did mind. I tolerated it because I supposed it would seem uncharitable to make a fuss at ten-thirty, before even the last traces of light had left the sky.) The noise continued. I lay in the tent and fumed. I hate to be disturbed at night. I have a thing about late-night noise and the lack of consideration from the people who make it. After several hours though, I must confess, it could have been my anger more than the noise itself that kept me awake, although they were still making a lot of noise.

I woke Sarah up.

"Listen to that," I said. "How can anyone sleep with that row going on?"

"I was managing okay," she said in a groggy, three a.m. voice.

"Doesn't it bother you?"

"Hmm."

"I'm going to go and tell them."

"Just go to sleep."

"Can't. Can't sleep."

"Try."

Ten minutes later.

"I can't sleep now," she said. "It is very noisy."

"Who is it? Can you tell?" I asked.

That was the problem. Lying in the tent it was hard to tell who was making the noise. There were tents all over the field and the noise seemed to be coming from all of them. This kind of put me off going outside for a confrontation. I didn't feel up to fighting by lottery, and I recalled there being some pretty big, muscular-looking specimens in some of those tents. So I just lay still, and fumed.

They went quiet at maybe four in the morning, but by then I was too wound-up to sleep. I tossed and turned.

An airbed is a seriously anti-social habitat when you're restless, where trampoline dynamics are brought into play. If you toss and turn, your partner is catapulted high into the air. This creates anger and the exchange of harsh words. Sleep becomes ever more elusive.

At five a.m. the sun came up and I abandoned sleep and left the airbed to Sarah so she might snooze through what little remained of the early morning until the children woke up. (They had slept through it all – how did they do this? As babies they never slept at night.) I walked around the site, whistling and deliberately tripping over guy ropes, hoping to hear the odd annoyed grunt of someone woken from sleep, but I heard nothing – and this annoyed me even more. When these people were finally ready to sleep, not even the Massed Bands of HM Royal Marines were going to wake them.

I spent the rest of the Sunday in a foul mood, unable to enjoy our surroundings, glaring at the campers around us. I blamed them all, but I couldn't definitively point the finger at anyone in particular.

I watched the caravanners emerge from their 'vans looking refreshed and relaxed from a good night's sleep. Evidently noisy neighbours didn't have the same effect on people who sleep in caravans. I was jealous. I was angry. The whole thing had spoiled my weekend. The only crumb of comfort came in the afternoon, as we were packing to leave. An ambulance arrived; one of the suspect campers was being delivered back to his tent. He'd a broken leg. He had fallen out of Thor's Cave. Ha!

Sarah told me not to be so horrible.

Ha ha ha!

The Cortina died. This was a sad time for us. We had grown to love the Cortina. We'd named her. She was Bertha and she had freed our souls and helped us to get out there again, but the MOT comes around each year, and each year we get the telephone call and the old air-suck-through-teeth communication that all mechanics learn during their apprenticeships.

This was always a time of anxiety and expense, but we usually survived. This time, however, the call was different.

"It's Bob, from the garage, Mr Wood. I've had a look at the car, and well"—big sucking noises on the other end —"I don't think there's a lot we can do."

As car owners, we are what I like to label, "End Users". That means cumulative depreciation equals cost. Net Book Value equals nil. There are to be no more owners. When we are done with a car, the world is done with it. I am well used to taking a car on its final journey, down to the "Borough Spares" yard, but this time it was a far more sorrowful journey. We'd had the Cortina for nearly five years, a record. Bertha had become a part of our family. I still recall the sense of betrayal that I felt, parking her in the yard, alone amongst all the scrap; the air, thick with the tangy smell of gearbox oil. I remember pointlessly locking the door for the last time and walking away, clutching the little bag with the thirty pieces of silver I'd just been given in payment (actually it was a fiver), then making the long and lonely trek back through Birkenhead docks towards the bus stop, a lone tear escaping from the corner of my eye.

It's difficult to buy a car when you don't have a car. I'd gone through the routine often enough, though usually we had a few days while time ran out on the MOT. This time we prevailed upon Sarah's father to run us around our usual route of cheap-and-cheerful back-of-the-forecourt dealers. We toured them all without success. We were facing another extended run as pedestrians, and our spirits were low.

On the way back home Sarah's dad took a different route to our usual one and we passed a Skoda dealership.

"Stop!" I shouted. I'd seen something out of the corner of my eye.

"What is it?"

"I'm sure I saw £245 stuck on a windscreen."

We walked back and there was our next car, an orange Skoda Estelle. Clean, shiny bodywork that seemed rust-free. I crossed my fingers and hoped that the engine worked.

We named her Wilma, because of the three letters in the registration number, WMA. Wilma was rear-engined, and it was a swine trying to fit her with a towbar. She was a temperamental starter and on a good day she could muster about ten or twelve horsepower, but she ran, and we were on the road again. Wilma was quirky and fun and we loved her.

For our main summer holiday we returned to St David's. This was our first time since the children had been born. We wanted them to see what a magical place it was.

We returned to Nine Wells, near Solva. We took Kevin and Amanda to see the sea, down our magical private valley, where Amanda stood in dog-muck and got it all over my shirt after I picked her up when her legs got tired.

The children fell in love with St Bride's Bay. They embraced it with the same enthusiasm that we had felt on our first visit; even despite the fact that this time the weather wasn't quite so good. St David's is a fair-weather destination. We didn't have fair weather. It rained. A lot.

The tent, now in its umpteenth year of diligent service (both to us and others before us), had started to leak. At first this only happened when we carelessly left the sleeping bags pressed against the inside canvas wall – like on the very first day – but later on it started to drip onto us directly as we huddled inside, in our cagoules and wellies. We bought waterproof spray, but you need to apply it onto dry canvas. We didn't have dry canvas.

We came home early.

The milkman laughed when he saw us the next morning. Andy was a caravanner. He understood. It had become a standing joke that whenever we cancelled the milk, he packed a raincoat, because every week or weekend that we decided to go away was, without fail, a total washout. Not just ordinary rain but pictures-on-News-at-Ten rain.

Wilma did well for us. We knew how to handle her, how to play the choke for the first fifteen minutes to keep the engine running – because if the engine ever stopped during that critical time frame it would never start again. We had weekends in Bala and Llanbedr, of course, still unable to break the stranglehold these places held on us, but we had to avoid hills; with a trailer-full of camping gear Wilma would not go up hills, and we often had to modify our routes. When we were coming home, and our gear was wet, Wilma struggled on the level and we had to pick routes that were mainly downhill, and this was kind of inconvenient. There was something else, too. The driver's door fell off. It wasn't all that critical, because I put it back, locked it, and used the passenger door, climbing over the seats for access. It was annoying, though, and we became conscious of the clock ticking on the MOT. We knew we wouldn't be paying for a second term, because Wilma's days were numbered. We needed more pulling power.

I tried a different tactic in selling Wilma. We had time, tax and a still-valid MOT on our side. I took her to the auctions. I parked her tight-in to the fence so that the lad who was to drive her through the auction room had no choice but to climb in on the passenger side. I'd never been to a car auction before and I found the whole experience fascinating.

There was a concrete building with a barn-door opening at each end through which the cars and the icy February wind were driven. The auctioneer on a high, Calor-gas-heated podium maintained a steady patter as bids came and went.

"Ford Escort. Full service history. Two-month MOT. B plate. What am I bid? Will anyone give me twenty?"

Nobody moved.

"Thank you, sir. Twenty-five. Thirty. Thirty-five... Any more for any more?"

Bang went the gavel.

"Your car, sir."

I hadn't seen a single bid. I stood in terror, not daring to scratch at any of the fiery itches that seemed to blossom all over my body. Car after car went through this surreal performance.

Then came Wilma.

"Surprising Skoda, nice-looking motor. No history but a full three months on the MOT. Who'll give me twenty?" He was quite chipper, quite positive. I almost felt like bidding.

Then the lad in the car broke the spell. He opened the driver's door. The door fell onto the concrete with an impressive crash. The lad rolled out after it. Wilma lurched, then stalled. There was silence in the room for a second or two, then...

Bang! Down came the gavel. The auctioneer couldn't speak

for laughing, he just waved the car out. Everyone was laughing. The lad jumped to his feet and willing helpers rushed to assist. They threw the door into the back seat and pushed Wilma out of the auction room.

I still had a car. I had three months left on the tax and MOT to find a replacement.

We paid five hundred pounds, by far the most we'd ever spent on a motor vehicle. It was a fifteen-year-old VW Golf. We called the car *Hitler's Revenge*, though not immediately; we needed a few weeks, first, for it to thoroughly disappoint us. Wilma and I went for our last drive together, to the scrap yard in Birkenhead Docks.

Our first outing in the new car lacked imagination but there was plenty of adventure. We strapped the children into the back of the *Revenge* and again headed off to Sarah's parents' caravan in Llanbedr.

From our home on the Wirral, Llanbedr is a distance of about 70 miles. They are not fast miles, and in the past we have usually taken about two and a half to three hours to complete the trip. On this occasion it would be somewhat longer. We broke down for the first time before we'd even reached Wales. It wasn't very dramatic, the engine just went silent and the car glided to a halt. I opened the bonnet and peered inside. It's funny how people do this, it seems better than just sitting at the side of the road and moaning, but invariably the bonnet-lift is an equally pointless exercise. Maybe one day I'll look under the bonnet and see a wire, marked "IMPORTANT", just hanging loose, with an obvious and accessible place for it be reconnected – but it hasn't happened to me yet. I looked under the bonnet and there was the engine. It seemed to be all there. I jiggled a few wires, shrugged, and climbed back into the car. I turned the key and it started. It sounded good. I felt very pleased with myself.

"What did you do?" Sarah asked, clearly impressed.

"Must have been a loose ignition lead," I blagged.

Should have been honest. Should have turned the car for home.

We continued on our way.

The next time we broke down was just outside the village of Hawarden. Same routine. Same result, though this time I didn't look quite so cocky. This time I *really* should have turned the car around.

We'd gone maybe another five miles before it happened again. Sarah suggested we call the RAC.

"The road's too narrow here," I said. "It's not a safe place to wait. I'll see if I can get it going again and we'll stop at the next safe place."

The car did start again, so we carried on to a lay-by that was maybe ten miles farther down the road and pulled in. I switched off the engine and we thought about it for a while. There was no phone; car phones were still only used by doctors and drug dealers. And we hadn't passed a call box anywhere. Ahead lay the Llandegla moors. They are nothing in a normal car, but in this car they were forbidding.

"I think we should go back," Sarah said. (I hate it when she's right.)

"I think we'll be okay," I said. "Let me have a look under the bonnet again."

Still no dangling wire.

The engine started happily enough, and we pressed on. We cleared the moors. We stopped twice more, but each time a short rest and a quick engine inspection proved to be enough to tease out a few extra miles. Two things were becoming apparent, though: the distance travelled between each breakdown was diminishing; and with each leg of the journey we were getting further from home.

We reached Bala after four hours. Four hours! Bala's a two hour run on the worst of bad days, and we were only a little over halfway to our destination.

The children, having been strapped into their seats all this time, were making it clear that they had had enough. So I turned into the large lakeside car park on the edge of the town; somewhere for them to run and play and get very wet, and where there was a phone. We sent the children into the lake and I called the RAC.

The car park beside the lake at Bala is very pleasant. The water was as smooth and reflective as liquid mercury. The view across the lake towards the summit of Aran Fawddwy was stunning. (I still vow to climb to the top one day.) The children played and got wet and I wondered what the hell we were doing. Why is the tent in the loft? Why didn't we bring it? We could have erected the tent beside the lake, then, stuff the car and the RAC and the stress, we could have stayed here. It would have been lovely.

The RAC man arrived after an hour. I explained our position. He looked unimpressed, turned the ignition key and the car started.

"Seems okay to me," he said.

I smiled patiently. Yes, it did seem okay, but I knew it wouldn't stay that way for long.

"I'll let it run for a while."

For fifteen minutes we stood, side by side, and watched the engine run.

"Getting a bit hot," he said. "Electric fan's not cutting in.

Must be that. It needs a new switch."

I nodded. I was unhappy. He didn't sound convinced at his own diagnosis. I was certainly far from convinced. I'd have been more confident in his reasoning if he'd told me that the problem was worn pedal rubbers. If it had been the fan, then the engine would be hot. It wasn't. I didn't have an engine that was hot and steaming, I had an engine that had stopped. But I was young, and I regarded RAC men as being in that same omniscient club as doctors and financial advisors. They told you stuff; you nodded; you did as you were told; you went back for more advice a week later when the first advice proved flimsy.

In this case we went back for more advice just half an hour later, calling from a car park just outside Dolgellau.

We waited for another hour, and the same man came back.

"Hmm," he said, and got his tool box out.

He removed the carburettor and stripped it down.

"Ahh, look. It's full of shi—" he looked at Sarah "—dirt. There's your problem."

It looked spotless to me. He cleaned it out, though. He checked the fuel lines, checked the ignition. He found nothing else but sounded positive, and I believed him. He fired up the engine, stood back and rubbed his hands on a rag.

"There we go," he said. "That's got it."

How did he know? The car always started when it had been standing for a while, but, as I say, I was young in those days, though ageing rapidly as the day wore on. He jumped into his van and roared off into the distance.

We continued. We stopped. We'd managed maybe fifteen minutes of driving this time. I waited for about five minutes and started the car again. It fired, as always, and I did the maths.

I could call the RAC every time we stopped, wait for them for an hour, then watch our friend do something utterly ineffective for a further thirty minutes so that we could set off on the next fifteen minute leg; or, I could simply park up for a few minutes each time the car failed, let it recover, then continue on our way.

We drove. We stopped. Drove, stopped. Always when we stopped it was in the narrowest, most dangerous stretch of road. We would slink down low in the car, waiting out the recovery time by enduring endless car horns, hand gestures and verbal abuse from the passing motorists as they came boogieing around the blind corners to find our little VW parked in the road.

In the back of the car the children – bored, tired and still wet from the lake – cried and fought. In the front Sarah and I argued and raged. It was not a good journey.

We arrived in Llanbedr and the caravan was waiting for us where Sarah's parents had left it. No struggling with canvas. No arguing over mismatched tent poles. We simply got out of the car and into the 'van, and it was lovely. All we had to worry about was how we were going to get back home. But we had a week, and I had my tools, and we had reached our destination – we were on our holidays. We had a nice cup of tea and a digestive. Things seemed much brighter.

I tried everything. I stripped down the carburettor. I followed the RAC man's regimen and eradicated every trace of the noxious substance called shi-dirt. I checked the points, the high-tension leads. I tested for a spark. Everything seemed fine. Indeed everything *was* fine, for about ten miles on each test run. For days I worked at it. As the end of the holiday loomed I began to accept that I was facing defeat. I needed an expert. We went into Barmouth for the day – only breaking down once – and, with high hopes, left the car in the hands of a mechanic.

We had good reason to be hopeful. The mechanic was optimistic.

"Easy," he said. "I'll have her fixed up in a jiffy."

Six hours later, we were sick of Barmouth. We knew every shop and back street.

We walked across the railway bridge that crosses the estuary; a pleasant walk on a fine day – but our day wasn't fine. We were worried. We worried about what we'd do if the car couldn't be fixed. We worried about what we'd do if the car was fixed, but we couldn't pay the garage bill. We had no lunch. We didn't dare spend the money.

At about four o'clock we took to hanging around the garage like petrol-head groupies. The car was still up on the ramps. I paced like an expectant father. Six hours. What were they doing to it? What was it going to cost? At last my resolve snapped. I couldn't stand any more. I marched into the office.

"Ah, there you are," the mechanic said. "I wondered where you'd got to. Finished hours ago. I'll get it down off the ramp for you."

I asked if he'd had any luck.

"Oh yeah, no problem," he said. "I stripped down the carb and blew out all the jets. Runs like a dream now it does." He charged me just eleven pounds. I felt like running a victory lap.

We drove back to the caravan without so much as a stutter. I had worked all through the week on that car. We'd been charged just eleven pounds by the garage. Why the hell hadn't I taken it to a garage on day one? Now the holiday was as good as over. The next day we would be going home.

The next day we got almost as far as Dolgelleau before breaking down. I didn't bother calling out the RAC this time, so, without all that waiting around, it only took us six and a half hours to get home.

Postscript: For those of a mechanical bent, who are dying to know what was wrong, the problem turned out to be muck in the fuel tank. As fuel was sucked up into the pipe leading to the engine, the muck would all be drawn around the filter, just above the bottom of the tank, until the fuel pump could suck no more. So the car stopped. Then, with the engine stopped and the fuel pump no longer sucking, the muck sensed liberty and floated away, so after a few minutes' rest the car would happily start again.

With much help from my father-in-law, once we were back home, I drained the tank dry, replaced the filter, and the problem never recurred. Mind you, now that the car could go more than ten or fifteen miles in one stretch, all of the other insurmountable defects began to reveal themselves: The oil-burning from damaged pistons, the un-repairable mistracking that caused the front tyres to polish-up to baby's bottom smoothness in mere weeks, and on and on. I took the car to the auctions a month or so later and was amazed to be offered fifty pounds from a shifty individual who was lurking in the car park before the auction even started. I was honest. I said to him, "It's not a very good car, you know," but he waved me off and handed me the cash. There was a gleeful look in his eye that suggested he thought he'd just pulled off a wondrous con.

Two days later I received a call from the police; was I still the owner of a VW Golf that had been found abandoned at the side of the M56?

I smiled.

"No," I said. "Not anymore."

I looked at the fifty pounds still sitting on the bookcase. No, I hadn't been conned.

We swapped the fifty quid for a brown car. We didn't have it long enough to form any kind of lasting relationship this time, but I remember it was brown, and it worked.

So to celebrate, we took the tent away for another few days at our favourite weekend retreat near Bala. The forecast was good and turned out to be correct. We had a fine evening sitting outside the tent sipping tea and admiring the view.

It was round about this time that I changed jobs. I saw dark clouds gathering in the bus scheduling world when the company began to lease time on a computer. A device called a VDU was wheeled into the office. It looked like a typewriter with a TV attached, a TV that only did green numbers. We called it Deep Thought, and put a Dymo label name badge on it. Here was a machine that did most of our work for us. It wasn't a very good computer, and nobody knew how to use it properly, but month after month it got smarter and faster all on its own, and it became obvious that the time to change careers had arrived.

I became an accountant. I still worked for the same company, who graciously let me move into the finance department and enter a profession for which I was woefully unqualified. I even got paid a little more. The downside to the career change was that I had to study and try to become a real accountant, when I realised that I could only fake it for so long. The study was hard and meant that my early (and so far unpublished) dalliance with Science Fiction writing had to go on hold.

Weekends became even more precious, but now I had to take study material away with me. What better learning environment though, than sitting at a camp table, surrounded by greenery, bathed in sunshine, with only the sound of tweeting birds to disturb me. Success in accountancy was assured.

August Bank Holiday loomed, and we thought, what about the Lledr Valley? We'd never been before. We had a painting on our landing that we'd bought cheap from the market, and it showed a shepherd lad looking down into the Lledr Valley. It looked lovely. A perfect setting for quietude and study. We found a site at Dolwyddelan Castle, booked, and straight after work on Friday evening I scribbled a note to the milkman, cancelling the milk, and we headed into Wales. The children were excited to be camping in the grounds of a castle, Sarah was excited to paint the castle and I was excited to be getting away in the tent again. We'd had a few bummy weekends as regards the weather, and we felt that maybe we were due a good one.

We arrived at the castle just as evening began turning into premature night. Black clouds were gathering over the mountains. The site owner gave us some advice:

"The camping field's on a bit of a slope, and it's a bit damp. I wouldn't take your car down there or you might never get it back up again. I suggest you unhook your trailer and wheel it down the hill by hand."

Now, you may ask, why, under such circumstances would you even consider going down the hill? Why not stay up at the top? A good question; one without a terribly sensible answer. Ok, the top of the field was really for caravans, and although none were there and none were expected we felt that, as campers, we should place ourselves well away from the cosseted hard-standing caravan area – that would not have been, well, uncomfortable or difficult enough for us. We began lowering our trailer down the slope in scenes reminiscent of *The Pride and the Passion*. (You know, that 1957 film where Frank Sinatra, Cary Grant and a cast of thousands drag this huge, unwieldy cannon across the mountains and valleys of Spain.) All the time we struggled we were conscious of the implications of letting it get away from us and having to watch our worldly goods go barrelling down the hill and into the stream below.

We achieved our mission without incident, parked the trailer across the slope of the hill, and started to unload. The trailer kept trying to turn and head south, so Sarah held it while I unloaded, then, in fear of being crushed in the night, I dragged it back up the hill and re-attached it to the car in the car park.

We started to erect the tent. We worked slowly and were quite laid-back at first, but then moved with increasing urgency as the clouds above thickened and boiled. We knew bad cloud formations – we'd seen a lot of them lately – and these looked *bad*.

The first spots of rain started to fall just as we got the last of the pegs in, so everything else, still scattered around the field in black bin bags, we gathered and tossed into the tent. I shouted at the children to come up from playing in the stream. They ignored me. I shouted again, louder, but it proved unnecessary – the first lightning bolt and clap of thunder arrived simultaneously. I saw the children's wide-eyed, open-mouthed faces lit by the lightning flash. The next moment they were fleeing up the hill towards us. Several more flashes and bangs exploded in the valley before they reached the tent.

Dolwyddelan Castle is really just the wrecked central keep of the original fortress. The outer walls are long gone. What remains is an imposing slab-like block standing high against the sky – and when lit by forked lightning it is eerily reminiscent of a gothic scene from Dracula.

The children scurried past me into the tent, but I stayed outside for a while to admire the drama of the light show. It was trying to rain, but up until now it had only managed the odd tennis-ball-sized raindrop. Another crackling, crashing artillery barrage ripped across the sky. It was a noise that made the ancient Welsh mountainside beneath my feet shake. Then the rain came; still the size of tennis balls, but now there were lots of them. The drops crowded the sky until there was no more room and they merged into a contiguous mass of moving water.

I ducked into the tent and zipped it up. Three wide-eyed, wet-eyed, horror-struck people ran to me and held me tight. I could feel them shaking. With each flash, bleaching the very pigment from the tent's canvas, they screamed, their faces a frozen-in-time blue-green tableau of terror.

Between each stab of light was darkness. *Total* darkness. And here was the thing – our lighting system for night time was a fluorescent tube, hung from a tent pole, powered by... the car battery. The car was in the car park at the top of the hill. Nothing in the tent was organised. We stood on wet grass, in the dark, amid heaps of anonymous black bin bags, visible only during each fleeting lightning burst, and visible to my eyes alone, because Sarah and the children had theirs covered. We couldn't communicate and discuss what to do, because the rain on the tent was a constant Niagaran roar, loud enough to obliterate all sound, except for the thunder and the screaming.

Groping around in the dark, assisted by the odd retina-burning flash, I hunted for the bin bag that contained the groundsheet, and had to open half the bags before finding it. Sarah realised what I was doing, and came to help, and we struggled to unfold the tarp and lay it out beneath the pile of bin bags. To do this it was necessary to move all the bags into a heap at one end, lay out half the groundsheet, then move the bags back onto the bit I'd laid, so that I could flatten out the rest of it. Only then would we have dry ground beneath our feet. Then again, the rain was so heavy, and we were on such a slope, that soon the water that had been coursing down the grassy slope began coursing across the top of our groundsheet.

We struggled on into the night; me cursing, Sarah and the children screaming and weeping. It was slow work, but by midnight we had an inner tent erected, an airbed inflated, and our bin bags were now heaped inside this new, still-dry inner sanctum. We huddled into our sleeping bags.

Still the rain hammered down. We could hear it lapping and gurgling across the groundsheet. Every few seconds came a crash and flash of thunder and lightning that echoed on and on around the valley. Sleep eluded us all. You only become fully aware of the vertiginous angle on which you've foolishly pitched once you're trying to sleep. Every movement sent us slithering together, down the slope, to the bottom of the tent. Being encased in canvas also makes you feel blinded as to what is really going on outside. Apart from the sounds, that seem doubly amplified, your imagination plays a part, painting graphic pictures of the probable state of affairs in the outside world. Imagination is really good at scenarios like flooding, mud-slides and electrocution from falling power lines.

So we fretted, awake, throughout the long night.

Morning came late, because, although the thunder storm eventually passed, the rain didn't. The rain got worse, occasionally turning to flurries of hail that bounced onto the roof of the tent like quarry stones, scaring the bejesus out of us.

Breakfast was a miserable affair. The milk was gone, probably the carton had been washed down into the stream with many of the other things we had not brought into the inner tent with us. We chowed down on cornflakes, sprinkled with Marvel powdered milk, and with water poured on top. Happy holidays.

We packed and went home.

Sounds easy in a simple sentence. It avoids details. Details like retrieving the trailer from the top of the hill; chucking everything in, whether in bags or not – everything was wet anyway. It avoids telling the heroic tale of our man-hauling the trailer back up the slick, muddy hill, a trailer now loaded with not only our tent and belongings, but also with about 50 gallons of Welsh water that had permeated everything. Then, our miserable journey home in a car full of steam and despondency. I'll even avoid telling of the massive cost of paying for three nights at a rate that included entrance to a castle that we only saw fleetingly as a storm-lit gothic silhouette. So, I'll keep the narrative simple.

We packed and went home.

We were home by Saturday lunchtime. We'd been away for just seventeen hours. I did my studying in the oppressive wet heat of the airing cupboard that doubled as an office.

Our final outing that year, a last-ditch stand against the elements, was to a small site in Llandudno. It was a pleasant enough site; a long garden with a duck pond at the bottom. Amanda was quite taken with the ducks, and gave them most of the bread for our breakfast toast.

Once again we got rain. Lots of rain. Our tent went into a sulk, conceded the battle, and began allowing rainwater to pass through without so much as slowing it down. When morning dawned, everything inside the tent was floating, and at some time during the night the ducks had swum in to take shelter and to eat the rest of our breakfast.

Again we packed and returned home after only one night. Andy, the milkman, greeted us the next morning with a pointed finger and howls of laughter. I laughed with him. It was funny. It was beyond belief.

But we'd had enough. We'd had enough of rain. We'd had enough of holidays. We'd had enough of camping.

The tent went into the loft.

"No more," I said. "Stuff it."

We had all that equipment, though. We'd been camping for years, and you acquire stuff. I looked for solutions. I thought about a trailer tent. We'd moved house in recent years (it had actually proved cheaper to move to a better house than to have our roof replaced; the slates were all loose and were now as resistant to water as Twinings tea-bags). Our new home had a lawned front garden; plenty of room to store a trailer tent. We went to look at some and became quite excited. It's still camping, but you get to sleep up in the air away from the cold wet ground, and the tent is pre-packed in a good roomy trailer. It seemed perfect, but then again, it was still canvas. I thought of all that rain, and noise at night.

Sarah, remember, was, from an early age, a caravanner. "Why don't we just buy a caravan?" she said.

I laughed. "Can't be done. No way. The cost!" I was adamant. "Besides, it's cheating. It's not camping."

It was a regular feature of our conversations throughout that autumn. I threw up all kinds of reasonable objections, Sarah countered them with all kinds of reasonable solutions, but the one obstacle, the one thing that Sarah could not counter, was the matter of cost. We simply could not afford a caravan. Finances weren't so bad as they used to be. I'd started passing exams and my pay was gradually beginning to reflect this. We even had some savings. It all boiled down to this, though: There are three groups. There are campers, there are posh campers, and there are caravanners. We still barely made it into group one.

Then on a gloomy Sunday in November, Sarah looked up from the local paper.

"There's a new caravan dealership opened in Moreton," she said. "Why don't we go and have a look around."

"It'll just get us depressed," I said.

"Maybe, but we'll get over it," she said. "Besides, it'll give us an idea just how far we really are from being able to afford a caravan. If they're way out of our league then we'll know for sure, and we can take our five-hundred-pound savings and buy a trailer tent, and we'll be happy with it."

It made sense, though I remained sceptical. I was still a camper. Caravan dealerships were enemy territory; a place for the weak and the pampered. I would have no truck with caravanning.

We walked through the gate of Moreton caravans and on seeing the four-figure price tag on the first row of 'vans I was ready to leave.

"See," I said. "Look at the price of these..."

I stopped.

I'd seen it.

Sarah saw the look in my eye even before she saw the caravan. An old Sprite Alpine. Five hundred and fifty pounds. I walked over to it and peered through the window expecting to see wreckage and mushrooms.

But it looked okay.

"Would you like to have a look inside?" The salesman had materialised beside my left shoulder.

"We might as well," I said, "but I don't suppose it's up to much."

I tried to sound nonchalant, but my stomach was churning with butterflies. Okay, so what if it was a mess inside. I could fix it up. When you've lived on nothing for years you get to know how to fix things up. We stepped inside. I expected to be overwhelmed by the mulchy smell of damp and mildew. But there was nothing. Outside it was a cold damp day; inside it was... cosy.

"Hmm," I said. "It's very small." This might be an insurmountable problem. We had two children.

"It is," the salesman said. "It's only twelve foot. Tiny by today's standards, but it is a four berth."

"What?" I was shocked. I had been thinking about how we might try to modify it to squeeze all four of us in.

"Oh yes," he said. "You drop the dining table between the two front bunks to make a double"—he demonstrated—"then you raise this post above the side bunk and pull out these tubes, so..." And before our very eyes there was a third and a fourth bunk.

Four berth.

"The thing is," he said, "We took this in part-ex, yesterday. It's taking up space on the forecourt and we're expecting the new models in any day now. Look, if you are interested I could let you have it for five hundred. Oh, and it comes with an awning."

Sarah looked at me, imploring me, her eyes dancing.

I smiled.

TRAVELLING IN A BOX: 1994

"Tiredness can Kill. Take a Break"

It's a fine sentiment, but in Britain it's every sort of flawed, especially if you are towing a caravan. Britain has motorway services every thousand miles, or so it seems. If you want good motorway services it's further. I know of only two or three that I would call good on the entire motorway network.

The signposting, once off the motorway, is at best cryptic, and you are given just one shot at figuring it all out. One chance. Get it wrong – miss that teeny, obscure little caravan symbol tucked away at the bottom of a totem pole that sways under the weight of obscure and irrelevant signage, and bam! Out you go, back onto the motorway. There's nowhere to turn, no second chance, nowhere to pause and regroup, nowhere to take your full-to-bursting bladder; you're just straight out and back on the road. Then it's another thousand miles before you get another single-shot chance at salvation. And if you miss that one...

—No. 27 from the Moanicles of Michael

It was the longest winter I can remember. Sitting on the grass outside the house was our wonderful new caravan. We spent a few weeks putting our mark on it – a new carpet, new curtains, a few minor repairs – but essentially it was ready to go. *We* were ready to go. Now okay, your modern caravan can be a cosy little home from home in early December, and there are many caravanners who regularly go away in the winter. This was different. Our Sprite was a thirty-year-old antique. It had no heating, precious little insulation, single-glazed glass windows and a mains electric system that was still little more than a plan at the back of my mind. We might have tried it, but the snow drifts in the road kind of put us off.

So we waited.

We let Christmas distract us. We waited throughout the post-Christmas poverty hole. January and February crawled past, and then, with March, came an early Easter.

We packed.

We didn't know where to go for Easter. We didn't want to go far on our first caravan outing. We knew plenty of tent-only fields, but we weren't so clued up on sites that allowed caravans. An old campsite book turned up a site near Llangollen. Only an hour away. Perfect.

The approach to the site is a white-knuckle ride, involving a near-vertical road up to and over a hump-backed canal bridge, a narrow single-track road and finally a long, steep, ear-popping drag up a monster of a hill. A wonderful introduction to caravan towing; but we managed it, the car managed it, we didn't meet any combine harvesters on the way (unlikely in March, but with us you never know), and the location was truly worth the sweating, the cursing and the cardiac stresses.

We pulled into the farmyard that leads into the site and made ourselves known at reception. The field, we were told, was very muddy and we'd have to be towed onto our pitch by the farmer in his tractor. The car would have to remain in the farmyard for the weekend – if we strayed onto the field with the car we'd sink. So, we unhitched the caravan, parked the car in the yard and waited. Soon enough the farmer roared into the yard atop a colossal Massey Ferguson; he backed up to the 'van and I hitched up.

"Where d'you want her?" he asked.

The field was sloping, and a position near the top of the hill seemed as if it might afford the best view. I said so much, and the tractor growled out of the yard with our little 'van in tow. This was the point where I noticed that the handbrake of our new home from home was working well. I'd forgotten to release it. The wheels weren't going round. The tractor roared, the caravan skidded and bounced along behind. Once onto the field the huge tractor came into its own and made relatively light work of it, even though a mountainous bow-wave of mud was building up nicely in front of the stationary wheels. Once they reached the seriously steep part of the hill though, the tractor started to lose grip, and a solid spray of stinking black mud plumed up from the wheels and splattered the front of the 'van. By the time the 'van was at the top of the field it was caked.

"Aye-aye!" he shouted down to me as I crawled about in the filth trying to un-hitch. "Don't know what you've got in there, but I've had less trouble towing the plough up here." Then a dismissive wave and he was off.

Over the winter I'd read up on how to pitch caravans. Most of the tips about getting the 'van level, though, involved having it actually attached to a car. There we were, sitting at an angle you could ski down, and there was nothing we could do about it. The corner steadies on the down side of the hill were vertical so we had to cannibalise a dry-stone wall and build a pair of mini-mountains under each corner in order to give us any kind of stability. It was very stressful.

Still, we were on site. The view was fabulous. Ahead, sitting on top of a steep-sided mountain that rose straight up from the bottom of our field, stood the ghostly ruins of Castell Dinas Bran, wrapped in tendrils of cold white mist. Behind it was the dramatic limestone edge of the Eglwyseg escarpment. I loved it. I vowed that we'd climb up to both the castle and the escarpment before the weekend was out, whatever the weather. I stood outside the caravan door, warming myself around a cup of tea. I watched the children laughing and playing in the mud. I felt content. I had one last job to do before being able to strip off my agricultural clothing and go inside to cosiness and warmth. I had to connect the electrics. I'd fitted a mains hook-up system myself over the winter. We had no gas heating, but a mains hook-up would allow us a small fan heater, and on this cold March weekend such an item would be more of a necessity than a luxury. I reeled out our brand new, twenty-five metre, gleaming orange hook-up wire, which was instantly sucked down into the black mud, and I plugged it in at the electric point.

I shouted to Sarah, "Try the fan heater!"

"Nothing!"

"You mustn't be doing it right!"

"It's a switch. It goes on or off. Give me some credit." She sounded a bit rattled.

"Try the light switch then." I was sure she was doing something wrong.

"Nope. It's not working. Didn't you check this before we came away?"

"Of course I checked it. It was working fine. I'm coming inside."

This wasn't easy, either. First I had to strip off my mud-plastered clothes, down to my underwear, all in the tight confines of the caravan doorway, and in the full face of the blasting icy wind.

The tricky part came when I began standing, heron-like, on one leg so I could free, first one, then the other of my feet. My trousers, stiff with caked mud, were wrapped around both ankles and wouldn't budge. I started to hop. A dainty little dance at first, but it gradually gathered momentum until I was jack-hammering and grunting around the caravan with scary, rotating arms. Things fell from shelves. Things smashed. Sarah watched me, open mouthed. She waited until I became an exhausted heap on the caravan floor. Then she threw me a tracksuit.

"Can you manage to put that on?" she asked. "Or is there something you haven't broken yet?"

I crawled under the end bunk to look at the RCD unit – the nerve centre for the electrics.

Everything seemed in order. The switches were thrown. The little red/green plastic tags that should show red, were showing red. I clicked the switches again just to be sure. Not a sausage. I stared at it. I shook my fist at it. It had all worked perfectly at home. I had been so proud. The job of fitting the system had been a difficult one that involved lots of unnatural contortions and swearing and bloodied fingers from errant Stanley knives, but it had worked, straight out of the box. No tinkering or head scratching had been required. I considered myself a genius of the electrical screwdriver. Now here's the thing with electricity; you can't see it. It just is... or in this case, isn't.

At home I had a nifty little electric test meter. I hadn't brought it. I had nothing to detect the flow of current other than perhaps by sticking my fingers down the socket, and I didn't fancy that.

Of course, we were only a short run from home. I could have been back in our driveway within forty minutes.

I just couldn't do it.

We'd come away on holiday. Psychologically it felt wrong to nip back home every few minutes for stuff we'd not thought to bring. The neighbours would lap it up. (In truth, the neighbours wouldn't have noticed, and even if they had they would certainly not have cared or even given it the slightest thought, but I had my pride.)

So, we accepted that, this weekend, we just wouldn't be quite as warm in the caravan as we'd hoped. Anyway, we were tent campers and we were here in a caravan. To campers this was still luxury.

We had our evening meal. It was fun. The dinner plates kept sliding down the Formica table top and onto our laps; caused in part by our precarious angle on the hillside and also by the buffeting motion from the angry wind that had started life in the afternoon as nothing more than a cold, searching breeze.

We were tough campers, but we went to bed early. Because we were cold.

As usual the children went straight to sleep and we didn't. We shivered. The wind howled and grew into a bruiser of a gale. Things crashed and broke; things that I'd missed during my earlier destructive de-trousering. Things crashed and splintered down in the farmyard. Big things, like buildings and trees! The caravan pitched and heaved and felt as if it might soon take us tobogganing down the muddy slope. The air became colder. In the light of our torches we could see our breath. We'd had all of this before, of course. We were well used to it. But what was new; what we'd never experienced before was the movement. In a tent, whatever the elements throw at you, you are on the ground, and on the whole, in our corner of northern Europe, the ground doesn't move much. This, on the other hand, was like being out in the North Atlantic. The swaying, the creaking, the wind – vicious and erratic. Three times I was sent outside with the torch to check that we weren't beginning to slide down the hill. From outside, the suggestion seemed ridiculous, there was no visible movement at all. The caravan seemed to be, if not level, then at least stable. Inside, though, we could feel rolling, heaving movement with every new blast.

The night stretched on and on. Perhaps we got some sleep; it can't have been much. We had sleeping bags, blankets, jumpers, coats, all the socks we owned, and still we froze.

In the morning everything was white.

It looked lovely. Dinas Bran Castle looked like an illustration from a Christmas card. Snow lay drifted against its ruined walls. Our field was an unspoiled empty canvas. I hopped out of bed – my head wrapped in veils of my own misty breath – and went to fill the kettle for a nice warm cup of tea. I stomped on the water pump (a twelve-volt unit with a foot switch on the floor by the sink) and nothing happened. A quick look outside at the water container confirmed that the water had frozen. I turned on the gas hob anyway; so as to maybe warm the caravan a little. It didn't work. We were using butane, and butane does not work much below zero, and it was *well* below zero.

So we stayed in bed. We stayed in bed until after the sun came up and warmed the gas bottles. Every half-hour or so one of us would hop out of bed and try the gas again. The children woke and became restless and complained of the cold. I told them to stay where they were – it was the warmest place.

The gas came online at about ten. By a stroke of luck we had a kettle full of ice left over from our supper, and, over a period of thirty minutes or so, we managed to coax it into becoming a pot of hot tea. I have always loved books and films about climbing in the Alps and the Himalayas. The Eiger. Everest. K2... and now here I was, clinging to the side of Dinas Bran, melting ice for sustenance. This was just like having my own "death zone" adventure, but without all the inconvenience of first having to slog up twenty thousand feet of rock and ice.

We had breakfast in a café in Llangollen and discussed strategy.

Another night like this was out of the question. I needed something with which I could test all the various circuits. We drove to Wrexham to visit B&Q, where I bought a cheap, simple-but-effective circuit tester. Back at the caravan I started work, beginning at the plug sockets and working backwards looking for any flicker of electrical activity. The sockets had no power. The RCD had nothing coming out or going in. The hook-up socket on the outside of the caravan showed nothing. I disconnected the hook-up wire from the caravan and tested it. Nothing. The fault must be in the wire. I disconnected the hook-up wire at the electric point end and checked it for continuity. It worked fine. Live, neutral, earth. Each was perfect. Maybe something had been loose. I connected everything up again and tried the electrics once more. Nothing. So I went through the whole checking performance again until, once more, I was at the electric point. A thought occurred to me: was any power coming out of the campsite's electric hook-up point? I stuck the point of the meter into the live hole and eureka, nothing.

"You having a problem?" It was the farmer, walking past with a bale of hay for his sheep.

I was fuming.

"Problem?" I said, my voice loaded with sarcasm. "No, not really. Just a night of having my nuts frozen off in Antarctic conditions because the bloody hook-up I've paid for doesn't work!"

The farmer looked puzzled. "Should be okay," he said.

He leaned over the socket, then took hold of the plug and

twisted it.

"You haven't switched it on," he said. "See?"

He pointed to the Dymo label above the socket that said, "Twist to the right to connect."

"It's a safety feature. Stops the little darlings sticking their fingers in it and electrocuting themselves. Most adults manage to figure out how it works though."

He tugged the rim of his cap in greeting, hoisted the straw bale back onto his shoulder and left me standing in the field, feeling as though I'd just grown a donkey's head.

The Easter weekend went better after that. We climbed up to Dinas Bran Castle. It's not a hard climb, though it's quite steep in places, and once you're on the uphill section the effort is relentless. The castle stands right on top of an isolated hill. It isn't high, it's just a mound sitting on the valley floor. On a map it is insignificant, but Dinas Bran is singular and impressive. Seen from below, from any direction, Dinas Bran is imposing. Back in the days when the castle was more than a heap of rocks, it would have been an intimidating sight to anyone with ambitions of conquest.

The views from the top are stunning, and on that cold Easter Day, after the overnight snow had carpeted the mountains and the valley floor with a frosting of white, all of our travails thus far receded into insignificance.

The wind was fierce, though. It was the kind of wind that could easily find its way through the weave of your woolly hat and freeze your ears off. So we didn't hang about. Below us, Llangollen looked snug and cosy nestling in the valley with a layer of protective mist that hinted at welcoming wood fires and tea shops.

We made haste. There was an abundance of tea shops. We

found one that was steamy and warm and made our toes, fingers and cheeks hurt as each slowly came back to life. We had tea and scones and it was wonderful.

It snowed again in the night, but this time we were warm. The little fan heater chugged away, and we were amazed at how quickly it made the caravan cosy and comfortable. Now we were cooking. Now we were *caravanners*.

THE CLUBS: 1994

So, you pull into the motorway services, and this time you spot the sign for caravan parking and, avoiding the foot-high concrete kerbs, you head off into the wilderness that is the caravan parking area. Do they allow you to park close to the facilities? Do you have line of sight from the restaurant so you can spot if anyone's trying to winch your 'van and possessions onto the back of a low-loader? Not a chance. Welcome to planet caravan. The lost world. A place where you exist at the very bottom of the motorway food chain. You get to park with the sixteen-wheelers. You get to wade through a cocktail of urine and derv on your long trek to the facilities. You try to unwind in the restaurant, while, at the back of your mind, there is that nagging awareness of the statistic that nearly one hundred caravans per week are stolen, and that yours, right now, is tucked out of sight between Eddie Stobart and Norbert Dentressangle, where any number of n'er-do-wells are free to compete for your possessions. So you relax and unwind? Like hell you do. You storm through the necessities – toilet, coffee and sandwich to-go — so that you can rush back to your car and 'van, praying that the brigands are having a slow day.

So now you finish your coffee, sitting bolt upright in your car, while Eddie's and Norbert's thumping multi-litre turbo intercooler power units tick over on either side, one in each ear, processing the air into a choking, toxic blue haze. You keep your windows closed. The July sun greenhouses through the windscreen and the temperature inside your car steadily climbs into regions that would have you thrown into jail if any of your passengers happened to be dogs.

Now you try to gulp down your scalding hot coffee before Argos or Asda, or Tesco or Texaco, park their juggernauts across the narrow gap ahead, thus compelling you to perform the dreaded reverse manoeuvre out of this thirty-two wheel polluted canyon from hell.

Take a break? Fat chance.

—No. 28 from the Moanicles of Michael

The May bank holiday weekend was hot. We took the caravan to Llanbedr, scene of so many camping adventures in the past. We stayed in a field beside the stream. The children loved it. They spent much of the weekend falling in the stream. It was very shallow but somehow they both managed to get every item of clothing they possessed soaking wet within the first hour. They managed to stay wet for the whole weekend without getting too wrinkly.

The site was good. It was very quiet – we were the only ones staying on it, but somehow it lacked something. Perhaps it was our having to walk half a mile up the steep lane for water from the only tap. Or maybe it was our having to dig a hole to dispose of the chemical toilet waste. We had a feeling that, just maybe, we might be able to do better. Granted, the site was very cheap, but did it have to be quite so basic?

So we thought about joining one of the Camping/ Caravanning Clubs.

Now I must digress at this point with a little explanation. There are two major clubs for caravanners in Britain; the Camping and Caravanning Club and the Caravan Club. To save ink I'll call them the CCC and the CC.

There are strong feelings of loyalty and competitiveness

within each club, members of each believing that theirs is the best. The CCC is "the friendly club" and allows tent campers; the CC seemed bigger, though I don't really know for sure.

Sarah and I are now members of both clubs, and I have to say that both clubs feel friendly, and both clubs have a relaxed atmosphere and offer a wide network of sites. I make this clear so that there's no sense of partisanship in what I have to say. We joined the CCC, initially, because we had only just migrated from camper to caravanner, and we had done so on the most precarious financial basis. We were unsure, at this stage, as to how long we might remain caravanners, so it seemed logical to choose the club that would permit us to return to canvas should the need arise. As our finances improved we didn't feel any temptation to switch, we stayed with the CCC because it is excellent, and later we joined the CC as well because it is also excellent, and now, as members of both clubs, we have a *huge* network of sites from which to choose.

So I hope that's clear. I don't want any wars over this.

Back to the story. We joined the Camping and Caravanning Club. We got a map, a monthly magazine, a copy of YBSB (Your Big Sites Book) and a glossy book showing all the club-owned sites, called *Your Place in the Country*.

We wanted to try a club site so we went to Bakewell in the Peak District.

The site is called "Bakewell", but it's actually located a few miles from the eponymous town; it's near a village called Youlgreave. We set out not knowing what to expect at all. We found our way to Youlgreave, then followed the directions that told us to take a right turn before the church, and at first you wonder what on earth you're letting yourself in for. From the village the road looks narrow and steep, once on the road you realise that, yes, it is narrow, and it is very steep, running down into Bradford Dale where it crosses the Bradford River over a narrow bridge. You wonder how the hell you are ever going to get back up that hill, but at this point it's hypothetical because there is nothing you can do about it; you've no chance of turning round and no way can you reverse. The entrance to the site is a farm gate that opens onto an even narrower rutted farm track. This runs for about three-quarters of a mile with few passing places, and with a caravan in tow, meeting another caravan coming the other way would leave you with some seriously limited options. As we crawled along the track in first gear, praying that we would meet nothing coming the other way, we wondered if we'd done the right thing this weekend.

Then we came to the site and we knew instantly that we had done the right thing. The CCC site at Youlgreave is wonderful. It's on quite a slope, so some pitches require a bit of care levelling the 'van, but it's quiet and it's pastoral and it's the kind of place where you can just drop down into a camp chair with a cup of tea in your hand and just soak it all in. It is total countryside.

We signed in at reception, where we were given hints about walks in the dale, teashops to visit, places to eat. We pitched the caravan and then we relaxed.

The site is on a lush hillside, with a picturesque stone-built farm at the bottom of the slope. At the top there is a footpath leading through a stone crush-gate. (A crush-gate is a kind of stile that's common in the Peak District, comprising two vertical stone slabs between which a lean hiker can squeeze but, theoretically, a sheep cannot. Less-than-lean hikers such as myself can find them to be something of a challenge.) The path leads up the hill for about two hundred yards, where it crosses

111

a narrow lane and continues up on the other side. (The narrow lane, by the way, is the only road in the dale and it carries almost zero traffic. The site at Youlgreave is quiet!) The path continues to climb quite steeply through meadows, up to a stile over a wall at the top, and from here the view back down the valley is lovely.

I like to think of this as Rupert Bear country. I grew up with Rupert Bear annuals and I loved the way Rupert and his chums would return to Nutwood after each adventure, not by bus or car, not by climbing chain-link fences and sneaking through dodgy council estates, but by running, swooping, free as the wind, down grassy green meadows and gentle slopes that led to the village below. Youlgreave is Nutwood. On our first climb up the hill it was late evening after a balmy summer's day. The clock on the church tower was reflecting the sun's rich evening glow in a blaze of gold. That wonderful light you get on summer evenings – photographers call it a warm colour temperature – was everywhere. The trees in Bradford Dale were nut-brown and verdant green. The sky was thick and heavy with blue. At any moment I half-expected Rupert, in his bright red jumper and tasteless yellow-check trousers to go dashing past, Bill Badger in tow, to complete the colourful scene. Bradford Dale is that elusive, truly peaceful piece of England.

We visited the town of Bakewell. Bakewell is the home of Bakewell tarts, sorry, Bakewell puddings. If you've eaten Cherry Bakewells, the sort that come in six-packs, and so you believe that you have already sampled this town's culinary offerings, well, I'm sorry, you're not even close.

There are several shops all claiming to offer the original pudding recipe, and they are all quite similar. There's no icing, no cherry on the top, and they don't come in boxes, or nest in crinkly red plastic trays. They are ugly and deformed, and they start at about six inches diameter, and go up to, oh, twelve, maybe fifteen inches across. So, one assumes, being so large they must be light and should be eaten in quantity. So we bought a medium-sized pudding each and took them down to a river-side bench where the puddings would form part of our picnic.

The first thing you notice, and I've said it before, is they taste nothing like you'd expect. The first mouthful comes as a surprise, and one that you're not sure is very welcome. A second mouthful and, mmm, it's not the Bakewell tart you expected but, hey, it's... nice. Third mouthful... actually it's better than nice, it's delicious, and... you're full. And you can not, under any circumstances whatsoever, find room for more. So, we've bought about four square feet of Bakewell pudding between us, and we've eaten about two inches of it, and we're not the only ones. We notice half the tourists in the town are walking around with paper bags full of ninety-nine percent intact Bakewell puddings.

We took them back to the caravan with us. Two of the puddings lasted the weekend, the other two went home with us and saw out the following week. They were tasty though.

Last time we came to the Peak District we stumbled upon the Manifold Way, that superb, traffic-free cycle route that winds up from Hulme End to Waterhouses. This time we brought our bikes – but we didn't do the Manifold Way, because the Peak District in the early nineties was traffic-free-cycling heaven when other places weren't. Nearer to our site at Youlgreave was the Tissington Trail.

The Tissington Trail is a cycle trail on the track bed of a

disused railway line. We parked at Parsley Hey, once a station on the line, took the bikes down from the roof rack, and with picnics strapped to our backs we pedalled south.

The great thing about disused railway lines is they are flat – more or less. You can make excellent progress with a minimum of effort. It's a wonderful run. There are splendid views across the Peak, you are never alone because there are hundreds of other cyclists sharing the route, and with them comes that special atmosphere of camaraderie shared only by the "doers" of the world. By the "doers" I mean those that get out there. They cycle, ride horses, climb mountains, sail... All along the trail there are cafés and tea rooms; places to stop and eat, drink or picnic. They are all populated by friendly, cheerful doers, happily aware that this is a special place and it's just for them.

We continued on as far as the village of Tissington itself. We weren't tired. Riding on level railway tracks was easy, and we'd done nearly twelve miles in no time, but the problem with railway tracks is that they are straight. You have to turn round and go back. So we turned round and headed back, and you know it's a strange thing: although it felt flat riding south, going north felt, well, it felt a bit like it was uphill.

I've always thought of going north in a car as like going uphill, because it's "up" on the map. I know this is just a psychological thing. Well *this* was more a physiological thing, because my legs were aching. It wasn't just me – we were all going slower. The children were starting to complain; Sarah was starting to complain.

It dawned on us that on our outward leg we had, in fact been going imperceptibly downhill, and we'd done it for twelve miles. It wasn't enough of a gradient to actually freewheel or anything – at least not consciously – but now we were going the other way, if we stopped pedalling we stopped moving. The true cyclists amongst you will pour scorn on my complaints about twelve miles at such a slight gradient, but we were very much casual cyclists. It didn't so much hurt in the way that a slog up Alp d'Huez behind a Tour de France peloton would hurt, but it became a chore. It soon turned from a chore into a miserable, cheerless grind. The children whinged. I whinged. Sarah complained at us all to stop whinging. On we slogged, for mile after interminable mile.

We made it back though, and there's no real moral to this story, just a mental note to get fitter and make it fun the next time.

We tried a few more of the club sites that summer and we were well pleased with the result. Disturbed nights seemed to be a thing of the past. We were quite happy with this type of site because we didn't think of ourselves as "clubby" campers and had no desire to try any of the "meets" that were regularly advertised in the CCC's magazine. To a shy and inherently unsociable family such as ours they sounded dreadful.

Then I had a hankering to visit the Elan Valley.

Three things made me curious to visit Elan. Firstly, I'd seen adverts for coach trips, and although I knew nothing about the Elan Valley there's something magical in the name that suggests pastoral scenes of peace and tranquillity; secondly, I'd never been to that part of mid-Wales before and I have a hankering for new places; and thirdly, my parents had just come back from a weekend in the Elan Valley and had brought back hours of video showing roaring torrents of water cascading over a sequence of picturesque dams, and... pastoral scenes of peace and tranquillity.

There was a problem, though. We couldn't find a site nearby. There were a few commercial sites round about, but we'd been down the commercial road before and felt that we didn't need any more exhausting all-nighters. There was a Caravan Club site nearby, but, as yet, we weren't in the Caravan Club.

Then, plop; through the letterbox came the CCC magazine with its supplement the *Out and About*, chock-full of weekend meets and temporary holiday sites run by District Associations, or DAs.

We wouldn't normally dream of joining in with the DAs, the slightly eccentric clubbies, as we saw them, but there, in the temporary holiday site section, was a one-week meet in Rhayader, the gateway to the Elan Valley. We sent off for details of the meet, but we'd decided to try it even before the leaflets arrived by return of post.

It's a good journey to Rhayader from the Wirral. It's interesting, straightforward, and there isn't much traffic. So we arrived at Gigrin Farm, the location for the meet, about a mile south of the town, feeling unusually relaxed after the journey. We pulled through the gates into the rally field and stopped beside the steward's caravan to be signed in. It was all very friendly and civilised. We were given a brief run-down on where the facilities could be found. We handed over a tiny amount in site fees – we were staying a week and I felt the need to remind the steward of this in case he'd made a mistake.

"No, that's okay," he said. "You just pay for your pitch. Children are free." He seemed surprised that I found it all so inexpensive. "I suppose this is why so many families come to the holiday sites," he said. "They don't cost much."

I'd just handed him barely enough to see us through two nights on an official club site. We were staying here for a week, including a bank holiday; nine nights.

We found a good spot for the 'van, at the top of a slope looking down the field, with views across Rhayader and over to the mountains beyond. It was a lovely spot. We had the kettle on and our camp chairs outside in no time. Kevin and Amanda were gone. The farmer had laid on a straw-bounce for the children on the site.

"You know," I said. "I feel really relaxed."

"Yes, I do too," Sarah said. "It feels really... I don't know. Really comfortable here."

Sarah and I have developed a theory; it's all about ley lines. It's a theory that evolved that afternoon in Rhayader as we tried to understand the peculiarly wonderful sense of peace that is associated with this place. Things have been said about the mystic spiritual powers of ley lines and we really have come to believe that there is some force that invokes a sense of peace, or of stress, or of something in between, and it is tied to particular places. We started calling that force ley lines – just to give it a name. We've no idea if it has anything at all to do with the things that mystics have long called ley lines, but it proved to be a good way to describe how we felt about it. Now, Rhayader, the Elan Valley area in general, and Gigrin farm in particular, has very good ley lines. It is a profoundly relaxing and peaceful place. Go there. See if I'm not lying.

Tea time arrived and I roused myself from a zen-like trance and went to fetch the children. They'd made friends. They were covered in straw. They'd found a farm dog that had just given birth to a litter of puppies and they'd named them all. They were insanely happy. They too had discovered ley lines.

After we'd eaten and the dishes were washed we returned to sitting outside the caravan, at peace, watching the lights come on in Rhayader. We smiled a lot. Even the air felt as though it was supercharged with extra oxygen. It was strange; it was like we were all on drugs.

Another quick lesson on Welsh pronunciation. Sarah and I

are clueless, and when we saw the word Rhayader, on the map and on the sign outside town, we adopted the pronunciation 'Ree-arder'. We went back each year and within our family this pronunciation has stuck. We later learned, however, that the locals pronounce it 'Raider', as in the Lost Ark. This came as quite a blow, because the town we have grown to love is, and always will be, Ree-arder. So we have reached a compromise, and we call it Ray-arder (when we remember to do so), with the merest hint of an aich sound after the R. Somehow this sounds more Welsh.

Anyway, back to the first time. During the week we discovered Ree-arder and Elan. The area has a network of reservoirs held back by mighty but picturesque dams – Caban Coch, Careg Ddu, Penygarreg; reservoirs that provide water for Birmingham. There'd been plenty of rain before we arrived and all the dams had water cascading over them. The road up past the lakes is a joy. Every turn brings new scenes of blue and white water, trees in multiple shades of green, mountains, and then barren wilderness.

We were there for nine days and we fell in love with the Elan Valley. We began a long sequence of return visits each May, when North Warwick District Association (NWDA) have their temporary holiday site at Gigrin Farm. We've seen changes. An off-road cycle route has been created. It runs from Rhayader, beside the lakes, all the way up to the top dam at Craig Goch. It has gradient, more than the Tissington Trail, but the scenery is breathtaking.

Gigrin Farm itself is home to the Red Kite Feeding Station. That first year we visited, there were Twitchers; strange people in khaki and green who would stand and stare at the sky through binoculars. They were looking for the elusive Red Kite; a magnificent eagle-like red bird with a distinctive triangular tail. That first year we saw one in the distance. Now, though, they are a constant presence. They are easy to spot. At three p.m. each day they are fed and you can stroll up and watch from one of the many bird hides in Gigrin Farm. It's an awesome sight – one of those not-to-be-missed moments. The birds are thriving there, and I'm sure it's because they too appreciate the feeling of well-being that comes from the favourable ley lines.

We went to a badger watch. There were night vision CCTV cameras installed outside one of the badger setts on the hillside, and the campers gathered in the barn in the evening to watch them emerge. As dusk approached we all got more and more excited, then a nose poked out of the hole. Before long three or four badgers were out and grubbing around in the dirt. The night vision picture was only in fuzzy black and white but twenty or thirty of us crowded around the screen to watch the show. This was live and we were watching nature taking place just a few hundred yards from where we stood and we were all spellbound. Then Mr Powell came into the barn, and said, "Ahh, you're watching the video from last month." He flipped a switch and the badgers blinked out of existence. The screen now showed just a black and white hole in the ground and the odd moth. We hung around for ten minutes or so, but somehow the moment had passed. We all headed out into the dark with thoughts of cocoa and warm beds.

When we found Rhayader we found a rare gem. We've returned many times. We also found a new type of campsite. We'd opened up the door to Temporary Holiday Sites and DA camping. A whole new form of super-cheap caravanning holiday, and it had been there all along.

THE GRAND TOUR: 1996

Sometimes the management at motorway service areas are considerate. They provide good signposting and the caravan parking is near to the facilities. It's rare and it's amazing and it's very welcome. Does this make life easier? Well, perhaps it would but for the Clarksons – the caravan-haters. The lazy sods who park their BMWs and Mercs and white Transit vans in the caravan bays, because it's easier to walk 50 yards rather than 80 yards. You, the caravanner, cannot reciprocate, however. The parking for cars is laid out with concrete bollards; flower tubs; tight, no-way-out corners; and other ingenious caravan traps – so it's back to the lorry-park for you, matey, and another carcinogenic lunch with Eddie and Norbert.

—No. 30 from the Moanicles of Michael.

When we planned our main holiday we reached for the *Out and About* and found ourselves spoilt for choice. Why go to just one site when we could go to so many? The concept of touring was about to be born.

It had never occurred to us, when we had the tent, to try more than one site in a single holiday. (At least not deliberately, that is. We had sometimes moved on as a matter of desperation – an escape route – but never as part of a pre-determined strategy.)

I fancied Norfolk. I don't know why, maybe because I'd never been before. We worked out a rough plan, one that would take us in a loop around the south Midlands and then east towards Norfolk. Our plan was loosely based upon what might be on offer from the list of temporary sites. Then, with true gypsy spirit, we hit the road, free from all the worldly constraints of planning and pre-determination. First stop was a temporary site near Stratford-upon-Avon.

The map showed the site to be in a field with a canal running through the middle. Actually the canal ran over the field, high up above, via an aqueduct. It sounds idyllic, but this was not one of those picturesque Victorian wonders of engineering, like the wonderful Pontcysyllte aqueduct near Llangollen; this was a rusty, utilitarian affair, where numerous leaks were evidenced by the red and green slimy dribbles that oozed down its stumpy legs. There was no art in this construction, not even a passing nod towards aesthetics, just a desire to move a channel of water from one side of the valley to the other, at low cost and minimum disruption.

No matter – it gave us somewhere to walk, and it wasn't objectionable if you didn't look at it. There was also the distraction of the railway. This did run through the field. The children loved it. They could watch canal barges going across the sky, and every fifteen minutes or so they could run over to the fence and wave to a fifty mph diesel train as it thundered through. I grumbled about the noise a bit, but secretly I rather liked it. Even now, after more than forty years of working in the bus industry, I've never quite understood transport cranks, and I've occasionally mocked their feverish passions and sixties' dress code – but, and here's the thing, if a train goes past – or an old bus – or a big ship – or a plane – or a tram, I can not help myself, I have to look. Something stirs inside. So maybe, deep down, I do understand.

Not the tank-tops and half-mast flairs, though. Come on, lads, get some style!

We went into Stratford-upon-Avon. It's a lovely town and we did the inexpensive version of the tourist trail, which involves looking at the outside of Shakespeare's birthplace, looking at the outside of the Royal Shakespeare Theatre, and, later, looking at the outside of Anne Hathaway's cottage. We didn't go in anything. Nothing that might involve the actual handling of money; we did rubberneck tourism.

I saw that the Royal Shakespeare Company were doing Macbeth. I would have loved to have seen Macbeth. That's what normal tourists do. I did Macbeth at school. I hated it. Perhaps, though, a tiny little grain of substance had lodged in my mind, because I regretted being able to see no more than the posters outside the theatre. Shakespeare has the power to do that. Even though, as a typical secondary-modern under-achiever, I had been bored to distraction by it all, the words themselves do have a power all of their own – a power that is quite separate from any ability on my part to extract any kind of meaning from them.

We go to the theatre quite a lot these days, Sarah and I, but in 1996 I was a realist. Kevin was a young thirteen year-old and Amanda was just ten. Macbeth has a lot of long hours in there for children whose metabolisms are controlled by green colourant from tinned peas. I couldn't do it to them. Okay, maybe it was much simpler than that: we couldn't afford it.

So we looked at history; we soaked up the special atmosphere of a town with class; we walked in the footsteps of William Shakespeare, hoping that some way-with-words might rub off, and we postponed beggary for another afternoon.

We had an evening walk. This was becoming something of a tradition for us. We don't miss TV on holiday. A holiday is an escape from the mind-sucking box. We don't take one with us, we do something else instead. Cards when it's raining (we play a lot of cards), but when the sun is shining on mid-summer evenings we like to go for a walk. That evening we walked along the canal. I'm not a big fan of canal walks. You walk and then at some point you have to make a decision to turn and walk back. It's all too linear; too mathematical. Walk out, walk back. There never seems to be a worthwhile objective, like a mountain top or the sea or the edge of a forest.

So, anyway, we set off along the canal. I have the annoying– in my children's eyes–habit of needing a goal. I have to have an ultimate destination, and it has to be worthwhile. So on a canal walk I tend to say things like, 'let's just get to that next bend and see what's round there.' I need to find some destination that's worth getting to. This inevitably leads to some quite long walks along canals, because there is never anywhere worth getting to. So, we argued and bickered, and eventually I lost and we turned around and began to retrace our steps.

It was getting dark.

Darkness is not really a safe state of affairs on a canal bank. There are no lights and on cloudy, moonless nights, such as that one, there is the ever-present risk of coming to a bend in the canal without realising, and continuing on into the murky depths. You can also add to this the risk posed by those indiscriminately placed iron hoops that canal people like to tie their boats to. They are just the right size to get your foot into. Of course I managed to do just this, but I was lucky. When I hit the ground and rolled, I somehow managed to roll away from the canal rather than into it.

I lay on the grass on my back and I saw lights. I said nothing, I just lay and stared at the sky. Sarah, of course, thought I was unconscious because of the lack of bad language that traditionally follows one of these events. I was fully conscious, though. I was just transfixed.

"Shh," I said. "Look up at the sky."

They all looked.

"What is it?"

"Shh."

"Why are you shushing us?"

"I don't know; it's just so... weird."

And it *was* weird. Lights pulsed in the sky. Some were a strange purple colour, others were just ordinary light. But they had shape. And sometimes they had rhythm. And then there was a perfect circle of light that shrank to a point and then burst out into six or seven circles of colour that grew and merged and overlapped. It was never bright but it was there. It all played out in silence. The silence was total, and eerie, and wrong, because such activity must surely be accompanied by some sort of sound.

I realised that I had made a mistake in shushing everybody, because now the silence had become oppressive and any sound we made seemed foolish; it seemed to draw unwanted attention towards us. We realised that we were whispering.

"I don't like it," Sarah whispered.

"It's just lights," I said, in a hushed voice. "Just a light show, nearby."

"Maybe it's aliens," said Kevin, under his breath, his voice cracking with the effort at staying quiet. "UFOs."

This was too much for Amanda. She started to cry, in a restrained and blubbery sort of way. I got back on my feet.

"It's not aliens," I said. "But let's get back, it's getting late."

Kevin won't thank me for mentioning this, but he was born in the same year that the film *ET* was released. When he was about six or seven we watched it on video. At that age Kevin was fearless, but ET, that cute little alien, beloved by all children, scared the pants off him. He had a reaction to ET that was akin to my own childhood fear of Daleks and vacuum cleaners (yeah, let's not go there). He hid behind the sofa, and to this day (he's in his thirties at the time of writing) he still cannot bring himself to watch the film.

Now, a lot of the "scary" bits took place at night, in the dark, with flashing lights in the sky. So it's fair to say that you could count him out if you wanted a hard-bitten, up-for-anything, scared-of-nothing teenager on hand for the spooky stuff. Kevin was not up for hanging around star-gazing.

It was Sarah who set the pace, though. A cracking good lick, too, for a dark canal-side littered with rusty, iron man-traps. She set a pace that would be immortalised in Wood-family lore as the "Hitler Speed March".

We had travelled far in my canal-side quest for a worthy destination, and now we were paying the price, with a delirious flight of terror, marching in near silence (apart from our rasping breath; our crunching, militaristic footfalls; and Amanda's terrified but stifled moans) and all the while we were accompanied by those strange, pulsating, unearthly lights.

We arrived at the caravan. We were awash with sweat and adrenaline; foot-weary, but comforted at being at last able to hide from ET in our safe and secure tin box on wheels.

As I fumbled for the keys, the lights stopped. Just like that. Show over. We each spent that night accompanied by our own private night-terrors, hiding beneath protective, armour-plate duvets, and wondering who or what was out there. Sarah and I relived our childhood monster-under-the-bed horrors. Our gift to our children was that we had given them a nice shiny new horror; something to darken their way through into adulthood.

The next morning we moved on. We packed quietly and quickly, and we laughed with rather too much hysteria whenever the previous night's adventure was mentioned. Somehow, though, we were each pleased to be on our way.

We headed into Cambridgeshire, to a club site at St Neots.

The location was fabulous, right on the banks of the river Great Ouse. The grassy pitches were all beautifully mown and it was a pleasure to put our camp chairs on the river bank and sit for hours watching the expensive boats go past.

We saw an unusual thing in St Neots. They mow the river. They do it with two boats, one is like a giant floating barber's shaver, with a man up front. This goes around cutting the weeds just below the surface. Close behind is another boat, with a giant mechanical rake, that collects all the bits of floating weed. It's all quite ingenious in a retro kind of way, and we spent a happy hour watching.

Two interesting things happened in the evening. The first concerned our own night-time habits. I don't know how it started, but since the beginning of our camping days, even before we had children, we had developed an unfortunate ritual. We always perform a reconstruction of the closing scene from the TV series, *The Waltons*. I'm the one who usually starts it all off with a 'Goodnight John-boy'.

Then Sarah will pipe in with either a 'Goodnight Jim-Bob', or a 'Goodnight Elizabeth', as the mood takes her. Kevin or Amanda will then take over with a string of weird but imaginative double-barrel names, with no connection at all to the TV series. I finally bring the performance to a close with a vocal impression of the single harmonica note that always signalled lights-out in the Walton household. Then I'd switch our lights out.

I mention this because we'd been for our evening walk. As we returned to our caravan we passed a nearby tent, lit by flickering gas light, that was home to a large family of six or seven – we weren't sure how many, they never remained still for long enough to count. As we passed we heard a familiar dialogue from within:

"Goodnight, John-Boy."

"Goodnight, Jim-Bob."

"Goodnight, Mary-Ellen."

"Goodnight, Jason."

"Goodnight, Erin."

"Goodnight, Elizabeth."

"Hmmmmmmmmmm." (The harmonica impersonation was considerably better than mine.)

With a final, stuttering pop of butane, the light in the tent winked out.

It stopped us in our tracks. We all looked at each other. We smiled. We were not the only hopeless nutters in the world. There were other families out there that were at least as crazed as we were.

I said that there were two things that happened to us. As I was about to open the caravan door there was a hushed and awed whisper from Kevin.

"Dad. Look up."

I looked. Up in the sky there were lights. Circles. Pulsations. Purple. All was silent. All was very, very weird. We had travelled 90 miles from Stratford, and here were those lights again. They must be visible right across the Midlands and Cambridgeshire, and yet I had scoured the paper that day and there had not been a single word about it. I looked out of the caravan half an hour later and they had stopped.

We didn't feel the urge to linger, so the next day our tour continued. We picked up our corner-steadies and headed for Norfolk.

Norfolk was a further ninety miles and they were unsettling miles. I have always lived amongst hills and have always longed for more. Our home is within sight of the Clwydians in North Wales, but whenever we feel the need for rarified heights and a view, we usually pass straight through and head for Snowdonia. I love Snowdonia and when there I dream of one day seeing the Alps. I'm comfortable with hills and thrilled by mountains.

Our journey to Norfolk took us through land that was flat. Flat as in – no contour lines anywhere on the maps. Flat as in – if you want a view, stand on a box. This was the Fen Country, and it was like being on the sea with no waves. The only relief came from the drainage ditches between fields. The land rolled on and on in two dimensions. The further we advanced into the flatlands, the more I felt the onset of an agoraphobia that I never knew I had. The sky was huge. I wanted to lie face down on the ground and cling to it.

It was also very hot. The air all around shimmered and fractured under the relentless sun. In the car we fried and bickered.

Our destination was a temporary site near Wells-Next-the-Sea. (Whatever happened to the "to"?) There was some elevation in this part of Norfolk, but to my mountain sensitivities it was still pretty damn flat. It made finding the site difficult. There were no reference points. We searched and argued and double tracked before finding a sign that we had passed several times that had blown over and now lay face-down on the grass. We approached along an arrow-straight, flat farm road that tracked along the edge of a long flat field. A collection of caravans appeared on the horizon. We had found our home for the next five days.

The field was the size of Texas. It was dry. It was flat (have I mentioned that it was flat?). It was also yellow and spiky; the aftermath of a freshly harvested wheat field. Our pitches were staked out, but where we pitched was immaterial; there would be a view of yellow spiky flatness. It was scary. It was wholly different from anything we'd seen before, but I liked it. It appealed to my outdoorsy need for wilderness.

First job, after dropping the legs, was to fetch water and put the kettle on. I towed our Aquaroll (a pull-along cylindrical water tank) over to the tap and began to fill. The trickle of water that came from the tap had the urgency of dew settling.

Another camper arrived with a jug.

"Have you seen the flow from this tap?" I said.

"Yes, you're right. It's much better today."

"What? It's usually worse?"

"Oh, god, yes. Didn't run at all yesterday. You'll be a while filling that big bugger. You're not planning to fill it right up to the top, are you?"

I allowed him to jump in with his diminutive little vessel, then I continued. It took half an hour to half fill it, then the flow stopped. Sarah came looking for me, wondering where I'd got to. "We have a problem," I said. "We should have showered this morning in St Neots."

Our mobile shower arrangements were rudimentary and involved a lot of preparation and a lot of water.

"We'll manage," Sarah said. "We can't skip showers, especially in this heat, and all this dust."

My heart sank. I have to confess that I had long been unhappy about our shower arrangements, but here in Saharan Norfolk it was a task filled with the likelihood of tears, harsh words and general gnashing of teeth.

Sarah walked me back to the caravan to ensure that I didn't run away; then she supervised and brewed tea while I fought for supremacy with the awning.

I dislike putting up the awning at the best of times, but on a hot and dusty day like today it was a terrible job. You'd think that with all my camping years it would be easy; after all, it's only half a tent when it comes down to it. It's a fiddly, messy job, though. You have to thread the beading into a channel and slide it round half the circumference of the caravan on one side. It never slides properly. It's too high, so you have to use the caravan step to reach, and so you have to keep stopping and moving the step along every couple of feet; and the stretch is just perfect for cultivating hernias and other interesting medical conditions. On top of all this it gets hot inside. Even on a dull day it can get as hot as Beelzebub's bakery in there. Today it was over eighty in the shade. Struggling away inside the canvas I wasn't so much sweating as making gravy.

I finished the task and accepted a cup of tea with gratitude. I rested in the shade and sipped my tea slowly, in subdued silence, while I considered the portents of showering.

"Right," Sarah said, clapping her hands together in a gesture of determination that suggested resistance to be futile.

First job was to secure the inside of the awning from watching eyes. Our little Sprite caravan of 1974 vintage came from the days long before fitted bathrooms and toilets. Our ablutions took place in the awning, which had to be rigged for privacy. The interior space must be segregated to allow a place for showering separate from the place where the water-boy performs his tasks. I, by the way, am the water-boy. The final tasks of preparation are to inflate the paddling pool and to heat the water. The paddling pool was my idea. At first we used to stand on the grass to shower, but if you are third or fourth in line, the mud bath that used to await would make the whole exercise kind of pointless. So we stand in a paddling pool.

The water is heated on the gas hob in an endless relay of pans and kettles. When it's hot enough it's added to the shower vessel in a fifty-fifty hot-cold ratio. This is the job of the water-boy. The shower device is a cylinder that is pressurised by frantic pumping, up and down, on a handle. It's hard work. The cylinder also has to be picked up and shaken to mix the hot and cold so as to avoid alternate scalding/freezing interludes – and god help the water-boy if this is not done properly. Then, while each family member is showering, the water-boy must fetch more water, fill the kettles, and re-pump the shower device to maintain pressure. But water was a problem in Norfolk. It came slowly. Tempers frayed. Children who were ambivalent about showers at the best of times roared their disapproval. Then, at the end of the whole sweaty performance, it was my turn. I had fetched my own water, heated it, shaken it and pumped it. Now for my reward – to stand shin deep in a paddling pool full of other people's dirt and sweat, cold water, and a topping of yellow grass and dead bugs. Then, after a totally disheartening shower, the water-boy gets to empty the paddling pool. It has to be somewhere discrete, and certainly not in the awning. How can you be discrete, and how can you be untouched by guilt when emptying a twenty-gallon paddling pool in a flat field where everyone around you has been dutifully making do with two-litre plastic milk cartons each day for the past week?

The other thing about this – it's heavy. Four people have luxuriated in long, refreshing showers. (Actually, make that three – the fourth has found the whole experience to be a gruesome ordeal.) So yes, some weight has been accrued here. To move the whole thing as a unit is going to involve hire charges to John Sutch Mobile Cranes. There is no way it can be dragged anywhere. So the solution is to move the water, one bucket at a time, but to where? Under the caravan. Sorted. All done in the privacy of our own home on wheels.

It must be said that we didn't get away with this without some suspicions from our neighbours. By the end of the week our pitch had become conspicuous for being a little circular oasis of verdant green in a desert of yellow stalks and dust. Eyebrows were raised, I can tell you.

Kevin and Amanda made friends in Norfolk.

"We've made friends," said Kevin.

"They're called Josh and Jessica," said Amanda.

"They're great," said Kevin. "They're twins."

"Do we have to go out?" said Amanda. "We want to stay here and play with Josh and Jessica."

An hour later Sarah and I were relaxed and having a quiet read and a cup of tea. It felt like we were on holiday.

The children came back.

"Tell us we have to go out," said Kevin, in an urgent whisper.

"Don't tell them we're here," said Amanda.

Two identical blond heads looked into the caravan. "Are Kevin and Amanda here?"

"Yes," I said.

I was given withering glares by both my children. Glares filled with hate and venom. They went off to play with their "friends". Sarah and I continued to read.

Ten minutes later they were back.

"Please. Pleeeease say we are going out now."

"Why?"

"Are Kevin and Amanda here? Can they play? Kevin says he has to go out. We don't think Kevin has to go out, or Amanda."

I looked at my children. My next words would turn me into a villain or a god.

"Yes, we are going out," I said.

"When?"

"Right now," I said.

"When will you be back?"

I paused for a moment to consider the interrogation I was

getting from these two ten-year-olds. I wondered how my children had been so easily deceived into thinking that they had made friends.

"We'll be back after tea," I said, basking in the adoring looks I was getting from both of my children.

"When do you have tea?" said Josh... or Jessica.

"Where are you going?" said the other one.

"Can we come?"

"We like McDonald's."

"We always have the nuggets."

I didn't even need to see the look of terror that passed across Kevin and Amanda's faces. I'd only known Josh and Jessica for two minutes and already I felt bullied and intimidated.

"Er, I'm not sure your parents would be very happy to-"

"Yes they would. They like us to make new friends and have meals with them."

(I bet they do. They'd probably offer us a bribe if we'd agree to adopt them.)

"Well, no. I'm sorry. We might be out late," I said.

"We don't mind."

"No, I don't think so."

"We'll wait for you then."

With that, Josh and Jessica settled down on the grass outside our caravan to await our return. I didn't even want to go out. I had been happy reading. Now we were being driven out of our home by a pair of infants.

We gathered up our belongings, all the while scrutinised under the relentless gaze of Satan's offspring, and we climbed into the car and drove out of the field.

"We might as well go and have a look at Wells-Next-the-Sea," I said. I wanted it to sound as if it was something I wanted to do. I didn't want it to appear as if I had been expelled by children. It was Sunday evening. Wells-Next-the-Sea was closed. There were places to eat but I didn't like the look of any of them, and I didn't want to spend the money. We wandered around aimlessly for a while until I exploded.

"This is ridiculous," I said. "I'm not being driven away by children. We're going back. Anyway, they will have got bored by now. They will have found someone else to bother."

I resisted the cries of dismay, and herded everyone back into the car. I would not be made a fugitive. We returned to the campsite. Josh and Jessica appeared not to have moved. They were staking out our caravan in the exact same place we had left them. As we climbed out of the car they came running up.

"You weren't very long."

"Did you have McDonald's?"

"Can Kevin and Amanda play now?"

I decided to put my foot down. "No, they're not coming out now. I think you'd better run along."

"Why aren't they coming out?"

"We don't have to go in yet, it's early."

"Well," I said. "We are going to play cards now. It's something we like to do in the evening."

"We'll come and play cards, too."

"No," said Sarah, trying to put a hard edge into her voice. "We'll see you tomorrow."

We moved into the caravan and closed the door. As we settled down around the table we saw with horror that Josh and Jessica had moved to a position outside the caravan window. They were standing watching us. I closed the curtains, even though it would remain light for another three or four hours. We played cards.

The next morning I lay in bed long after waking, unwilling to move. I didn't want to open the curtains. I felt certain that Josh and Jessica would still be there. I wasn't the only one who felt this way, and although nobody said anything there was a certain carefulness about the way we eventually rose, washed and dressed. There were no sudden movements and noise was kept to a minimum.

The absurdity of our situation struck me again and again, but what could we do? Complain to the parents?

"Excuse, me. Mr and Mrs Satan? Would you speak to your children please, they are misbehaving."

"Oh dear. What have they been doing?"

"Well, they keep asking to play with our children and sometimes they sit in the field near our caravan."

"That is terrible. We'll see that they are soundly thrashed for their behaviour."

Somehow I couldn't see this approach working.

Or we could take baseball bats to them, but this seemed to open up possibilities of a long spell in jail.

"We'll just have to be firm," said Sarah. "We can't allow two children to control us like this. Next time they come you'll have to speak to them."

I didn't have long to wait. They arrived halfway through breakfast.

"Are Kevin and Amanda playing?"

"No, not today."

"Why not?"

"We are all going out today." I separated each of the words so that I sounded firm.

"Can we come?"

"I'm sorry, no."

"Why not?"

"We don't have room in the car."

"Why do you have to go in the car? We could walk. We can show you the way to the beach. We've been before."

"No, we're not going to the beach."

"Where are you going?"

And so it went on. Endless contradiction. Nothing I said they accepted. Always a question in return. I felt helpless. Kevin and Amanda were of no help. They hid. We went out in the car to escape them again. We probably would have gone out in the car anyway, but now it felt that we were being ousted. It cast a pall over the day.

We visited a stately home called Holkham Hall. It was probably very interesting. On another day I might have enjoyed it.

Would they still be there when we got back? What else could we do to delay our return? Should we eat out tonight? Should we stay out late and party? Was I the most pathetic and impotent male on this good earth? Why was I allowing myself to be so tyrannized by two little children?

We found a chippy and ate out; a large dent was made in the holiday budget. Fish and chips for four was seriously above and beyond.

We found a bench overlooking the harbour in Wells-Next-the-Sea. There was a cold wind that cooled our chips faster than we could eat them. The tide was out and as harbours go, it didn't look much; more like a cutting through the mud flats, but it was something to see while we ate. I felt low. I felt dispirited.

"There's something about this place that isn't right," I said.

"What do you mean?" said Sarah.

"I don't know. It's not what I expected."

"There's nothing objectionable about it," said Sarah.

"It just doesn't seem to have the atmosphere of a real fishing port."

Sarah shrugged. "It's got fishing boats, lobster pots..."

"Yeah, but, where are the seagulls?"

"I'm sure we've seen seagulls. Do you think maybe you're just feeling a bit down about, you know?"

"No. I'm not letting them get me down. This is real. There are no seagulls here. In a proper fishing port there are seagulls, hundreds of them. They circle around. You can hear their cries. They give a place atmosphere."

As I spoke a seagull appeared. It was huge. It was like an Albatross. It swooped down. It seemed to have purpose. It seemed to be diving straight for me. Then, at the very last moment, it pulled up and as it did so it released the biggest dollop of seagull crap ever seen by mortal man. The bird's aim was immaculate; most of it caught me full in the face, the rest landed in my chips.

"There you go," said Sarah. "Now you've got atmosphere."

Josh and Jessica were not waiting for us when we returned. It was probably just as well. I was in a thunderous mood, and I'd have probably tried to run them down with the car. I wanted to fill the caravan sink and finish the job that a flimsy, half-used tissue had failed to complete, but Sarah wouldn't have it.

"You are not washing your face in our sink. I use that sink to prepare food. Go outside and use the fire bucket."

That completed my day. There I was, my head jammed in a bucket of cold water, on my hands and knees outside the caravan, my hair caked with the most enormous gob of dried seagull excrement. And then I heard the voices.

"Are Kevin and Amanda playing?"

And, moments later:

"What's your dad doing in that bucket? What's that stuff all over his head? Can we stay and watch?"

We saw a wonderful thing the next day, while eating breakfast. We saw a blue Honda towing a caravan out of the field. Sitting in the back of the Honda were Josh and Jessica. They waved to us. We waved back, wearing wide, genuine smiles. They were moving on, out of our lives forever. There was a carnival atmosphere. Bran Flakes have never tasted so good.

I had heard that nearby there was a place called Blakeney Point where seals could be spotted. It's owned by the National Trust and I'd seen enthusiastic leaflets and posters extolling the area's natural wonders. Blakeney Point is a spit of sand that is wild and untouched and has all manner of wildlife. I'd never seen a seal in real life, so it sounded good to me.

We headed for Cley-Next-the-Sea, another grammatically challenged town, only about five miles away. Cley has a windmill. I'd seen images of it on postcards and hanging in the windows of art shops everywhere, and rightly so. Cley Mill is exactly how you would expect a Norfolk windmill to look. Red brick, white sails, a white encircling balcony at about quarter height, and I could not stop photographing it. Some things are notorious camera magnets. I defy anyone who has driven down this coast to honestly claim not to have ever photographed Cley Mill. The BBC couldn't stop themselves; they showed it on the telly every night for months as a programme trailer; with a big orange hot-air balloon painted like a globe, floating in the sky next to it. Sarah didn't photograph it; she's an artist. She gave a little squeal as we approached, and was reaching for her sketch pad even before I'd parked the car. We were nearly an hour capturing it from various angles on various media. The children spent the hour rolling their eyes and giving out huge, shuddering sighs of boredom. I pleaded for patience and promised them seals.

We drove on to the car park at Cley beach. There was a display showing photographs of seals in their thousands basking on the sand. The children perked up.

We walked to the beach and turned left, per instructions. The tide was in. We were walking, not on sand, but on shingle or gravel that sloped down to the sea on our right and swallowed our feet at each step, in a way that was reminiscent of those bad dreams where you try to run but your legs don't seem to get you anywhere.

The view ahead was not encouraging. The same featureless ribbon of shingle stretched to infinity. No seals could be seen, but we had known that this would be the case. This was the beach that led to Blakeney Point, and Blakeney Point was where the seals where, and Blakeney Point was three and a half miles away. We are good walkers, though. Three and a half miles is a mere stroll for the Wood family, and a bit of soft gravel was not going to discourage us. We walked.

I read in one of the leaflets that Blakeney Point has doubled in length in only the last thousand years. This, say the scientists, is through a process called accretion, in which material is gradually moved along the coast by wave action. Well, I'm sorry. I have to differ with the scientists. The material – the gravel – has been carried along the coast, not by wave action, but in the shoes of the poor sods who walk. Every few yards the pressing urge to stop and empty our shoes would get the better of us, and yet another few grammes of "material" would thereby accrete. You know how annoying it is when you get a stone in your shoe? Imagine how it is to collect a cupfull. Imagine the extra effort of heaving those weighted boots, step after step. Imagine the relief of being free from stones,

139

then the heartbreak after just one short pace when the whole geological accretion process starts over again. We tried barefoot. One step. It hurts. We tried walking near the top of the beach – it was softer and much harder to walk. We tried walking nearer to the sea where the gravel was more compacted. We got wet feet and we moved wet gravel. Wet gravel is heavier than dry gravel and harder to empty because it sticks in your shoes.

We walked. We transported rock from east to west, by the ton. Each step caused pain. Each single pace demanded a monumental act of will and a display of stamina and strength. Our calves burned. It was hot, and our necks fried and sizzled in the sun as we bowed our heads to the task. We did not have drinks with us. We should have brought drinks, but we preferred to save weight. Besides, we knew that there were light refreshments at the Old Lifeboat House at the point. But first we had to get to the point.

Why were we doing this? To see seals? To marvel at the wonders of nature? No. The desire to see seals had evaporated after only the first few hundred yards of toil. This was now the old problem. My problem. This was personal. Destination Fixation. The need to get there, to see what's around the corner. Sarah didn't want to see seals any more. The children definitely did not want to see seals, but they knew the futility of argument. They could see the steely light in my eye; the set of my jaw. They understood. It was the destination that mattered.

"We will get to Blakeney Point." These were the words I had spoken, and the children knew, Sarah knew. They had seen me in the grip of Destination Fixation many times and they had felt its power. No matter what hardships awaited us, I would bloody well march us to Blakeney Point!

We were fading fast, though. We stopped for a breather and looked out at the featureless grey sea. The constant white-noise sound-track of crashing waves and rolling gravel was starting to jangle our nerves, when Kevin suddenly shouted.

"There!"

We all jumped and cried out.

"It was a seal. I saw one."

"Where, what did it look like?"

"Like, like a grey football floating on the water."

We desperately searched between the waves, hoping against hope for a seal. If we could see one, then we'd be off the hook. Our "destination", our goal, was "to see seals". Reaching Blakeney Point was secondary. If we could see seals we could mentally tick a box, mission accomplished, and turn back to the car park. We stared out to sea until our eyes hurt. Every strange-shaped wave, every floating log raised our hopes for short seconds, then dashed them as their true form materialised. Optimism turned to desperate hope then turned to dismay.

I faced west and peered up the beach. I could make out a building through the spray.

"Can you see that?"

Everyone looked.

"It's a building. It must be the Old Lifeboat House. Can't be far now. There's drinks there."

Sarah, Amanda and Kevin looked at each other, then nodded. They'd reached the same silent conclusion that continuing now, and getting drinks, would provide comfort much sooner than turning back.

We continued our march. A pound of rock in each shoe. Step after heavy step. Our eyes were fixed on the building ahead. There was no more searching out to sea. Stuff the seals. We each had only one thing in mind. One goal. For the children, their fixation was for Coke, in ice-cold bottles, with drops of condensation meandering down the neck. Sarah held a vision of tea. A pot of Darjeeling, on a tray. A china cup and saucer, and plenty of milk, for multiple refills.

I dreamed of Carlsberg. My dream was the more fanciful; I was driving, so I'd probably end up with warm fizzy pop, but it was the dream that kept me moving.

The building got nearer and nearer. I wiped the sweat away from my eyes and realised that my hair had gone stiff with salt. I could taste the salt on my lips and it made the craving for beer all the more urgent.

We started to angle up the beach, into the softer shingle where the going was heavier but the route shorter. An uneasy feeling began to gnaw away at my insides. Where were all the people? There must be customers. The guide leaflet said that boats came across and dropped people by the score just outside the Old Lifeboat House where they could partake of "Light Refreshments". So, where was everybody? Where were the tables with umbrellas, the chinking sounds of china cups? Where was the Walls ice-cream sign that should be hanging above the door, or the Carlsberg sign? More importantly, why was there no glass in the windows and why were weeds growing out of the doors?

We stopped. I looked at my family and I saw eyes filled with malice and accusation. They didn't have to say anything. I opened my rucksack and took out the crushed and mangled guide leaflet that was stuffed in the bottom. I read:

"When you pass a disused building on your left, you'll know you're halfway there."

Sarah was loyal. "Look, I know you want to get to the end. If you really want to see these seals, well, we'll carry on." She said it with a sigh and a downward inflexion that showed that she didn't mean a word of it. She knew I was defeated. She knew that there wasn't a chance in the boondocks of hell that the children would ever go for it. And she knew that I knew.

We turned and headed east.

Into the wind.

Here was a factor that we had never considered, though the clues had been there, all along. On the walk out there had been very little wind – unusual for a coastal location. Furthermore, I had lectured the family on the geological principles of accretion, how waves moved along the beach from east to west. For waves to do this there must be wind, moving from east to west. The wind had been on our backs, all the way, pushing us along, making the going easier. Now? Now, it was hard.

Oh, yes. An apology to the scientists. My error. Accretion has nothing at all to do with gravel transported in shoes. All those tons of rock that we had moved along the beach? We were now moving it all back.

We never saw the seals.

Back at the car park. Hours later. Dehydration. Physical exhaustion. Heat exhaustion. The car park café had closed. Everything was shuttered up. Our car stood alone, with just the dust and the sighing wind and the tumbleweeds for company. It was a scene from a Spaghetti Western. Inside the car we found half of a small bottle of Evian mineral water. It had been sitting on the parcel shelf, in the sun, all through the afternoon. It was like drinking straight from a kettle. There was enough liquid for one disgusting mouthful each. I realised that some serious sucking-up was required. I owed big. I made a magnanimous gesture.

"We'll eat out," I said.

We drove a short distance along the coast until we saw a brown tourist sign drawing attention to a place called Walsingham. I'd never heard of it, but it was a big sign, full of touristy symbols. The clincher was the little white knife and fork. I pointed the car towards Walsingham and we pulled into the first pub/restaurant that we came to.

We pushed through the swing door and everyone inside went quiet. It was like in the Westerns when the honky-tonk piano stops. But this room wasn't full of cowboys, it was full of vicars and priests and nuns. We took a table. Every now and again we stole glances over our shoulders. What was this?

We ordered our food and drinks. We felt like interlopers; strangers in a strange land.

Was this fancy dress? It certainly didn't seem that way – there was too much fervency in the air. These weren't ordinary Christians. These were hard-nosed clerics with a steely glint in their eyes. You could smell the holy water.

We ate to the sounds of clicking cutlery, and with little enjoyment. Every scraping chair-leg brought unwanted attention. The atmosphere was intensely uncomfortable.

We finished our meal, paid our bill and fled. To fully appreciate the magnitude of what had just happened, you must understand, as a family we only ever eat out on birthdays – grandparents' birthdays, where the grandparents pay. This might happen once, maybe twice a year. It is a huge event. We never go for a meal ourselves, just the four of us, except for the very occasional and desperate fish and chips. To go out, as a family, and buy a meal in a real restaurant was simply unprecedented. It should have been a monumental occasion. It turned out to be profoundly unsettling. We craved voices and revelry. All we got was the foreboding of the bill to come. It was a meal we couldn't savour; one that we rushed through with the sole objective of getting out of there as quickly as possible.

When we hit the street, the credit card bill felt as weighty as an encyclopaedia in my pocket.

We set off to explore Walsingham, and we found that the weirdness was not confined to the eateries. It was late evening and the light was fading from the sky, causing the trees and buildings and churches to silhouette, and pulling the narrow lanes down into the dark and gothic, and everywhere, nuns, monks, assorted clergy, floated along the dimming streets, pausing to look in shop windows that were lit from within by subdued lighting. These weren't ordinary shop windows. Here was a town bereft of Next or WH Smiths or Marks and Spencer. Every shop window was filled with religious artefacts: icons, crucifixes, rosaries, porcelain statues of the Virgin Mary. There were clothes shops that sold nothing but clerical vestments. I wondered about the rules here. Could I enter a shop and kit myself out as a bishop? There seemed nothing to stop me. Would I be asked for a union card, a secret sign or some other form of ID? Would exorcists spring out at me from the dark corners of the shop, wielding crucifixes and shouting psalms, unmasking me as an imposter?

Not everyone in Walsingham wore the full regalia, but we were certainly the only ones dressed in shorts and T-shirts. My sweat-stained Newcastle Brown Ale T-shirt felt particularly inappropriate. We were Everton fans in full blue kit, teleported into Liverpool's Kop on match-day; we were Persian Grey show cats, loose at Crufts; we were a Country and Western combo amongst musicians.

What's more, this was bi-partisan religion. Catholics and Anglicans rubbed shoulders, presenting a united front. The only true outsiders, here, were the ungodly Newcastle Brown Ale T-shirt wearers.

We did not linger in Walsingham. Some would say it is a deeply spiritual and moving place. Others, like me, could be totally creeped out by it. I've dabbled in religion. I was christened and married in churches, and as a boy scout, I was coerced into wasting a good twenty-five percent of my weekends attending church-parades.

Walsingham, though, was not religion as I knew it. This was full-on, hell-or-redemption religion.

We hurried, nay, fled, back to the car park, feeling ecclesiastical eyes peering from every dark corner. With trembling hands I managed to get the keys into the ignition and we headed out of town. On both sides of the road, nuns, priests, vicars and bishops paused in their devotions to watch us leave.

We came out of town on a different road. It was a narrow road, it was dark, and I had my headlamps on full beam. We had gone no more than half a mile when the headlamps reflected back at me from a pair of eyes. They belonged to a deer, standing in the middle of the road. I slammed on the brakes and missed hitting the animal by inches. It did not even flinch. It just stared at us. I couldn't pass so I inched forward to give it a hint. Eventually it turned and walked slowly into the bushes at the side of the road. This was not normal deer behaviour. Deer are supposed to be nervous and skittish. This one acted like it was on Valium.

It shook me up, though, and I'd had enough already to scare me this evening, so I took things a little slower. It was just as well, for around the next corner were dull-minded rabbits. The pattern continued with more wildlife than I have ever seen in one place. Pheasants, badgers, owls, stoats – all calm and serene, waiting in line to become road-kill.

After the deer, we'd all gone through the usual near-miss dialogue, expressing shock and surprise; but now, as we engaged in each new wildlife encounter we took it all in, in stunned silence. It was like watching a Walt Disney wildlife feature through the car windows. There is only so much weirdness one can take in a single day. I said this to Sarah when we arrived back at the caravan site.

It was late, and out of respect for the other campers (and following the rules) we left the car in the late arrivals area at the bottom of the field and walked the three or four hundred yards up towards the caravan.

"It has been kind of strange today," said Sarah.

I said, "I think the animals were deliberately placed in our way."

"Why? By whom?"

"Forces," I said.

That was when the sky lit up.

It was like Stratford, and St Neots. This time it was way more intense. The circles were sharp and defined, the pulsation was more rhythmic and urgent. This time there wasn't quite the silence as before. Deep down, at a sub-sonic level, was a sound that could be felt but not heard; Vincent Price playing pedal notes on a great organ. The four of us stopped halfway up the field and were mightily afraid. Amanda was the first to say it.

"Daddy, I'm scared."

I reached for her hand and gave it a squeeze.

"It's only lights."

We continued walking back to the caravan, where we would be safe. We tried not to walk quickly so as not to transmit our own fear to the children, but it didn't work, and gradually our pace increased towards Hitler-Speed-March velocities. Then we were running, all the way back to the 'van.

Once inside, the differences between this display and those at Stratford and St Neots were clear to see, for this time we could see the lights through the drawn curtains and through the skylight. Now we could hear the noises, no longer sub-sonic but a soundtrack for Armageddon. Deep booming chords and explosions shook the field and intense flashes of light bleached the colour out of the curtains. I imagined the paint peeling from the outside walls of the caravan, and the tinder-dry straw in the field spontaneously combusting around us. The children cried. Sarah gripped my hand. I tried to be brave but failed. We made the beds quickly and hid beneath our duvets. We closed our eyes. We all hoped that the world would still be there in the morning.

It was. Nothing was different. Everything seemed good in daylight. The weirdness was over. We decided to do a food-shop in Wells-Next-the-Sea. Something ordinary, something routine with which we could re-embrace reality.

We found a mini supermarket and we quickly stocked up. While we were queuing I began earwigging a conversation between the lady in front of me and the checkout girl.

"Did you go last night?"

"Ooh yes, it was lovely."

"A bit noisy at times, it got my tinnitus going."

"Yeah, but the lights were amazing."

"Excuse me," I butted in. "You're talking about lights? Last night?"

"Yes, did you go?"

"Go? Was it some kind of... performance?"

"Yes. You missed it? Oh, you missed a treat."

"What was it?"

"A touring show. Lasers and fireworks and all kinds. Here, we've had a poster up in the shop for weeks."

She pointed to a colourful poster on the notice board. It was not unlike a circus poster, and I realised I had seen them around for several days. In fact, had I been seeing them since the start of our holiday in Stratford? I studied it carefully.

Firework & Laser Display.
See the Sky Light Up.
Fun for all the family.
Admission £3.00

At the bottom was a list of the dates and venues. It was a touring show that started in Solihull, moved to Stratford, then Cambridge, Great Yarmouth, Wells-Next-the-Sea, and tomorrow, Skegness, then...

I checked the dates: Stratford, yes that was right. Cambridge. Cambridge was only about fifteen miles from St Neots, then last night, Wells-Next-the-Sea. I started laughing in the shop. I howled. I slapped my thighs. Everyone stared at me, especially Sarah, who had wandered over to the freezers before I had reached the checkout.

"Lasers!" I shouted. "Ha! Lasers and fireworks."

The mystery was solved. I did a little dance.

The rest of the Norfolk stay was routine. We cycled a lot. The roads were flat and fairly quiet and the cycling was easy. We would have preferred some off-road routes, particularly with Amanda who, at twelve, could still be quite erratic on the roads.

We visited Sandringham. It was good but it was expensive, and I was beginning to rack up a mental account of the financial predicament we would be in when we finally returned home. I wondered if I was starting to sound mean, and preoccupied with money. Sarah reassured me.

"No, not at all," she said. "You've always been mean and preoccupied with money."

She said it with a smile, though. We both knew the truth. When things are tight everything you do and say has its core in finances. It's how we both were. We had a history. Every decision, no matter how seemingly insignificant, had to be weighed against the financial impact. A visit to Sandringham would, we knew, be expensive. We had to mitigate it by packing sandwiches and drinks, even though there would be plenty of places to buy food when we got there. We had to do a recce of the car parks at every destination, and find which was the cheapest, or even find a free one that maybe involved a bit of a walk.

It didn't get us down. We were seeing new places; we were giving our children the opportunity to see new places, things *were* getting better, and in the meantime we were managing. There was a sense of achievement in that.

Our time was up in Norfolk. We'd been longer, here, than anywhere in the tour so far – five days – and it was time to move on. Next stop on the tour was Clumber Park in Nottinghamshire, where we spent our time cycling, relaxing and avoiding expense.

The tour finished in familiar surroundings at the site near Bakewell that we had all grown extremely fond of, and we had pre-booked. The reasoning was: if the first part of our holiday turned out to be a disaster, and we'd hated all the places where we stayed, then at least we could ensure that we ended the holiday on a high.

As it turned out we enjoyed every part of our first tour and Bakewell concluded things in the best possible way. Our final night was dramatic. We had the mother and father of all thunder storms. So we did get to see a real light show in the end, and once more we were all relieved to come out of it alive.

The Norfolk tour had been such a success we tried a similar thing again the next year, 1997. We toured Yorkshire, sticking to temporary sites and cheap farm sites. Yes, we were frugal, but more than that, we were starting to see a slight change in our finances, perhaps as a result of the passage of years. At the end of that summer there was even a little money left over.

THE LAKES: 1996

Am I the only one who gets annoyed by pelican crossings? I'm talking about the kind with the red and green man, and I'm talking now as a pedestrian, because sometimes I am one of those, too.

So what happens? You press the button. The man is red. You are sensible, you wait. And wait. There are plenty of gaps in the traffic but you stay on the kerb, observing the empty road, enjoying the tranquility, waiting for the green man.

Still red. You wait a little longer and begin to feel self-conscious, standing at the kerb watching an empty road. In the end the sight of other people going about their business is too much. You have a good look around, mindful of your kerb drill, or green cross code, or whatever other mantra you learned as a child, then you go for it. No problem. You reach the other side of the road in safety, and just as your foot touches the kerb you hear that beep beep beep sound as the green man appears. Suddenly there is traffic, and they have been forced to stop at the red light. They're glaring at you with malevolent, Clarkson eyes. Why have you stopped them? If you were able to cross, why in God's name couldn't you just do it, without pressing the button?

You feel their rage as you walk away.

Note – pelican used to be pelicon. PEdestrian LIght CONtrolled crossing. So there. Now you have learnt something from my rantings.

—No. 57 from the Moanicles of Michael.

152

In addition to our excursion into the flat-lands of middle England we had also started to venture a little further north. From the Wirral, the Lake District had always seemed to be such a distance. There was also a psychological barrier. Looking at the map it appeared such a hard, uphill journey. This was the thing about always putting north at the top of maps. I knew this to be nonsense, of course, but still.

I'd only been to the Lakes once, as a very young child, so maybe my parents felt the same about travelling up maps. Sarah had been several times and now she was exerting pressure.

"It's beautiful," she kept on saying. "It has inspired artists and poets for centuries. We should go."

"But it's so far away."

"There are mountains."

"I know, but..."

Sarah convinced me. We went to the Lakes. It wasn't far – two hours to the southern lakes even on a bad day, and it wasn't uphill (although it still *felt* uphill as I mentally traced the route along the map in my head).

We became hooked. The Lake District is a special place. Much has been spoken and written about the Lakes and all the words fall short of describing that tightening of the heart that always accompanies each new panoramic view as it unfolds, whether it be from the passenger seat of a car or from a picnic spot high up in the fells. The walking, of course, is exceptional.

Two locations in particular have enticed us again and again: Keswick and Coniston. They are places of very different character yet we couldn't decide which we liked best. If we were going for a week we invariably spent half the week near Coniston and the other half near Keswick. These two bases then provided access to everything in between.

Our Coniston home was at Torver, at a CL that offered a wonderful sweeping view of the lake itself. (A CL, by the way, is Caravan Club speak for Certified Location, a small site – a farm site in this instance – licensed for up to five caravans.)

From the Torver site it is possible to walk along the lakeside into Coniston where we would invariably end up in the Bluebird café, by the lake, for tea and scones. The Bluebird name crops up a lot around here, after the boat used in the water speed record attempts (including the final, fatal one) by Sir Donald Campbell in the sixties. (My favourite iteration of the Bluebird name, by the way, is in the form of Bluebird Beer that comes from a local micro-brewery.)

Whenever we are in the Lake District Sarah's artistic side comes to the fore. She becomes possessed. On our first visit she was determined to paint the centre of Coniston village, and because of the traffic she found it safer to snap a dozen or so photos and work on them later. The result was one of her finer efforts, but when I looked at it closely I was drawn to a lone figure standing slightly to one side of the bridge.

"Look at this man," I said, after staring at the painting for several seconds.

"What about him?"

"Well... he's urinating against a wall."

"No he isn't, he's..."

"He's what?"

"I don't know what he's doing but... He's not, is he?"

"Well it looks like he's urinating against the wall."

"No, it's the way I've painted him, he's... let me get the photo."

We both peered at the photograph. We stared. Sarah was the first to speak.

"He is, isn't he?"

"I'd say so, yes."

"But how could I have painted him without realising? Oh my god, I can't leave it like that, I'm putting this one in for the November exhibition in the church hall!"

The exhibition is run by Sarah's art group. Each artist can exhibit up to three paintings. Sarah sold two of hers that year, a flower study and the one that had become fondly known, to us, as "The Urinating Man of Coniston". Someone somewhere has a painting hanging in their lounge showing a view of Coniston Village. There's a tub of flowers in the centre of the village that doesn't belong. If they were to look closely they would see that the tub of flowers has been added and that it conceals an interesting secret.

There are some fine walks around Coniston. One of the most popular fell walks is to climb the Old Man of Coniston, and there are several routes. The one that has so far eluded us, though, is via the Walna Scar Road (it's not a real road, it's a track made from boulders) and then takes the ridge over Brown Pike and Dow Crag.

We do seem to be unlucky with this one. We've called it off for poor visibility on three attempts so far. The first two failures were for conventional poor visibility when the cloud ceiling dropped and we were socked in by mist. A lot of people don't mind walking in clouds. I'm not impressed. It's not a fear of getting lost or anything, my map reading skills are up to it, it's just that it seems an awful lot of effort to climb a mountain when all you can see from the top are your own feet.

Our third attempt seemed more hopeful, because as we were approaching the top of the Walna Scar Road (the point after which it begins to descend into the Duddon Valley) and from where the relatively short slog up Brown Pike begins, the sky was a uniform blue and there were no clouds. Visibility was not going to be a problem today.

Then the wind hit us. I leaned forward and pressed on. I'd gone fifty yards or so before I realised I was alone. I turned and looked back and there, far behind, were Sarah and the kids, all of them bent double at the waist and shuffling around in circles. I went back.

"What's happened? What are you all doing?"

Kevin stood up and shouted something that was lost in the wind, then bent down at the waist again and resumed shuffling. I grabbed Sarah's arm. She didn't seem to recognise me at first, but then she handed me her glasses, or rather, the frames of her glasses.

"Wind's blown out the lenses," she shouted. "Can't see a thing. They've got to be around here somewhere."

We searched for half an hour or so before admitting defeat, then we led her down off the mountain. (Three-nil for the Walna Scar Road route.) Back at the caravan Sarah found some prescription sunglasses that she then had to wear for the remainder of the week. She looked like one pretty cool dude, especially in the rain and especially at night.

Our Keswick site is the Camping and Caravanning Club site that sits right on the northern lake shore. It has wonderful views down the length of Derwent Water, to Borrowdale and diminutive but impressive Castle Crag. A thing we do, it's almost compulsory, in fact, is to take our camping chairs and our biscuits and evening mugs of cocoa down to the lake-side to sit and relax and watch night fall. We sit in companionable silence, sipping our hot drinks and munching our biscuits, ignoring the evening midges that come to join us for supper, sipping our blood and munching our flesh.

Despite this tranquil scene, the Keswick site is only a ten-minute walk into the centre of town, and this is always worthwhile because Keswick is buzzing and cool, full of chocolate shops and classy mountain equipment shops and other establishments that beguile us into parting with money. Yes, Keswick is a town contrary to our ethos of avoiding spending temptations, but we can't help it. We love the place.

Again there are so many choices for walking: a circuit of the lake is just far enough to be challenging but do-able; Cat Bells, on the western shore, is probably the Lake District's most rewarding easy climb; and if you want a real beast there is always Skiddaw, looming behind the town – a fell-walker's pain-magnet. (To date, I haven't tried Skiddaw. It's on my list, but there's so much else in this part of the world. So many fells to climb and always so little time.)

Here's the dilemma. We love finding new places. We still love to return to favourite old places, but the more new places we find, the more we add to our list of new favourite old places, and there's only so many weekends and holiday days in the year.

LONDON: 1998

Why does Clarkson have such a downer on caravans? If you want emptier roads why not ban all the cars that don't have caravans on the back? It makes sense. Take bank holidays. We head for, say, the Lakes, on a Friday night, pitch the 'van, and will not be seen on the roads again until Monday evening, when we return home. The rest of the time we are crunching up and down the fells in our boots, and you could close the roads for all we cared.

The Clarksons, on the other hand, drive up to the lakes on Saturday morning. They queue into Ambleside for two hours on the off-chance that someone will pull out of the car park early. They drive around the roads looking for a stretch where they might get out of first gear for a few yards, then queue up again to get back on the motorway to head home. Come Sunday, same routine, different National Park. Same on Monday. Who's the polluter? Who's the clogger of roads? Next time you're in a traffic jam, count the caravans. Okay, now count the cars. See?

—No. 42 from the Moanicles of Michael.

"Do you know," I said one evening, "the children have never seen London?"

"There's probably a reason," said Sarah.

"Amanda's twelve and Kevin will be sixteen soon, and we've never given them the opportunity of seeing the capital."

"Can we afford it?"

"We could do it on the cheap, you know, look *at* stuff rather than look *in* stuff."

Sarah put down the book she had been trying to read and

looked thoughtful for a moment.

"I suppose there's plenty we could do without actually spending much; Tower of London, Houses of Parliament, Buckingham Palace," she said.

"Why don't we look into it?" I said.

The deal was done. I booked us into a site at Chertsey in Surrey, and we spent the winter making plans. It would be a challenge. Every part of the trip would have to be investigated with an eye to minimal expense, but it proved to be easier than we first thought. As the days began to lengthen into March we became more and more animated with excitement; neither I nor Sarah had been to London since we were in our teens, and the children were full of questions about what they might see.

Easter fell late in 1998, creeping into the second week of April. We'd had some mixed Easter weekends in the past, but on the whole we found that when Easter managed to stay clear of March you could hope for reasonable weather.

We were not allowed to arrive at the campsite until after ten o'clock, but we didn't want to waste Good Friday, so we built in some slack and left home at about four-thirty in the morning. It was a fine but dark morning and we chose to avoid the M6 and travel down the A41/M54. This was an option we'd used more and more for travelling south. It's shorter, takes no extra time, and is much less boring than the motorway.

Just south of Shrewsbury we stopped, put down the caravan legs, and had breakfast in a lay-by. It was just starting to get light. We hadn't breakfasted en-route like this before, and we felt it was a nice touch to add that extra dash of excitement to a long journey.

"Look at that, it's snowing." Amanda sounded excited.

"Did we bring the sledge?"

I didn't bother to answer Kevin's question.

"It won't do much," I said. "It's probably not unusual to get the odd flurry in April."

"I don't know, those clouds look heavy," said Sarah.

"Nah, it's just because it's early morning. The dawn light makes it look like that. It'll stop soon enough."

We had our cornflakes, then boiled a kettle for tea and Sarah put some bread under the grill for toast. The sky and the air and the road were all one colour: white.

"Are we going to get stuck here?" asked Sarah.

"It's localised," I said. "Half a mile from here you won't know there's been any snow at all."

The view from the caravan window was now only half a view. Snow had stuck to the bottom of the glass. I rushed my toast and gulped my tea. I encouraged the others to follow my lead without saying so much. I wanted to be off. If this was localised I was starting to feel vulnerable sitting here and watching it. I didn't relish spending my Easter weekend sitting in a lay-by on the A41 in Shropshire. We quickly tidied and I went out to switch off the gas tap in the storage box at the front of the caravan. I could hardly lift the lid, such was the weight of snow that had settled on it in the short time we had been stopped.

The snow underfoot was deep – deep enough to find its way into my shoes, and it made that squeaking noise peculiar to new snow. I switched on the headlamps, started the car, and we crept gingerly out onto the road. It was still early and there had been few cars and no grit, so the snow was smooth on the road. I took it very slowly.

"How is it?" Sarah asked.

"Iffy," I said.

"Should we stop? Should we turn back?"

I wanted to do both. A car in snow can be quite scary. It has a mind of its own. When you are pulling a caravan you have two minds, each pulling in different directions. Driving in snow is something many people do, but it was not something I was enjoying.

"There's nowhere to stop. I can't chance another lay-by, who knows what the snow might be hiding – pot-holes, farm equipment..."

"Well, should we go back?"

"Probably, but how do we turn with the caravan?" I said. "If we push on, carefully, to the M54 we can choose to go round the roundabout and come back, or we can go on the motorway. There'll be more cars there, so it's bound to be better."

"I suppose," said Sarah. "If this is local, we'd be going through it twice if we go back."

It was a reasonable point. I'd never seen snow like this before – we don't get proper snow on the Wirral – and for April this was ridiculous. It must be a local blip in the weather. If we carried on it would get better.

We came to the M54. From the approach we couldn't see the condition of the motorway. I didn't have time to think about it. I headed down the slip road.

The M54 was a carpet of white, save for two single tyre tracks. I put our wheels in them and followed in what I presumed approximated the centre lane, there was no way of telling for sure. We chugged along at about twenty-five mph. A red Astra swept past doing about fifty. A plume of white snow-ploughed ice pelted the car.

"Grip must be better than it looks," said Sarah.

It wasn't. The Astra, although still travelling in a straight line, began to rotate around a central point so that we were looking at the passenger door as it headed on up the road. Then it found grip, and its direction changed abruptly. It went diagonally across the road, across the hard shoulder and slumped to a halt in a drift beside the embankment.

All through this dance routine I didn't brake or change course or even lift off the accelerator. I knew that to do so would be disaster. Any attempt at a change in momentum would put us into a spin. From time to time we would come out of the tyre tracks we were following, only by inches, and I could feel everything begin to slide, all six wheels. My mind was flooded with lurid images of what might happen to the car and the caravan and the four of us if it all got away from me.

"I think we need to leave the motorway," said Sarah. "This is not safe."

I agreed. Then again I wasn't sure. The motorway was quiet and in the middle lane we would have a lot of room to slide about before hitting anything solid. Our minds were made up at the next exit. A car had attempted to quit the motorway – the same one that had laid the tracks we were following. It had managed to get halfway up the sloping exit road before losing traction and slithering into the barrier where it was now stuck fast. We both looked over at it without saying anything. We knew that we were now staying with the M54 until we either reached the M6 or we crashed. There were few other choices. I toyed with the idea of pulling onto the hard shoulder, but we had now seen several spinning cars and we weren't sure we'd be any better off parked, just waiting to collect an errant high-speed nutter.

A few cars were passing us, and while we felt they were irresponsible in the extreme, we were also grateful because they gave us tracks to follow.

"Put the radio on," I said.

"Do you really–"

"Yes, do it. There may be traffic reports. We need to know what to do at the M6. Do we turn south to London or north back towards home?"

We tuned to a local station. The traffic reports were continuous. The M6 around Stafford was closed. So that solved that one, we wouldn't be turning north. The Midlands, generally, had become an inland sea. The snow, sleet and rain had been coming down for a long time and a number of homes and villages were cut off. It was like being in a disaster movie.

We came to the M6 and turned south. Here the going was better. There was, as always, a lot of traffic on the M6 and the snow had turned to very wet slush and deep puddles, and the tyres seemed to have something more substantial to hold on to. We still kept our speed down, and most other vehicles were now doing the same. The hard-shoulder casualties were drowned engines rather than nob-heads parked on crash barriers.

As we squelched through Wolverhampton and Birmingham another decision needed to be made. Our plan called for a switch to the M42, then onto the M40. This was the shorter route and it gave us less of the M25, which is wise in anybody's book. Now, though, I had my doubts. I was relishing the security of slushy tarmac under my tyres. What was the M40 like? It's quieter than the M6 and M1. Would it be a repeat of the M55 nightmare we had just left behind?

We talked it to death. All four of us chipped in with opinions. We were starting to sway towards sticking to plan. The M40 route was shorter so we would be exposed to danger for less time. A radio report talking about flooding on the M1 seemed to swing it for us, but then we missed the M42 exit, because we were so busy discussing it, and it became a *fait accompli*.

The radio tales became ever more desperate and lurid.

"Does anyone out there have a small boat or canoe? We're putting out requests for small sailing vessels. Rescue teams are trying to reach a trapped family..."

"We're putting out an emergency help-line number, ring it if you know of someone who is..."

"...food and blankets. I repeat, anyone who can help with food, warm drinks and blankets, please could you report to the leisure centre at...."

There was no music. No inane DJ banter. Every station carried pleas for help and heart-warming tales of neighbour helping neighbour. We drove on in silence, totally captivated by the scale of human travail that was being enacted around us. On some stretches of the M1 the flooding was on both sides of the road, and was so extensive that we appeared to be creeping along a narrow ribbon of tarmac that crossed an ocean – an ocean with treetops and pylons sticking up.

And we were going on holiday!

As we neared London the rain eased. We looped onto the M25, where we joined the ceremonial on-road car parking for twenty-five minutes. Then we took the Chertsey exit. We had arrived.

We moved through the booking-in formalities in a daze, and were shown to a pitch close by the river with a fine view of Chertsey Bridge. We set up quickly and brewed restorative tea. The sun was shining. Birds were singing. Swans plied up and down the river. It felt good to be alive. The normality of the scene felt unreal, like a movie scene. At last it penetrated our fuddled brains: this was not just a river, this was the Thames! London beckoned.

We drove into Windsor, after lunch, and commenced our

"look-at-but-don't-go-in" brand of tourism. We looked at Eton College, we looked at Windsor Castle. The Royal Standard was flying so the Queen was home.

One of the things you do a lot of when you're a "look-at" tourist is walk. In Windsor there is a place where you can do this, it's called the Long Walk. The Long Walk is about three miles and feels like fifteen. It's straight and there are trees. On the way out you get to see a statue of a man on a horse who never gets any nearer. On the way back you get to look at Windsor Castle for hours and think about what you're going to have for tea. If you're into plane spotting there is a lot of scope when the wind is in the right direction. We saw planes. Lots of them. Kevin, in particular, was fascinated by the conveyor belt of jumbos and 737s that stretched up into the sky until all that could be seen was a jewelled string of landing lights. It was fun for an hour or so. I wouldn't want to live there. You'd think the Queen would be a bit miffed about it all. She probably gives the duty manager at Heathrow down the banks from time to time.

"Ah, hello, this is Mrs R. speaking, from Windsor. Would you mind closing runway 2 for a few hours, we have a splitting head-ache."

We only had a few hours at Windsor, but it was sufficient, and we were time-pressured enough to avoid feeling down about having to do all our tourism on the outside. Besides, the main event was tomorrow.

Back at the caravan we spoiled our appetites by munching Easter eggs before tea. I know, it was Good Friday and you're not supposed to eat Easter eggs until Easter Sunday. We changed this rule years earlier when the children were tots. It seemed better to help them to pace themselves across the whole Easter Weekend, rather than have them stuff themselves against the clock all Sunday morning and afternoon; then bring it back again in the evening. I don't buy in to the religious arguments either; there doesn't seem to be a great deal of correlation between the crucifixion and the marketing strategies of the UK confectionary industry, and their mission to convert all of Britain's children into spotty, obese vomit factories.

We woke early on Saturday morning. Our train into London would leave before ten, and there is much to be done in a caravan in the mornings. Shower, shave, breakfast, fetch water, dump water...

The train took us to Waterloo. We walked to the river and crossed Westminster bridge, gawping in awe at the Houses of Parliament and St Stephen's tower. No, it's not Big Ben. Big Ben is the bell that hangs in St Stephen's tower. I kept telling the children this and they kept rolling their eyes.

"Does it matter?" Kevin said. "Everyone calls it Big Ben. You're so picky."

"I'm not picky. I just get annoyed when people choose to ignore an obvious fact. It's lazy thinking."

"Kevin, don't start him," said Amanda. "He'll be off on the one about the Millennium again."

It was 1998. In less than two years a monumental mistake would be made. I could see from Amanda's eyes that she was baiting me. She knew I could never hold back on that one. I decided to defy her. I bit my tongue and looked out over the river to take my mind off their taunts.

"Don't wind your father up," said Sarah. "Anyway, he's conceded the Millennium thing. He's accepted that he is wrong."

"I have not conceded! The new millennium does not start

until 2001. I have never backed down on that one." I was incensed. I could also see, from Sarah's expression, that I had been played.

"That's okay, dear," she said, beaming a smile of satisfaction. "You are, of course, correct and all the rest of the world are wrong."

"I am right, that's just it! I can't understand them. They're all idiots. The whole world is going to celebrate the wrong year. They are going to have concerts and parties and Jools Holland, and they are going to let off billions of pounds' worth of fireworks *a year early!* What is it with them?"

I cannot let it go. Sarah knows it. Kevin knows it. Amanda knows it. They can wind me up and set me off like a clockwork train. They love having that power. But you know what? About the Millennium?

I am bloody right!

We walked down the Mall to see Buckingham Palace.

"Is the Queen home?" asked Amanda.

"No," I said. "We know where the Queen is. She's standing at the window in her front living room in Windsor Castle, shaking her fist at all the planes."

We hung around for a bit, though, to see if anything would happen, then turned and headed back up the Mall. It began to rain. It was a cruel rain, slushy, wind-driven and very cold. It drove full into our faces as we walked. We fought with umbrellas, but the wind wasn't having any of it, and our exposed hands became red and raw. We passed through Admiralty Arch without interest, and we headed into Trafalgar Square feeling cold and miserable and not in the mood for stone lions or pigeons at all. We found a Deep Pan Pizza that was advertising an eat-as-much-as-you-like buffet deal for a reasonable sum. It had just opened and we went for it without preamble. Inside it was warm and cosy. There was a wonderful cheesy smell. We sat down and waited to order. When we were given empty plates the full impact of this deal hit home. We could eat... As... Much... As... We... Liked!

It's not that we were out-of-town hicks and knew nothing of city life, I'm sure they did these things back home in Hicksville, too, but before 1998 we had simply never eaten out. Pizzas came in a cardboard box, frozen, from Kwik Save. Eating out was chips in paper, and that was a rare treat. For our London adventure, though, we had saved. Eating out was part of the plan. We were here, in the capital, and this showed that we were scraping together some kind of wealth. Dining out in Trafalgar Square would have been incomprehensible to us a couple of years earlier.

We watched what others did so that we wouldn't do anything stupid, then, empty plates in hand, we attacked the pizza buffet with naivety, and wide eyes, and Guinness-World-Record-breaking determination. Between Kevin and me there was also a competitive element. It must be a male thing. Sarah and Amanda were quite sensible. They knew when to stop. Kevin eyed me, and I eyed Kevin and we let slip the dogs of war. It was unclear who we were challenging, each other or the entire worldwide Deep Pan Corporation, but of one thing we were certain; today there would be winners and losers. The duel raged on. If one of us left our seat for the buffet the other would respond. There could be no cheating – no returning to our table with half-full plates; when there wasn't room on them for more pizza we grouted the gaps with pasta. Everything that came back had to be eaten. No signs of weakness would be tolerated.

Sarah saved our lives.

"Stop! For heaven's sake, you've eaten enough. You're like a pair of pigs, the two of you."

We both protested, but without putting heart and soul into it. We couldn't stop yet, could we? It was too soon. We hadn't bankrupted the Deep Pan shop yet. I was secretly grateful for the intervention, though, and I'm sure Kevin was, too. I suspect, also, the Chief Executive Officer of the Deep Pan Pizza Corporation breathed a sigh of relief as he lifted his hand away from the red, profit-warning hot-line telephone.

We ordered coffee. I must have looked terrible. I certainly felt terrible. I had a raging thirst from the aftereffects of all that dough and salt and fat that had sucked all of the moisture from my body, yet it was a thirst I couldn't quench because there was no more room inside. Any liquid would have simply topped-off and dribbled back out of my mouth and nose. Kevin looked as green as I felt.

We continued our tour. It had stopped raining but it was cold. The cold felt good; it took some of the feverishness away. I staggered around London in a haze of gaseous exhalations. Trafalgar Square pigeons dropped and died at my feet.

We looked at the National Gallery and the National Portrait Gallery. These were in the days before the British Enlightenment, when national galleries became free of charge, so we admired the buildings from the outside. Sarah's eye held a wistful tear. As an artist she would have loved to have spent a leisurely afternoon strolling around inside. We could have afforded it, too, but we knew that it would have been a waste trying to drag our teenagers around an art gallery. Besides, she knew that tomorrow there was a bigger treat in store on our itinerary, one that the children were just going to have to live with.

I took Sarah's hand, promising to return in a few years, just the two of us, when we would hit *all* the art galleries, and with the same kind of zeal as I had shown in ridding the world of pizza. So, as gently as possible, I led her away.

We went underground and the children experienced, for the first time in their lives, the roaring, rushing, manic, subterranean world of the Tube.

Once through the turnstile we were propelled through a dynamic system powered by seething humanity.

Nowhere to stop.

Nowhere to think.

Just put your ticket in the slot, snap, out of your fingers and up the other side.

Don't pause, don't breathe, just move with the flow.

A human log flume.

Don't stop for the beggars. Don't stop for the buskers (catch a few bars, he sounds good, too late). On and down, hold hands, don't get lost, eastbound or westbound?

Where are we going?

Onto the platform... Time to breathe, but no, there's noise and wind and the end of the world? A silver bullet blasts through at warp speed, then brakes squeal. It stops. Doors open. Hiss. Slam. Closed in seconds. Barely time to get a family of four through safely.

Nowhere to sit.

Acceleration.

Spread your feet to keep your balance, hang onto the straps, face inches away from strangers: whites, Asians, West Africans, Eastern Europeans.

One stop. Two stops. This is us, off the train, quick, before the doors close.

Back into the tide. Ride the current. Up, up and out of the pit.

We stood, panting and wide eyed, looking at deserted city

streets. This was the business end of London and it was Easter so it was closed. No matter, we weren't here for business. Which way to the Monument?

The Monument is a good tourist stop. You can go up it and it's cheap – relatively. We started to climb the spiral staircase, round and round, up and up, and soon our thighs were burning and our hearts were pounding. For me it would have been hard enough, anyway, without having to carry aloft twenty-odd pounds of undigested pizza.

Now and again on the narrow staircase, it becomes necessary to pass someone coming down, and this is good, because it gives you an excuse to pause, or stop, while you figure out a passing manoeuvre.

We reached the top before a myocardial infarction felled me, and once I'd managed to quell the dizziness and blink away the purple spots from my eyes, I cast my attention on the view. It's pretty dammed impressive. The complaints about high-rise buildings spoiling the traditional views were rife even then, but for my money the view from the top of the Monument was worth the climb. The Thames can be seen winding into London; brown, murky and thick with historical significance. The Tower of London, Tower Bridge, St Paul's dome... Every direction, every angle of view is filled with iconic landmarks. There can be few cities in the world able to boast so many immediately recognisable pieces of tourist candy, and from the top of the Monument you can see most of them. Okay, there are a lot of big buildings going up, and these have and will continue to obscure some of the views, but for the most part these buildings are impressive in their own right, and worth seeing, and if you didn't have progress and development I would, on that day, have been standing in the mud looking at a bunch of squalid, burnt-out timber-framed buildings, with plague victims being hauled out by the score.

As we circulated around the balcony, I noticed something else. We were the only ones up there who were speaking English. I heard French, German, various oriental languages whose exact origin was way beyond my guessing, and some tongues that I couldn't place by hemisphere, let alone country. It felt like we were abroad. It was exotic. We all noticed and we were thrilled. Imagine if one day we could go somewhere that had a different language and we were the foreigners. How cool would that be?

We had to tear ourselves away. There was much more to see. We unscrewed down the spiral staircase, and when we reached the exit the kids were given certificates stating that they had been to the top of the Monument. I thought that was a nice touch, and a far better souvenir than a plastic London Bus or a snow-dome of Buckingham Palace. We'd seen Buckingham Palace in the snow and we hadn't been all that thrilled.

Back down into the human meat-processor that is the Tube, and the next time it spat us out we were at the Tower of London. Plenty to see here without spending money. We saw the queues of affluent tourists lining up to get in and felt grateful that we would not be amongst them.

We crossed Tower Bridge with eyes boggling, then walked up the other side of the river to look at HMS Belfast and the Globe Theatre. You can walk right along the South Bank these days, but back in 1998 it was all a bit iffy, and we found ourselves down alleys with stray cats and dogs and dodgy-looking people foraging in bins and mushed newspapers sticking to the shiny cobbles. These days this is one of my favourite parts of London, but in 1998 we were happy to find a bridge and get back across the river.

The day was coming to a close. We'd seen about one percent

of the interesting stuff. London is a big place and we knew that we would be back for more. Our plan was to have our evening meal before heading to Waterloo Station. We found a McDonald's and Sarah and I had tea and coffee. My appetite for food might be back by, oh, late August? The children had McNuggets and fries. Large.

Our train from Waterloo whisked us away from the capital. We returned to the caravan and fell into our bunks exhausted.

On Sunday we went to Kew Gardens. I'm not a fan of gardens, but there is something else at Kew that Sarah had wanted to see for many years, and Kew had thus been high on our hit list since we first thought of London as a caravan destination.

You have to pay to get into Kew, and £13 seemed way pricey in April when everything's dead – but it did get us into all the hot-houses and stuff, so maybe it was okay. In the summer it would be worth every penny, but I grumbled a bit because I thought there should be some kind of discount for looking at dead plants.

I stopped moaning, though, when we went into the Princess of Wales Conservatory. This was quite something, with different climates in different sections. I liked the temperate sections best because it was warm, and outside there was an arctic wind that would have had penguins pulling on woolly jumpers. It was nice to dawdle a bit here and to feign an interest in all things horticultural.

You can't do this all day, though, so eventually we left and headed for the warmth of the Palm House. The great thing about the Palm House is the building itself. It's big and wonderful to explore, especially since you can climb up to balconies high in the roof and look down on the plants. I wanted to find a banana plant. I had a point to prove. I once

173

told Sarah how bananas grow pointing up, not drooping down.

"That's ridiculous, how could they?"

"They do, honest. I know it seems to defy logic but they definitely grow pointing up."

I think, secretly, she had come to accept the truth – but she would not admit it. I believe this was a ploy to wind me up, and it worked. So here was my chance to prove, once and for all, that I was right. I raced around the Palm House on a frantic quest for bananas. I knew there was one here. I needed to find it. Sarah was in less of a hurry because she enjoys getting me agitated and didn't want to see any physical evidence that would spoil the game.

I found my banana tree. It was all leaves. Not a single hand of bananas to be seen. I was devastated. Sarah was delighted, and now, seeing the opportunity to raise my blood pressure, the children ganged up on her side.

"Of course they grow downwards. It's gravity. You can't convince us. Prove it."

This was before Wikipedia. The children somehow sensed its absence.

They drove me mad.

There was an unexpected surprise that we all enjoyed. One of the smaller palm houses was themed so that you walked through time, with plants chosen to represent those that grew on earth millions of years ago. There were plastic dinosaurs, jets of steam and smoke and pre-historic sound effects. It all worked rather well and provided another diversion that kept us out of the cutting wind in the real world.

Then came the big moment. Sarah's moment. In the nineteenth century there lived a painter who specialised in botanical art. Her name was Marianne North. She headed out to far-flung continents, remote islands and deep jungles, where she would paint. She travelled alone, and in those Victorian times this was simply not done. She was brave, independent, and had no time for dogmatic views on what was done and what was not. She thumbed her nose at Victorian niceties and travelled, and on top of this she was a fabulous artist. Marianne North has been Sarah's number one heroine and role model for many, many years.

In a corner of Kew Gardens there is a medium-sized, insignificant building in which her paintings are displayed. Marianne North had the gallery built in 1882 as a place where she could show her work, which she donated to Kew. She did not believe in the popular method of carefully hanging each painting on an open wall where it could be admired individually; she was a jaw-droppingly prolific artist, and she wanted to show as many of her paintings as wall space would allow. So in her headstrong and unconventional way she got to it and stuck the lot up.

As you walk through the doors of the gallery, the sheer volume of her work takes your breath away. There are 832 paintings, produced over a period of just 13 years. Every inch of wall space, every foot of elevation, is covered in paintings. Not only paintings but panels of 246 different types of wood that Marianne collected from her travels. Even the wooden door surrounds are decorated by flowers that Marianne hand-painted herself while preparing the gallery.

A few of the paintings were familiar to me. Sarah has been regularly borrowing a book from the local library which show many of them. The book was withdrawn a few years earlier, though (much to Sarah's horror and disgust), and it's one that the local pre-Amazon bookshops do not seem to stock.

But you can buy it at Kew.

Seeing the look in her eyes as she drifted around trying to

absorb nearly a thousand paintings crammed onto the walls, I knew that an early birthday present was required. This, also, was not extravagance; it was part of the plan – my plan. She objected and fussed and tried to stop me, but I could tell that, deep down, she was hoping I would be stubborn. I can be stubborn when I need to be. The copy I bought also happened to have been signed by its writer, Laura Ponsonby. I knew I'd done right by the starry-eyed, dream-like trance that Sarah slipped into for the rest of the day.

Easter Monday was a short day. We had to be off the site by noon. We decided to have a look around Chertsey. We crossed the bridge and went to see the locks that allowed river boats to by-pass the weir. We walked down the river and marvelled at the miles of rickety, damp houseboats. Do people live here? All year? Are the chest clinics a growth industry down here?

On our way back towards the site we crossed Chertsey Bridge again, and passed by a modern but dull office building with no character or architectural merit whatsoever, and I have no idea which companies are housed in it. Outside there is a small piece of corporate art. It is a bronze statue (by the sculptor Sheila Mitchell) that depicts a young, pretty woman in a flowing dress hanging onto the clapper of a bell. Her face shows determination and an inner strength. It is a captivating piece of work. On the plinth on which the statue stands, there are brief details of her story. We read it, slowly, and were enthralled.

The girl's name was Blanche Heriot. In the fifteenth century, during the Wars of the Roses, her lover, Herrick Evenden, was imprisoned and was awaiting execution. The execution was to take place at the sounding of the Curfew Bell in Chertsey Abbey. As curfew drew nearer, Blanche, in desperation, climbed the bell tower and thrust her body between the clapper and the bell, thus preventing the bell from ringing. Her intervention saved Herrick's life; a pardon, granted by King Edward IV, was subsequently delivered and Herrick was freed.

We packed up the caravan and returned home. We were quiet and subdued; each of us lost in our own thoughts. I suspect we were thinking about the same thing, the story of Blanche Heriot and that marvellous sculpture.

HOPPING IN WALES: 1998

Consider our motorways. They carry large volumes of traffic travelling at speeds of up to (and often more than) 70 mph. They are dangerous places. Certainly not an agreeable setting for a picnic, and we are rightly told – never, ever, stop on the hard shoulder. If your car breaks down you must get everyone out of the car, over the crash barrier and up the embankment. I have no argument whatsoever with this sage advice, it is sensible stuff. Hard shoulders are a deadly, life-threatening environment.

Now, consider duel-carriageway "A" roads. They carry large volumes of traffic travelling at speeds of up to (and often more than) 70 mph. How are they different to motorways? Well, they have lay-bys! Places where we can stop and eat lunch. The children are allowed to open the car doors and step out onto a narrow strip of tarmac where the very air explodes from the onrush of thundering juggernauts. We can take our camping chairs out of the boot and assemble a family group beside the car. We can eat sandwiches and take afternoon tea mere inches from hurtling projectiles of steel and iron driven by time-pressured and road-weary travellers who have not yet found the time to relax and unwind.

Let's be quite clear about this. We are not merely permitted to partake in this suicidal activity; we are actively encouraged to do so. Giant blue signposts with the letter "P". Trailers selling tea and coffee. There are even count-down enticements to make sure that we have plenty of time to make a decision.

Can this possibly be the contender? The most stupid inconsistency in the whole UK road network?

* * *

—No. 49 from the Moanicles of Michael.

"Now, what seems to be the matter?"

"It's my toe, I think I may have broken it." I looked up at the nurse with a forlorn expression.

"It seems quite swollen. Does this hurt?"

"Aaaaaaaarrgh!"

"Hmm. I think it's broken. What did you do to it?"

I wriggled uncomfortably on the chair. I didn't want to answer. The nurse looked at me and raised her eyebrows. An answer was expected.

"I had a problem opening a can of peaches," I said.

We were on the second day of our main summer holiday. We had arrived at a site in Rhandirmwyn, in mid-Wales, when I made a grand announcement.

"I will cook the tea tonight."

I do this from time to time. The meal is usually edible but often there comes an unwelcome aftermath.

On this occasion the main course had gone well – spaghetti Bolognese – and although I had brought every pan, plate, dish and item of cutlery into play, there had been few incidents. I pushed my luck, however, when I volunteered to go the whole distance and produce a dessert. I reached out for a tin of peaches.

It was July. It was hot. I was wearing shorts and my feet were bare. Sarah had warned me about cooking in bare feet. How did she know? From whence had she drawn such powers of prescience, to be able to make predictions like, 'Don't cook in your bare feet, you might have an accident.'? I think even Sarah would have found it difficult to foresee the dangers

179

lurking in a tin of peaches, though.

I took out the can-opener, began to wind, and spilled a tiny drop of the juice. It made the can slick and it popped out of my hand. I grabbed for it and, like a wet bar of soap, it leapt free again. As it headed for the floor my lightning reflexes came into play and I tried to catch it on my foot. I kicked out but the edge of the bunk was in the way and I toe-ended it. I went down like a sack of turnips, howling in pain. My beloved family laughed, heartily. They had apparently seen something funny in my performance. I lay on the caravan floor in a pool of tears and peach syrup.

The pain didn't ease. I tried to go for a walk in the evening but didn't get as far as the site entrance. I had a wretched night listening to the snores of the family while trying to keep the duvet from settling on my toe. Next morning we headed for the cottage hospital in Llandovery.

"Are you going to X-ray it?"

The nurse shook her head. "No point, really. We can't do anything for it. It might just be badly bruised, in which case it will ease in a day or two, but it looks broken."

"If it's broken what should I do?"

"Limp."

"Can't you put a cast on it?"

"That would hurt more than if we just leave it alone. Just keep your weight off it and take Paracetamol if it gives you trouble."

I looked up at her with beseeching eyes.

"If it's bruised it will be okay in a couple of days. If it's broken it will be okay in a couple of weeks, okay?"

This was the start of my two-week summer holiday. With luck it would be okay by the time we headed for home. Sarah drove me back to the caravan. The children were waiting with unsympathetic enquiries.

"Will we have to go home?"

"No," said Sarah, "but your dad won't be doing much walking or cycling this holiday."

"Good, what's for dinner?"

Rhandirmwyn was only a stopover. It looked nice. A river ran through the site and all around there were pine forests and hills that had huge potential for walking. I saw it all from the caravan window. Monday morning I hopped around the awning, pulling pegs and howling, then we hitched up and Sarah took us south to the Gower Peninsula.

The journey would have been alright except for Swansea. For some reason the providers of roadside signage in Swansea didn't want people to find the Gower Peninsula, but it was okay because I was reading the map. Everybody knows that only men can read maps, which is the reason for all the route-finding problems on UK roads, because usually the men drive and then expect the women to fly in the face of evolution and read maps. We came to a nasty junction that was followed by a very sharp downhill section. This was fine for us but I commented on the difficulties it might present if we had to come back that way. It wasn't just steep, it was the kind of slope best tackled with ropes and harnesses.

"Don't fancy that hill-start with the caravan," I said, with a smug laugh. "I'm glad we're going the other way."

Ten minutes later we found ourselves on a familiar road, heading up a familiar hill.

"Isn't this the hill that you were glad we didn't have to come up?" said Sarah.

This was her final word on a heated exchange that had raged

since entering the Swansea No-Sign Zone.

As if the hill wasn't bad enough on its own, there were traffic lights halfway up.

"Try and time it with the lights so we don't have to stop," I said. "They're on red. Go slower. Give them a chance to change. Slower. *Slower.*"

The car began to bunny hop, then stopped. The lights changed to green. The hill-start needed both of us on the handbrake and a great deal of shouting. With a juddering and a rattling and a rich smell of burning clutch, Sarah got the car moving and we carried on to the next roundabout where we did a 360 degree turn and headed back for another pass.

This time we tried a completely different route through the town, and again found ourselves on the same hill. Again we missed the lights, and once more we performed screaming heroics with the clutch and handbrake.

Our third attempt took us through a housing estate where speeding had become a problem. The solution was speed bumps. Speed bumps are the worst thing in the world when you are towing a caravan (apart from hills and Clarksons). This estate had dozens of the things and each one was like South Africa's Table Mountain.

We cringed as we crashed and bumped through mile after mile of secluded housing. At last we came to a T-junction.

"Which way?" asked Sarah.

I was busy rotating the map on my knee and getting red in the face.

"Left, I think," I said.

"I don't know, it looks kind of familiar."

"No, I think it's definitely left."

"Right seems to take us back to Swansea."

"Yes, and we don't want to go back to Swansea. It's left." I was sure now. I had the map. I was male. We know these things.

Sarah shrugged and turned left. Within fifty yards we knew where we were. We could see the hill climbing ahead of us, as familiar by now as our own road at home.

Sarah was dying to say, 'Told you so.' I could see it in her eyes. She's good, though. She just stared ahead and grasped the wheel in a white-knuckle grip. I swallowed. I wasn't sure how much of this the car could take. We'd had the Sierra for four years now. It was a good car, especially after necessity had us fit a new engine. We were also now on our second clutch, and I had hoped that a replacement would solve our hill-start problems. It hadn't. Any hill-start in the Sierra was uncomfortable. When towing the caravan, it felt as though we were trying to relocate an anvil warehouse. I had tried all ways: Revving like mad, low revs and prayer, different gears. Always the same result. The car would rattle and vibrate and protest. Double vision was not uncommon. This was on slight inclines. Serious hills were scary. This one in Swansea was the mother of all hill-starts, and we missed the lights every single time.

The fourth time through Swansea I had my head buried in the map. I was determined to get us through this place. I looked up and we were on a different road.

"What happened? Where are we? *What have you done?*"

"I saw a sign that said, 'Gower'. I followed it."

"This road is not on the map," I said. "The map is wrong."

The site in Gower was at Port Eynon. It was a temporary site run by a DA, so it was cheap, but they were using a field at the back of a large commercial site, so if you didn't mind a short walk you could use all the facilities.

We stayed at Port Eynon for five days, and I was able to see some of it. I found that I could limp around if I squeezed my toe into my walking boots. It hurt a bit but the boots didn't flex so I found that I could walk.

We didn't see much of Kevin in Port Eynon, because he made friends with someone on the commercial part of the site. Kevin was sixteen, now, and sometimes prone to moodiness.

He was acting a little strangely – not wanting to come with us to explore the Gower. It was strange because there was a lot to see.

We went to Worm's Head, a spectacular promontory of rocks that reached out into the sea. It was great for walking (or hobbling) and equally inviting was the beach alongside it – Rhossili Beach – that had all the important factors in a beach that we craved: it was clean, it had scenery and it was largely empty, owing to the Himalayan staircase that had to be scaled to get back up to the car park.

I struggled with the swimming here, because once the boots were off I was largely disabled again. Bare feet, a broken toe and a half mile of those painful hard-sand ripples did little to encourage me into the water. I tried paddling, though, hoping that the numbing cold of the sea water would ease the pain, but it didn't. I also tried swimming, in the hope that taking the weight off would help, but flapping my feet around in the water flexed my toe and was even worse than walking. So I hobbled back to base camp intent on doing a lot of reading.

Kevin came back with me. He had become disinterested in swimming and seemed to want only to return to the campsite. I couldn't understand him. Yes, it was a pleasant enough site, but not *that* good. At times, in Gower, he seemed really cheerful and chatty, but always keen to wake up early and be off. He'd been sleeping in his tent for the last two years; he found that this gave him more of his own space, so we didn't know what time he was getting up in the morning. He was gone when we awoke and only returned for meal times.

Then we learned that his friend's name was Anne.

We were happy for him, but we should have guessed at the trauma to come. When we said that we were moving on, after only five days, there was trouble. We had little choice, the tour of Wales was planned and we were booked in at our next site.

"Leave me here," he said. "Come and get me next week. I like it here."

There were never any direct references to what it was, exactly, that he liked about the Gower, but he was adamant that he should stay and we should leave. We really felt for him. We knew that he wasn't being logical – but what is logic when it stands in the way of true love?

We began to discuss the options. Should we stay and let things run their course? Would that turn out to be harder and more difficult for him in the long run? Should we leave him behind and provide instructions on how to get home by train or coach from Swansea? Should we lay down the law and point out the futility of trying to conduct a romance separated by the hundred miles of country between Solihull and the Wirral?

It was our last day. We still hadn't decided. Kevin decided for us. He came back to the caravan with a face like thunder and began packing his tent. I looked at Sarah. What had happened? We hardly dared ask. We put up with silence all though lunch, then Sarah cracked.

"What's happened, Kevin? Have you decided what you want to do?"

"I'm coming."

"We don't want to force you. We are open to options here."

"I'm coming with you."

"What about Anne? What does she...?"

"Anne's gone home, with her parents. Holiday's over."

We were relieved. We shouldn't have been. The next week was hell. He had a picture, and a letter. He kept it with him all the time. He unfolded it and read it and refolded it so many times the paper began to tear. Our hearts bled for him. We remembered; sixteen sucks.

We moved on to St David's. This was the third time for the children and the fifth time for Sarah and I, and St David's was still a special place for us. This time we opted for a different site. We wanted a change of scene.

Our last visit to St David's – to Nine Wells, near Solva – had been two years earlier, in 1996, and it had been marked by the incident with the electric hook-up.

Ah, the electric hook-up. Okay, I'll tell you all about St David's 1996. We had electrics in the caravan so we were determined to use them. The trouble was we had no fridge, no TV, no need for lights in June. All the electric hook-up did for us was charge the battery, but it was still a novelty for ex-tent-campers and we wanted to use it.

We'd been there a day when another caravan arrived next to us. We were fascinated by these people. They reversed the caravan into their space, dropped the legs, and before anything else, before getting water or even closing the car doors, the father, a frail and pasty-faced soul, set about hooking up the electricity. The rest of the family, a mother and two children, scampered into the caravan and took up what seemed to be well-rehearsed positions on the two front bunks, and began to wait. The father then retrieved an enormous TV and manhandled it onto the flat space in front of the window. Now we understood the seating arrangements. These were the family positions for viewing.

There was more to be done. Next came the aerial. The father raised a substantial, ex-Goonhilly-Downs aerial on a pole and began pointing it every which way. Each move was greeted by wails of disapproval from the family within, until, some thirty or forty minutes later, a satisfactory alignment was found. There were no cheers from within, just approving silence. The father scurried round and we soon saw him sliding into the remaining empty seat. Then the four of them adopted a zen-like trance, with hanging jaws and wide, staring, pupil-dilated expressions.

Outside, the sun shone and cast sparkling reflections on the sea. The whole blue expanse of St Bride's Bay could be seen from our caravan. Next door the view was obscured by the box in the window. Four faces hovered in semi-darkness, illuminated only by the ghostly, coloured moving lights of TV death.

They stayed like this. As far as I could tell they didn't go for water. I don't know if they ate. The temperature outside pushed eighty degrees. God knows what it was like inside with the doors and windows closed and the TV belting out heat by the gigawatt.

I dare say this would have gone on for the week or fortnight, whatever the duration of their holiday, if I hadn't gone and spoiled it for them.

It was three days later. We had been to the beach and had a car full of wet towels and polystyrene body-boards and inflated inner-tubes.

For some reason, I don't know why, I decided to reverse into our space rather than drive straight in. I always drove straight in – much easier – but today I reversed, not too slowly, and *crunch*. I hit something. Something hard.

Oops.

Then I noticed that the TV family were on their feet and looking dismayed. There was a lot of anxiety and the father seemed to be getting the brunt of it. Faces were dark. The TV was off.

I hurried round the car to find that I had hit the concrete post that supports the hook-up box for both our caravan and next door's. I hadn't just knocked it, I had creamed it. It lay, shattered and sad, on the grass with wires splaying out in all directions.

Mr TV appeared at my elbow.

"Oh my god. Look what you've done."

"Ahh."

"What are you going to do?"

Voices came from inside.

"Dad, it's still off. What's happened?"

"What are you going to do?" he repeated. "We've paid for electricity."

"I'll go and tell them at the farmhouse."

"Can they fix it now? Tell them they have to fix it now."

"Do you want to come down with me?"

He began wringing his hands and looking over his shoulder at the blank TV screen.

"No. You go. I'll... I'll just..."

He reached up and, unbelievably, he began adjusting the aerial.

"I don't think that's going to help," I said.

"I've got to... it might... I'll try..."

I left him to it.

I returned a few minutes later with the site owner. He laughed when he saw the state of the post.

"You've certainly buggered that up," he said.

"Is there any chance that..."

"None at all. I'll have to get a sparks from Haverfordwest. I'll ring him on Monday. I'm afraid you'll have to do without for a few days."

He leaned in the open door of the TV people.

"May as well put the telly away. It'll be a few days, I'm afraid."

He laughed and said to me, "It'll kill 'em, you know."

Mr TV was outside again minutes later. He began adjusting the aerial. The family remained inside and stared at the blank screen.

That had been St David's two years ago. This time, for our return to St Bride's Bay, after a history of midnight door-slamming and weird TV zombies, we felt that we might try somewhere else, somewhere normal.

We arrived at Penarn Farm in Treginnis. It hadn't been an easy journey. Kevin had moped and sighed the whole way. Amanda had lectured him about pulling himself together. And the exhaust pipe had fallen off the car just outside Carmarthen.

Penarn Farm was populated by goats and hippies.

We were a little alarmed at first. There were two other caravans on the site and they all seemed a bit odd. There was a penchant for long hair and sitar music and long periods of vacant inactivity. Had we done it again? Maybe it was Pembrokeshire. Maybe the entire coast attracted the weirdos.

It grew on us, though, and the location was fabulous. St David's is only about two miles from where the coast path faces Ramsey Island, and Penarn was in between, within an easy walk of either, and I was getting better at walking. I could now manage a mile or two at a pinch. It's also a very quiet part of the region with very little traffic, so it was well-suited for cycling.

Our first priority, though, was to drive to Haverfordwest and get a new exhaust. It had started to blow on our way from the Gower. Probably the repeated hill-climbing antics had rattled all the good, solid rust off it. The exhaust was completely gone now. It hadn't fallen off as such, it had just kind of turned to brown dust and been blown away in the wind, and the car was sounding like a Lancaster Bomber. It was embarrassing. The car was also proving difficult to start, and my theory was that the loss of the exhaust pipe was affecting the way the engine breathed.

Haverfordwest is often worth an afternoon when you need to buy stuff. It's small, and it can be difficult to find somewhere to park, unless you want to leave your car at ATS and buy a new exhaust every time you visit, but it is an island of civilisation in a part of Wales that is really quite remote. It's the place to go if you need to buy things outside of the usual staples like tea, milk and cornflakes. Haverfordwest is the place to go for car parts and tools.

We had to leave the car for a few hours so we decided to eat out. This was something that we were starting to do more and more, but it was still a rare enough treat to be held up as being special. So we stomped up and down the shops looking for somewhere to tempt my wallet, somewhere exciting, somewhere that might even bring Kevin back to planet earth for an hour or so. We failed. We bought pies from a pie shop and ate them sitting on a wall overlooking the river.

They are trying their best, the council, the town elders or whoever. There is an attractive new shopping arcade fronting the river which is home to the same old shops (WH Smiths, Boots, you know...), and the bus station is quite attractive, but, I don't know, trying your best is sometimes not quite enough. Haverfordwest is not an unattractive town. Many other towns are worse, but somehow I wanted it to be better.

We picked the car up from ATS. We had trouble starting it, so scratch that theory. Our starting problem had nothing to do with the exhaust, after all. It would be okay, though, I thought, slamming the door in the face of that sensible me inside that said, 'Oh, no it won't.'

We didn't need the car at Penarn, however. We walked. My foot was getting stronger so we did sections of the coast path. It really is the most beautiful stretch of coastline.

"One day," I said, "I will get a small tent and do the whole route, Pembroke to Fishguard."

"Yes, dear."

Sarah had heard this before – every time we visited this coast in fact. I also plan to walk the Pennine Way, the West Highland Way and the Appalachian Trail... one day.

The Pembrokeshire Coastal Path is a great place for Twitchers. I know this, although I'm not a birdwatcher myself. It's not a good idea to overtly carry binoculars here, if you're not a birdwatcher, because the Twitchers stop you and engage you in incomprehensible conversations.

"Did you hear the Lesser Spotted Googledicks?"

"???"

"Back there a way. There's a mating pair. You can hear their call. Cawooop Cawoop."

"Ahh."

It's difficult to extricate yourself from this kind of conversation. Do you go along with it until you make a blunder, showing your ignorance in all its glory?

'Are you sure they're not Greater Spotted Googledicks?'

'You are a fool and a philistine! There is no such creature as a Greater Spotted Googledick.'

Or do you admit to being a fool and a philistine right from

the outset?

'I'm sorry, I know nothing of birds. I am but a fool. I'm minding these binoculars for a friend.'

Or,

'Actually, I am an astronomer. I'm waiting for dark.'

Trust me. Buy a rucksack. Put your binoculars in there. It's also a handy place to keep your sandwiches.

The other good thing about Pembrokeshire is the seagulls. (See, a philistine. There are probably ten thousand species of seabird around the Pembrokeshire coast. I see seagulls. Grey ones and brown ones.) Yes, anyway, the good thing about Pembrokeshire gulls is that they are still wild. They know nothing of sandwiches and pies. This cannot be said of the genetically-modified Cornish seagulls, which are intelligent, hunt in packs, and are devoted scholars of Daphne du Maurier. On a recent visit to St Ives, two seagulls drew our attention to the right, with lunges and feints and hesitant attempts to seize my lunch, while a third crept up on the blind side and made off with Sarah's vegetarian Cornish Pasty.

So in Pembrokeshire you can stop anywhere and have a picnic without fear of being molested by gulls, and on the coast path you will be spoiled for choice, because everywhere there is a view to make you weep. It's a wild coast. Waves crash in amongst the rocks sending spray high into the air. There are beaches, at Whitesands Bay and Newgale, that are amongst the best on the whole British coast.

We saw seals. Heads bobbing about in the sea, no more than a few yards away. At last we had seen seals, and without the need for a route-march to the ends of the earth as in Norfolk. They are here. Hundreds of them.

It's also a fragile coast.

Two years earlier the oil tanker Sea Empress had cocked up its approach into Milford Haven, and got itself into difficulties. 72,000 tonnes of crude oil spilled into the sea and found its way, inevitably, to Pembrokeshire, where it proceeded to put the seals and seabirds into difficulties. Actually, it killed most of them. Whitesands Bay had become Blacksands bay. The bracing sea breeze had become a stinking death-laden shroud that tainted everything. We had returned to this coast harbouring real concerns about what we might find here, but it was gratifying to see that it had all cleaned up nicely, after a lot of hard work by many good-hearted volunteers. Wildlife was back and the status quo was restored, but it shouldn't have happened. It should never happen.

It was time to move on. We said our farewells to the goats and the hippies... and the car wouldn't start. I cranked it and cranked it. Nothing. Then the battery died and it wouldn't crank. I tinkered for a while. Then, with Sarah steering, Kevin and I managed to push it to the farm entrance and from there to the top of a hill that went down a narrow little road to the sea. Once we were at sea-level there would be no pushing back.

I climbed in. I set the choke. I selected second gear. I switched on the ignition. This was it. I released the brake and the car started to roll. Timing would be everything, if I left it too late I would get fewer opportunities. If I went too early the car would not be moving fast enough and I would have wasted the first part of the hill. I let the car accelerate until I felt it would accelerate no more, then I popped the clutch. At first nothing, then I heard a burbling kind of noise from the exhaust, but the engine was still on life support. Around narrow, twisting blind turns. I was running out of road. The sea was coming up fast. I would soon be past the point of no return. I would soon be in Porthclais harbour.

The engine fired.

Clouds of blue smoke billowed from the exhaust. I tap danced around the pedals: Brake, so I didn't go into the harbour. Clutch, so that I didn't stall. Accelerator, so that the engine didn't die again. Three pedals, two feet and a heel. The car stopped and I revved it, scared to lift off. Let it warm. Push in the choke, gently. Not too early. Not too late.

At last I felt confident enough to try a three-point turn. I returned to Penarn in triumph. We hooked up, without stopping the engine, then we headed north.

"It's the battery," I said. "It's got to be the battery."

"Where can we get a new one?"

"A good run should charge it a bit. Once we're pitched in New Quay, we'll drive into Cardigan and get a new battery. No problem."

New Quay was our next destination. Not Newquay in Cornwall but New Quay in Cardigan Bay, between Cardigan and Aberystwyth. I drove slowly. I concentrated hard. I didn't want any slip-ups, no stalling before the battery was charged. I had no intentions of trying to bump-start the car with the caravan on the back.

We arrived at the club site at New Quay without incident, and we raced to set up the caravan before the engine went cold. I didn't want to leave the engine running because club wardens can be a little fussy about such things. I needn't have worried. The battery was good and the car started first time. We drove to Cardigan.

This wasn't tourism, this was survival. We cruised around the town looking for the trappings of motor parts hanging from shop windows. It took half an hour before we struck lucky.

"Are you sure it's the battery? I don't have anything here to test the old one."

"I'm sure it's the battery."

"Do you want a standard battery or a heavy-duty? The heavy-duty's a bit pricey."

"Oh, give me the heavy-duty. I want something that will start a bus."

We were parked about half a mile away from the shop. Every Christmas there is a TV programme where big tough men compete at carrying impossibly heavy and awkward objects around short courses. They don't usually curse as much as I did. There's nowhere to grip a car battery except for these tiny little ledges for your finger-tips to cling to, and after about ten seconds your fingers tell you that you are not going to make it. I had to stop many times. Each time, bending to the ground then back up again, I came closer to popping a disc, and each time I became more inventive with the English language.

At the car I just wanted to get away from Cardigan. I didn't want to do car-mechanics in the car park. I prayed that the car would start. It was tentative, but it fired. We drove back to the campsite where I swapped the batteries over. The new battery was truly heavy duty. I only needed to look at the ignition key and the car would start. I was well pleased with my efforts, and quite happy to turn a blind eye to another serious outflow of cash.

The site was good but not really near to anywhere, in any meaningful, on-foot kind of way. It wasn't good for cycling, because you could either cycle down to the coast, then you'd have to push the bike back up the hill, or, if you wanted to walk, you could follow the "short" footpath down to Cwmtydu, on the coast – the warden's recommendation – if you have a full day (and thighs of steel) to donate to the project. Otherwise you have to drive somewhere. Maybe I'm not giving the area full credit. I was not at my best. I'd spent far too much un-budgeted money in the past two weeks and it was preying on my mind. I also had a little worm of an idea wriggling away at the back of my mind. What if it wasn't the battery? What if it was something else?

We drove to Aberystwyth, partly just to see if we could – to see if the car would get there.

I adored Aberystwyth. It's funny, because there is a lot wrong with the place. It's past its best. Many parts of it are quite run down, but, I don't know, I love the place. It has atmosphere. There's the old Victorian university building on the front, with its mosaics set in the wall. There's the stump of a pier that seems destined to get shorter each year. At the far end of the promenade there is the funicular railway that creeps up the side of the cliff to a ramshackle building on top filled with dubious attractions: slot machines, a camera obscura through which you can see... Aberystwyth. I didn't really get it, the camera obscura. It's like a pinhole camera that you make as a child, only this one is big enough to get inside. Once your eyes acclimatise to the dark, faint images of the seaside town can be discerned on the walls. The question is, why? I suppose it's a Victorian thing. I don't know if it's still there, it seemed to be on its last legs when we visited. Maybe it's been superseded by digital. It was quirky, and different, and we were perfectly happy to part with our coin to go in and have a look.

Aberystwyth shouldn't work, but it does. It has shops and tea rooms and a youthful feel, owing to the numbers of university students who should have been home for the summer, but who somehow feel the tug of a place that they don't really want to leave. Aberystwyth is the epitome of the Victorian seaside resort. It has fared less well than many others, but still has that certain something. I was sold. We all were. It's had its knocks, but now life is creeping back, and it feels good.

Our fortnight's holiday ended. This time we packed to go home. Awning down. Tent packed. Caravan legs up. Car... didn't start.

It had started every day in New Quay. Today it didn't. This may be something to do with it having been sunny every day, but today it wasn't. Today the rain was coming down like it had been missed by loved ones.

I put in a call at the pay phone, to Green Flag or RAC or AA or whichever motoring organisation I had chosen to antagonise that year.

"We'll be about an hour. You'll need to meet us by the site entrance and show us the way in."

I tipped off the site warden, who didn't seem very happy about car maniacs coming on site, then I took my umbrella and limped up the half-mile lane to the entrance on the main road, where I waited.

An hour came and went. The rain continued to fall. I was bored. There was nothing to see, except for a road with no traffic. Another half hour. I wasn't sure what to do. If I walked back to the pay phone I might miss them, then again, the girl on the phone had said an hour.

After two hours I'd had enough. I sloshed back up the muddy track and made the call.

"Ah, glad you rang, Mr Wood. The mechanic we called said that there are about fifty campsites near New Quay and he wasn't going to drive round aimlessly trying each one. Could you be more specific?"

"Okay, which direction is he coming from? I'll give you directions."

"Right, one moment." There was a shuffling of papers. "Here we are, he's coming from Truro."

I was silent for a moment while I digested this.

"Truro? Truro in Cornwall? When I called I said, clearly, New Quay. Near Cardigan. I am not in Newquay in Cornwall."

"One moment, Mr Wood."

I waited while there was muffled conversation.

"Thank you, Mr Wood. Someone will be with you in about one hour."

I met him at the site entrance fifty-five minutes later. I was bored with the site entrance. I'd spent almost three hours there, in the rain. The mechanic arrived in a huge truck. He introduced himself as Gareth. I climbed in and told him the Cornwall tale. He said that this was always happening.

He hammered down the little rutted lane at about forty mph, smashing into low-hanging tree limbs as he went, and leaving a trail of debris in his wake. I wondered what the fussy, paint-all-the-stones-white wardens would make of him.

Gareth soon had the bonnet of the car up. He connected jump leads to the truck and began to rev the big diesel like crazy. The noise was appalling. Campers came out to see what was going on. The warden came running up the field.

"You can't do that. How long will you be?"

Gareth spat on the grass and muttered, "Won't take long, soon have her running."

Jump leads didn't work. After half an hour of trying, Gareth was ready for something more dramatic. "We'll bump start her behind the truck," he said. He attached a steel towing bar and gave me instructions.

"Keep it in second. Stay off the clutch until it's running properly."

The campsite has an oval road that runs in a circuit through the four separate sections of the site, each divided by hedges.

It's about a quarter-mile lap. The road is shale, and immaculately tended and raked, with, of course, white-painted rocks marking the corners. There is an obligatory five mph speed limit everywhere on site. Both caravanning clubs are rather fond of green notices that tell you what not to do, and rightly so, because these sites are meant to be a haven of tranquillity and rest.

Gareth set off. He had no time for green signs and rules. Besides, as far as I could see there were no signs prohibiting stock car racing. We were soon doing thirty or forty on the straights, barely slowing for the corners. Curtains of shale sprayed up from our wheels on each corner, sand-blasting the tents and caravans that were unlucky enough to be camped there. I was mortified and utterly powerless to do anything about it. Gareth was enjoying himself immensely. Stock car racing was obviously a lost childhood dream, and he was in his element here. The car fired, but still Gareth circulated, just to be sure. Each time we passed the office I could see the warden at the window, red with rage but evidently a little afraid of Gareth and his disdain for regulations.

At last we stopped. I dipped the clutch and the engine continued to run. Gareth had skidded to a halt on the grass, ploughing two deep furrows into the immaculate lawn. He came round from the truck with a beaming smile, evidently delighted with his day's work.

"Keep the effing engine running," he shouted. "If you stop it you might never start it again. Best thing is to get yourself home and get it seen to." He unhooked the tow bar and helped me to attach the caravan.

"Remember," he said. "Do not stop that engine for anything, not until you are in your own driveway."

"What's wrong with it?" I asked.

"Haven't a bloody clue. Coil, dizzy, carb, battery... could be anything. Get it seen to."

Gareth jumped into his truck and sped off, doing another lap of the site for good measure, then bombing up the lane, taking out all the overhanging trees that he missed on his way in. I jumped into the car and we followed, fearful of bumping into the warden now that the scary mechanic was out of the way.

It was four o'clock in the afternoon and the rain continued to pour. We hadn't eaten since breakfast. We couldn't stop the engine, so, in Aberystwyth I pulled up outside McDonald's and Sarah ran in while I revved the engine to keep it lively.

She came out with McChicken sandwiches, moments later. Not exactly veggie, but white meat is close enough for us on occasion.

I carried on driving with the plastic burger box on my lap. McDonald's are not designed for one-handed eating. I struggled on while more and more of the McDonald's sauce migrated onto my shirt. Eventually the burger itself dropped into my lap and I was left with the bun and the fries. I couldn't stop. We had to keep going. Across the winding road through the Cambrian mountains, rivers were swollen and brown and whole trees were being swept along. This was not the time or place to break down. I drove with total concentration, keeping the engine running by sheer force of will. Mile after mile. Llangurig, Newtown, Welshpool, Oswestry, Wrexham. Then Chester, nearly home. Through Ellesmere Port onto the Wirral – we could walk home now if we had to – but we didn't want to.

At last I drew up outside our home. With the engine still running we unhooked the caravan and pushed it into its slot in front of the house, then I pulled the car onto the path and switched off.

Experimentally, I turned the ignition key again. Nothing. The car was dead. I had had enough of crap cars. I vowed that before we went anywhere, ever again, we would have a decent car.

THE SMELL OF ONIONS AND ACCORDION OIL: 1997 – 2000

Don't you just love getting stuck behind a tractor? It's even worse when you're towing a caravan. None of the motorists behind you can see the tractor in front of your caravan so you are the target of their ire. You can feel the beams of hate on your neck. With a caravan you just don't have the acceleration to pass. You have to wait.

So, where are all these tractors going? I know they have to move from field to field, and I accept this, it's okay, but today I was behind a tractor for over an hour, and I have to ask – how big are these fields?

—No. 81 from the Moanicles of Michael.

It was November. Outside, the rain was driving down and the wind was howling. I was sitting in the window leafing through a book about conquests of the Eiger. I've always enjoyed books about mountains and adventure. It's one of those escapist things, to dream about places you know you can never visit.

There was a thump from behind the front door. Something heavy had landed on the mat. I tried to ignore it but I couldn't. Whenever something comes through the door I have to go and see straight away, in case it's interesting. It usually isn't. It's usually junk mail.

This time it was interesting; it was the Carefree brochure. Carefree are the Camping and Caravanning Club's international bookings section. Each year they mail out a glossy colour brochure detailing all the European campsites in their network. We also get similar offerings from the Caravan Club and from Select Sites. Usually I do no more than skip-read through them all – they're full of pictures of sandy beaches and pools with chutes and blue skies in impossible-to-reach places across Europe. They might as well be on the moon; no way could we ever even consider a holiday abroad. It was impossible.

Impossible.

Or was it?

This was the back end of the 20th century. It was a time of privatisation, flotation, share-ownership and windfall payments, and a windfall payment was coming my way! The company I worked for, and in whom I held a bunch of free (but initially worthless) shares, was talking about a flotation. Big money might just be heading my way. Most of the potential cash had already been earmarked for long-deferred essentials; new carpet in the lounge, new sofa, new telly, but...

I picked up the Carefree brochure again and had another look. Normandy. Now that wasn't too far. I looked at the inclusive price. Found a few different sites. My heart began to beat a little quicker. Maybe a short tour taking in a few sites. It might just be possible. In fact this was definitely something to think about. Could we do this?

I had never been abroad!

I called Sarah downstairs. She had been in her studio, painting (studio is a posh word for our bedroom). She came down all grumpy and interrupted and multi-coloured. We talked. We did sums. We discussed until our throats hurt. Over the years, imperceptibly, we had been getting more affluent. We now had a better car; a Mondeo, and it actually ran. We had never really considered taking the caravan abroad, but we were suddenly looking at prices that, with a bit of budgeting and care, were almost affordable.

I continued to flick through the brochure, a knot of excitement in the pit of my stomach. The floatation was almost a certainty. We might just do this.

A germ of an idea began to form. Paris. We could go to Paris. There were sites nearby and we could do Paris as part of a tour of northern France. I began to study French using a cheap set of language tapes I bought from a discount bookshop. I was surprised at how much I remembered from four years at school doing French CSE. I was really serious. I annoyed the hell out of everyone at home by insisting on having French days; days when, in the house, only French would be spoken. These "days" usually lasted little more than 20 minutes over breakfast, but they got us excited. The enthusiasm for the idea was growing with each week. The whole preposterous idea was taking shape.

December stretched on and on with no announcement about the flotation. January came. Nothing. As the end of January approached we agonised. Should we book anyway? Could we risk losing the deposit? It was, to us, a big deposit. Could we afford to lose it? The answer was assuredly no, but should we take a risk? News about the floatation had not been forthcoming for a few weeks but we were still confident enough to take a chance so as not to miss out on the early booking discounts. On the last Thursday in January we decided we could wait no longer. We filled in the booking form, wrote the cheque, and put it into an envelope. Sarah would post it in the morning. We were going to France.

The next morning I arrived at work to be greeted by a fax that had been pinned to the notice board:

The floatation was off.

Indefinitely.

The market climate was no longer conducive, blah, blah...

I called Sarah. "Don't post the envelope! The dream's over." The envelope was in her handbag. She'd been in the act of leaving the house and heading for the post box when I'd called.

It's hard to put into words the magnitude of our disappointment over that fax. Colleagues at work had made similar plans; new cars, cruises, deposits on new homes... The feeling of depression that blanketed everyone and every aspect of work is difficult to describe. The world was suddenly a very grey place.

Time moves on. We adjusted. We had a holiday in Britain. It rained, but hey, no change there, we were waterproof now, anyway, and at least we had a reliable car.

Then came 1999. Our 1999 holiday was already booked. It had been booked seven years in advance. 1999 was the year of the eclipse.

Cornwall 1999. Hmm. What a strange and conflicting suite of experiences. Grid-lock had been expected. There had been fears of food and water shortages and dire prophesies of mass blindness on an apocalyptic, Day-of-the-Triffids scale. In the end it was the scare-mongers, the doomsters, who had prevailed. They got their wish and all but bankrupted Cornwall. People had become so terrified by the lurid predictions of desperate, dehydrated, sightless tourists, in their millions, staggering about, bumping into the Cornish landscape and stepping into the void off the Cornish cliff-tops, that, in the end, we pretty well had the whole county to ourselves. It got a bit busy on the big day, but for the rest of the week it was all rather subdued.

So, what of the big day? We had waited in our temporary camping field, on a hill just above Falmouth, cameras and viewing equipment prepared and poised, Mylar glasses at the ready, and we saw... nothing. The day dawned and the sky remained a uniform grey all morning. At 11:12, on 11 August 1999 it went dark. Then got light again. It was all very spooky and interesting, and I would not have missed it for anything, but it was yet another astronomical event spoiled by the British weather. There was an upside; for the most part we had the beaches to ourselves, albeit not a lot of fun in the rain, but disappointing? After waiting and planning for seven years? Yeah.

It all just went to convince us that it was time we had some good weather on holiday.

We so wanted France.

Another season passed us by, and once more the Carefree book arrived on the mat. Three years on from the aborted flotation, and financially, things were still improving, still looking better, and, well, those seeds had been sewn. We had been allowed to dream, once.

So I opened the brochure, all casual, no expectations. I took another look at those prices. I did some sums and, yes, with some saving and a bit of belt-tightening...

I didn't say anything to Sarah yet. I thought about it. I performed surreptitious maths on scraps of paper where I worked through the sums again, and yes, it was possible. We could have borrowed, of course, but we have both been pathologically debt averse for many years; ever since a nasty episode with a three-hundred-pound credit card bill that we had struggled to pay off. Seems like loose change in these days of rampant personal debt crises, but it scared the hell out of us, and it cured us. If we were to do this thing then we would bloody well have to save for it. And the thing was, no matter how I turned it, it appeared to be possible. I reached out the two-year-old itinerary from those heady, pre-floatation days. I tweaked it a bit. I changed a few dates. I went back to the cost estimates. By the time I showed it to Sarah I was regarding it as a *fait accompli*. (There, I was already thinking in French.)

Then Sarah, casually, nonchalantly, threw in a rogue idea that was so preposterous, so... absurd.

"What about Switzerland?"

I nearly choked.

"What? Are you off your trolley? We can't go to Switzerland."

"Why?"

"Well, it's... it's... there's snow, and steep hills, you know, the Alps."

"Yes?"

"And the cost. Everyone knows it's so expensive in Switzerland."

"Do they? What, exactly, is so expensive in Switzerland?"

"Well, food – eating out and stuff."

"How often do we eat out? Couldn't we take food?"

"Yes, but... it's miles away and... it's Switzerland. We couldn't possibly..."

"Why don't you look into it? Before we plan anything. Wouldn't harm."

I was left opening and closing my mouth like a demented goldfish. I'd run out of arguments. All I knew was that the idea was crazy and impractical and this was because Switzerland – the Alps – was the place I'd fantasised about for so long, and fantasy is different to reality. Fantasy never happens.

I agreed to think about it. I set about the task with negative expectations. I flicked through the Carefree book not even believing there'd *be* any sites in Switzerland. I found three. I looked at the prices, expecting to find them way out of our league. The prices are generally shown for seven nights inclusive of ferry costs. You then add any other nights on a per-night basis. I found I was looking at prices not dissimilar to those in northern France. I must have mis-read. I looked at the small print. Then I realised that mileage and petrol were the missing links, but our three-week plan for northern and central France included a number of sites and quite a few miles going round and about in France. Switzerland was indeed further, but in the scheme of things, not *that* much further. The more I worked at it the more possible it began to appear. I noticed that I was beginning to feel something unusual in the pit of my stomach. Could it be the beginnings of an ulcer? No, it was the beginnings of a deep and gut-wrenching sense of excitement. It was the realisation that something important, something incredible might be about to happen.

I worked up a plan. Stop off near Paris. Visit Paris. Continue south-east, another stopping place in the Marne Valley. Take a day, look around.

Then... head for the Alps.

I got out the maps. I reached out the old school atlas that I'd inadvertently acquired on leaving school. A thought hit me like a shock wave. Oh... my... god... I was planning a caravan holiday using a world atlas!

This time there was no procrastination, no waiting on the affairs of others; we booked. We sent the deposit.

We saved like mad then paid the balance. Exciting things started happening. We received a pack with all kinds of swag. GB plates, one for the car and one for the caravan. I'd never had GB plates before. Just fitting them was, for me, part of the holiday. We received a book about driving in Europe, and this prompted a quick trip to Halfords for a couple of yellow plastic things to stick onto the headlamps so as not to blind the French and the Swiss. There was an envelope filled with tourist information about the places we would be visiting. We bought Swiss vignettes. These are tax discs that you need for driving on Swiss motorways, and you need one for the car and one for the caravan. Annoying but not hugely expensive, and they're a fantastic affectation once they are stuck on your car and caravan.

Best of all, we got a yellow Michelin road atlas of France and a road map of Switzerland. Now, it has to be said, I love maps. I can sit and stare at an OS map for hours, lost in the detail, the colours and the names of places. The road atlas of France might not have contours and familiar OS symbols, but to make up for it, it is huge. There is just so much, so many pages, so much atlas and so much France. The sheet map of Switzerland is thin and flimsy by comparison, but oh, what a map. I would unfold it with care and reverence, and spread it out on the floor, then stare in wonder at that vast, white-and-blue expanse at the bottom where roads did not reach and where names leapt out at me: Eiger, Matterhorn, Jungfrau.

I must have spent days with scraps of paper and my dinky little measuring wheel. I'd planned it all once before, of course, but now I had a real map and I had the exact locations for each campsite. I could do it all over again, and this time I could do it in detail. I could stare at the maps and imagine the places I would soon see with my own eyes.

Six weeks dragged. It was difficult to concentrate on other things, like the day job, and sleep, but eventually the days passed.

An abiding memory I have of that day – the day we took our

first steps abroad – is that of standing on the promenade at Dover. It was after midnight and it was very dark. We'd parked-up on the prom for an hour to calm our jangling nerves after the appalling thirteen-hour road journey south, the details of which are both in the prologue to this book and etched into a dark place in my brain. The four of us looked out to sea. We were starting to get a little nervous. The English Channel looked dark and cold and endless. It isn't endless, of course. Had the weather been a little clearer we'd have been able to see lights over in Calais, but on this occasion the narrow twenty-mile strip of water looked, to us, as daunting as a vast rolling ocean. None of us spoke for several minutes.

"Okay," I said. "Let's go to France."

FRANCE: 2000

Hmm, empty roads, clear and sensible signage, service areas every few miles. It seems somehow unpatriotic to be in Continental Europe with all these millions of kilometres of road... and I have nothing whatsoever to moan about!

There are no cat's eyes!

My first experience of France: driving at 2 a.m., in total darkness. I hadn't really known what to expect about the foreign-ness of arriving in Europe, but in the dark, *because* of the dark, it felt alien and far, far removed from night-driving in Britain.

We had left Dover after midnight, and made the crossing to Calais with P&O. The plan was to park-up in the first available lay-by, or *aire de repos* as they are called in the Michelin guide, then sleep in the caravan until dawn. I'd been disappointed that our plans had prevented a daytime crossing, I had wanted to *see* it all, feel it, straight away, but the ferries are cheaper at night. I would have to wait until morning for my first sight of Continental Europe.

My disappointment faded after only ten minutes of driving. It hit me like a train and I wriggled in my seat with excitement. This road was not a motorway, it was an *autoroute*. Blue signposts flashed by in the headlights: Paris, Reims, Dunkerque. The whole of Mainland Europe lay at my feet. The darkness, though. That was the biggest surprise. Complete darkness and the absence of traffic. In Britain, few roads are empty at 2 a.m. This was the A26, a main artery. Some cars, all with GB plates, passed us after leaving the ferry but now we were alone. Nothing to see but the grey concrete road ahead, lit by our headlamps. No villages, no distant street lights... *no cat's eyes*. Nothing to see but so, so different.

We pulled into the *aire de repos* at Zutkerque and stopped. It was bigger than a lay-by; almost the size of a motorway services, except dark. We could see nothing so we got out of the car, lowered the corner steadies on the caravan and stumbled into bed.

What would daylight bring? Couldn't wait.

I opened my eyes and I felt disorientated. Usually in the caravan I know exactly where I am; this time it took a moment before it fully sank in. I was in France. It was daylight. What strange new things were out there for me to see?

I had to wait, though. There were still the sounds of some seriously heavy sleeping coming from Sarah and the children. I didn't want to start our first morning in a new land with a row. It was only 5:30 a.m. I had woken early like a child on Christmas Day. I would just have to delay gratification for a little while longer.

I lay and listened to the sounds coming in from the outside... from France! First, and strangest, was the lack of vehicle noise. We were camping in a motorway service station. There should be zooming traffic, hissing air brakes, shouting and cursing, but here there was birdsong. Nothing else. The road was still empty of traffic – and we were only ten or fifteen feet away from the edge of the A26. I've stayed on expensive sites that were noisier than this. A car or lorry door opened and closed, quietly. A muted conversation that I couldn't understand. It was in French. The Christmas-Day butterflies did an extra lap of my stomach. I wanted to wake everyone up. How could they sleep at a time like this? I wriggled a bit, and coughed. I scratched my head noisily. Nobody moved. I tried to peek out through the curtains but from my position all I could see was the grey sky.

I waited like this for an hour, then in the end I had to disturb everyone because I needed to go to the toilet – the one in the caravan, because I wasn't ready for French toilets, not just yet. I'd heard all about French toilets.

We put the bed away and tidied up the inside of the caravan. My hands shook as I rushed. I did things wrong, I fell over things. By the time I finally opened the caravan door and placed a foot on French soil I felt a little like Neil Armstrong. I'd stepped on French soil before, of course, last night, moving from car to caravan. But now it was light. The sky was grey and there was a slight mist which gave everything a flat and colourless look. We were in a line with three other cars, two with caravans, one with a trailer, all with GB plates. A couple of lorries also shared the service area, one French and the other Spanish. It was just a car park, really, with a toilet block in the middle. Just like in England. No, not like in England, not at all. It was small. There was no litter. The road surface was clean, no broken fan belts or shredded tyres or pools of black diesel melting the asphalt surface into suspension-snapping potholes. The hedge that bordered the parking area from the carriageway was trimmed and cared-for. The ground beneath it was weed-free, and had obviously been worked on quite recently. This was a haven of tranquillity. It could not have been more different to British motorway services.

First job, while I thought about it, was to attach the headlight beam deflectors. I should have done it in Dover but our journey south through UK motorway hell had been so fraught that I'd run out of time. Halfway through the job there was a cough from behind me.

"How do you do that, then?"

I turned round.

"Excuse me?"

"I've got the sticky things, but I didn't keep the packet with the instructions. Could I borrow yours?" He nodded over to his car, an old Ford Escort with a trailer on the back.

I finished putting the stickers on the lamps and passed him the instruction sheet.

"Where are you heading?" he asked.

"Ultimately, Switzerland," I said, feeling like Columbus or Livingstone. "How about you?"

"Oh, we're taking the trailer tent down to Corsica."

I gaped. I looked over at the car which seemed to contain four grown adults, not including their driver. They appeared to have spent the night in the car, sleeping upright, shoulder to shoulder.

"Where are you staying on the way down?" I asked.

"Oh, no time for that," he said. "We have a ferry booked from Genoa tonight." He looked at his watch to emphasise the urgency of his plan. "I suppose I'd best be getting on." He jumped into his car and scorched off down the slip road. His upright passengers hadn't even got out of the car to stretch their legs. They must have been as stiff as corpses. I shook my head in horror at their plan. It must be over seven hundred miles to Genoa, and they'd need some leeway if they were catching a specific ferry. They'd have to average nearly seventy all day without stopping. It made our adventure seem like a trip to Asda by comparison.

A man came out of the toilet block and walked over to one of the lorries, the one with the "F" plate. He nodded at me as he passed and muttered a quiet "bonjour". I nodded back. Nodded. I'd worked on my French all year and suddenly I felt self-conscious in the extreme about actually speaking in

French to a French person. At a subconscious level I felt that maybe I'd been kidded, that really everyone in the world spoke English; that I'd learned French in the same way that people learn Latin, because it was of scholarly interest but had little practical value. Now, with one casual word of French, one *bonjour*, a lorry-driver had opened a chasm of fears and self-doubt. People here really did speak another language, and if I were to survive in this land for two weeks I was going to have to overcome all my reservations and speak back to them.

A van pulled up outside the toilet block. Two men got out, unloaded cleaning equipment and began to clean. From where I stood the toilet block already looked spotless, but, at six-thirty in the morning men were here cleaning it again, and it was being cleaned to hell and back. They kept at it for nearly an hour, really giving it loads. They cleaned with love and with passion. Let me just say, this wasn't a Charnock Richard, or a Hilton Park with parking for umpteen thousand. This was, effectively, a lay-by with room for maybe a couple of dozen vehicles. It had one small toilet block, and by the time we'd finished breakfast and pulled back onto the road it had become a holy shrine to toilets. In my mirrors I saw that one of the men had now pulled out hedge trimmers from the back of the van. He was about to start on the garden. I was in awe.

We drove. My eyes were everywhere. The central reservation of the motorway... *autoroute*... had rose bushes. They seemed cared for and, oh my god, the soil beneath them had been mulched. I'd never seen anything like it. I kept comparing things to their British equivalent. The centre of British motorways are forbidding linear deserts, inhabited by only the most hardy and ugly weeds that struggle for survival beneath endless rails of galvanised crash barrier.

The evidence of care and harmony, here, was everywhere. Each road bridge we passed under was subtly different to the last. In Britain a bridge is a means of crossing one thoroughfare with another, as cost-effectively as possible. What we were seeing here was a cultural chasm; for the French, a bridge is simply another opportunity for artistic expression. It's the same with lamp posts. Each little orchard of lamp posts was different – as if they'd been re-invented every time a fresh cluster of them had been required. I thought it was wonderful.

In truth, and after subsequent repetition, driving through northern France is, I suppose, quite dull. But that first time... I was amazed. We were all amazed. It's sad that the wonder that comes from doing a thing for the first time inevitably fades. It can never be repeated, for then it is the second time – and second, third and fourth time is never as magical.

Absently I switched on the car radio. The pre-tuned channel for Radio 2 was just emitting static so I scanned. Cheri FM. French. So different. It's funny to think that we were naïve enough to be surprised by this, but we were.

"Whoa!" I said. "The radio's in French." We were less than a hundred miles north of Paris, so this must go down as one of the most stupid things I've ever said, but I was, genuinely, surprised and delighted.

I noticed that the fuel gauge was getting low, and a thrill of unease gripped me. Yes, I was in France. Yes, they did speak French here. And yes, I was going to have to buy petrol, and for this simple little task I was going to have to communicate.

A sign indicated that I was ten kilometres from a service station, an *aire de service*, that sold petrol. I licked my lips. They'd gone dry. In my head I was practicing, over and over. *Bonjour. Pompe numéro*, whatever, *s'il vous plaît. Merci beaucoup.*

Shortly after joining the A1, the Autoroute du Nord, I saw the signs for Aire de Wancourt, which showed a petrol pump icon. I pulled off the *autoroute* and eased into the filling station. It all seemed very familiar. I quickly recognised the *sans plombe* pump as being unleaded, and filled up. Credit card in hand I made my way across the forecourt to the shop. Inside there was another British tourist trying to pay. I knew he was British because I could hear him from afar and he was shouting, in English. He was red, both in the face and all the way across his bald head, where the veins were standing proud.

"Don't you understand! Pump Five! F-I-V-E!" He spelled it and counted each letter off on his fingers – which of course came to four, not five. I'm not sure how this was meant to help the poor girl, who was looking very rattled by the encounter. I watched him rant and felt both ashamed and even more determined to make a reasonable effort. There were two tills and I went to the one that didn't have the loud, ignorant bald Brit slowing things down.

I gave the girl a smile. "Bonjour," I said. "Pompe numéro sept, s'il vous plaît." I felt very self-conscious, and my pronunciation was terrible.

She smiled back at me. "Oui, trente cent et un francs, s'il vous plaît." She rolled it all together, like weetrnsoaunfroncseelv'play. I don't really know if this was the actual number. I didn't know how much she asked for then, so I certainly can't remember now, but this gives a flavour of how it went. I handed over my credit card, signed the slip, she said *merci*, I said *merci*, she said *au revoir*, I said *au revoir*, and I left. The bald ignorant Brit was still there and still shouting.

Now okay, it wasn't much of a conversation, I know, but the thing is this; years later I can still remember it, every word –

well, my words, at least. It was the first time ever that I'd spoken to another person in another country in another language, and I felt so damn proud. Maybe it was partly the bald ignorant Brit as well – the comparison – but it felt good. Yet at the same time I felt ill-prepared. I had studied and listened to tapes and stuff, but I just didn't feel ready.

But I had tried. I had every intention of trying throughout the holiday. I got back to the car and Sarah asked, "What are you smiling at?"

I *was* smiling. I'd spoken French.

Aire de Wancourt also has a restaurant, so we pulled over into the car park and went in search of food. Another first – our first dining-out in France. We chose a fast-food counter and bought sandwiches. Again there was novelty; in France it is virtually impossible to get square bread – a sandwich is a baguette. Easy to ask for, *un sandwich fromage s'il vous plaît*, and wonderful to eat. This kind of sandwich is commonplace now, in England, but back then it was unusual – certainly for us – and we enthused about how this was the way sandwiches should be. Amanda had Coke with her food and she got a free Coca-Cola duffel bag as part of a promotion. She'd have probably got the same bag anywhere else in the world, but she got it in France, and she was all – 'France is wonderful! They even give bags away with the food!' – and to the best of my knowledge she still has that bag somewhere.

We continued on our way, and we neared Paris. Our route had us veering just north of Paris and coming out on the A13, then leaving the *autoroute* and heading to our first campsite near Saint Illiers la Ville, about 45 miles west of Paris. I remember little about the trip around the north of Paris. I remember that my grip on the steering wheel became ever tighter, that my eyes grew wide, and that overall I became quite damp. But we did it, we didn't hit anything, and soon we were on small country roads where driving now became even more difficult. There was two-way traffic, difficult left turns, traffic lights that did odd things, like go from red to green without passing through amber. I had stuck a post-it with a big red arrow pointing to the right on my steering wheel, just to remind me which side of the road I should be on.

We came to Saint Illiers la Ville, passed right through, continued along for miles. No sign of any campsite. I turned the car in a wide gravel driveway. It's always difficult to retrace one's steps with a caravan wagging around on the back, because you can't three-point turn, you need space. We returned back towards, and through, the village. A few more miles back the way we had come, then I turned at a roundabout and headed back again. Nothing. I saw two men walking along the road and stopped to ask directions (after practicing in my head three or four times).

"Excusez-moi, monsieur. Ou est le camping? Prez de Saint Illiers la Ville?"

I asked beautifully. They understood my request without difficulty. They both replied together, agreeing, disagreeing, correcting. They spoke for a good five minutes, waving arms, arguing, pointing. I nodded and smiled throughout. When they reached a point where I believed them to have reached a consensus, I gave them a *merci beaucoup* and a wave and drove on. I didn't have the faintest clue what either of them had said. We drove back through Saint Illiers la Ville, carried on for a few miles, then turned again in the same gravel driveway that had proved useful fifteen minutes earlier. Our repeated manoeuvre was digging a sizable furrow in the gravel and I felt we'd soon have to find someone else's driveway to destroy if this carried on much longer. Shortly after our third trip through the village we passed the two Frenchmen again who waved at us and pointed in the direction we were coming from. We waved back and continued again to the roundabout, where we redirected ourselves yet again, for a fourth pass through the village. When we reached the two Frenchmen this time they were waiting for us just on the outskirts of the village beside a very large and clear sign that said "Camping Domaine D'inchelin" and which had a large, obvious arrow pointing up a lane on the right. They were alternately pointing to the sign then the lane and shouting and laughing. The sign was clearly visible from both directions and we had driven past it five times. We waved our thanks and hoped to never meet them again, and two minutes later we were pulling up beside the reception in our campsite.

We had pre-booked so registration was easy, a quick *bonjour* and a wave of our paperwork, and we were quickly shown to our pitch. The site was good. Plenty of room around us. Our pitch actually had a hedge all round to mark our territory. This was particularly welcome to Kevin because he had chosen to use his pup-tent in France, rather than sleep in the caravan with us, and I could tell that he was a little apprehensive about it. He'd been doing this for a couple of years in Britain, the beginnings of teenage rebellion, but I wondered how he'd feel waking up in the morning to hear nothing but foreign tongues around him. I could tell, though, that he felt much easier about it when he saw that we had our own distinct plot of land.

It was easy to find everything on the site and we set up quickly. Sarah and I dropped into camp chairs outside the caravan. A feeling came over me. We were far from home. Remote. Far from everything and everyone we knew. Our family had only each other to depend upon. It was a scary thought. I turned this idea over in my head a few times until Amanda broke in with a request.

"Dad, is it okay if I go and play with Helen?"

"You've made a friend already? That was quick."

"No, it's Helen... Helen Smith from down our road."

"Don't be ridiculous, Amanda. It's just someone who looks a bit like..."

But it *was* Helen Smith, Amanda's friend. She was standing with her, both of them smiling at me. We'd driven over five hundred miles to a far and distant land, and within fifteen minutes of our arrival had bumped into one of my daughter's best friends, who lived only a dozen houses away. I don't know what amazed me more: the mind-numbing coincidence of it, or the calm and matter-of-fact way that Amanda seemed to accept it.

After a few seconds I realised that my mouth was still open. I closed it with a snap, then said, calm as you like, "Yeah, sure. Go and play."

We woke early and drove to Breval, a little town that had a railway station with trains to Paris. Ours was the only car parked outside the station, which I thought, for a Monday morning, was a little strange and a little unsettling. But I had confidence in my research. Transport was what I did. I'd worked in the bus industry for nearly thirty years and I knew timetables. I'd worked out the train times into Paris long in advance.

My mind was put at rest once we reached the booking office. The train, as I'd expected, was due in less than ten minutes. I bought each of us a Paris Mobilis ticket, and we were shown where to cross the track to reach the other platform, and where to go to punch the tickets (in France the rail tickets have to be punched at an orange punching machine on the platform before boarding the train). All of this was bravely but successfully transacted in my stuttering French. I paid using my credit card, though, because I continued to be baffled by the built-in mathematics that form the French numbering system. Eighty-two, for example, is sixty plus twenty-two. It's hard enough learning the language without having the odd bit of mental arithmetic thrown in along the way. It's far easier just to accept the mystery cost, smile and hand over the plastic. The tears and recriminations could come later, back home, when the credit card bill arrived on the door mat.

Outside, the platform was heaving. There were hundreds waiting for the train. On the other side of a fence I could see a packed and sprawling car park, with cars jostling for position in a frantic bid not to miss the train, due any moment. I thought this seemed just a little odd; why not park in the car park on our side of the tracks? It was empty.

We settled into a space on the platform, and straight away there was shuffling and anticipation. The train had pulled into sight. It was a monster; a massive electric traction unit followed by an enormous snake of carriages that just kept on coming. It seemed so much bigger and intimidating than our trains, though this was partly down to the fact that French station platforms are only about six inches high. In France you see all of the train, not just the top half that we're used to seeing in Britain. The train stopped and we joined in the jostling and elbowing for position. That's when we heard the shouting and commotion. The ticket clerk had run across the tracks, right in front of the train, and was now dodging down the platform waving something above his head and shouting. We watched him, fascinated, and wondered what was going on. He was coming in our direction. Then, as he got closer I realised he was coming straight for us, and he seemed quite agitated. I started to get warm round the back of the neck. From blending in with the crowd we were becoming the focus of everybody's attention. What the hell had I done? He ran up to me, panting for breath.

"Voila, monsieur. Votre carte."

My credit card. I had left it behind in the ticket office. I mumbled an embarrassed and very grateful *merci beaucoup* and we rejoined the queue. My mind started to assimilate what had just happened here. We were, the four of us, on our way to a large and unfamiliar foreign city. We had hardly any cash with us. (We didn't want to be lumbered with bag loads of French and Swiss Francs after the holiday, so we'd chosen to pay our way mainly on plastic.) However, we only possessed one credit card between us. This was the very first full day of our three-week holiday and we had been the merest tickle of a bug's bum-fluff away from losing our one and only source of funds.

Oh... my... god!

Three weeks in Europe with zero money! What's French for 'Where are the offices of The Big Issue please?'

What will be our first stop in Paris? Forget the Eiffel Tower. Stuff the Arc de Triomphe. We hunt down a cash machine and we withdraw cash.

The train pulled out of Breval on time. When I say on time, I don't mean about on time. I mean, the timetable said 8:09; I kept an eye on the platform clock, and as the second hand socked home at nine minutes past the train began to move. My watch said eight and a half minutes past. My watch was wrong. Now that is how to run a railroad.

The train journey was great. For the locals it was nothing more than a regular, Monday morning commute. Most looked just about as miserable as Monday morning commuters do in England. I was like a big kid though; peering out of the windows; playing with the overhead reading lights; pulling down the seat-back trays. I tried to eavesdrop on the conversations around me; tried to understand what was being said, but failed. They were probably the usual journey to work conversations: my job sucks; Jean-Claude knows nothing, how come he's paid so much more than me? And, did you see Grand Frère last night? (Well, maybe not that bit, I hope.)

The train journey was wonderful. I love train journeys. I love the way you can see into the back of people's houses. You get a view of their private lives that you cannot get from the front – from the road. These were French houses and French lives and so it was doubly fascinating. I spent miles with my nose pressed up against the window and my breath fogging the glass and spoiling the view. Then our route took us through the Renault factory. Miles upon miles of shiny new Renaults parked-up outside. I couldn't get over how big it was. Areas this vast in Britain are given names like Shropshire. The Renaults just kept rolling past. What do *we* have now? Morgan. They make about five hundred cars a year. They don't have to be parked outside.

The train arrived at Gare St Lazare. We were arriving in an exciting and evocative capital city, and to arrive in such a place by train is one of life's great experiences. I love trains, I love railway stations. I love the way people meet or part; wait or hurry; blend in or pose. I love the cross-section of life that can be found in railway stations. I love to see the huddles of people beneath the information displays, eyes aloft, brows furrowed in concentration. They are people with goals and expectations;

they have places to go and reasons for going.

Gare St Lazare was all of this and more. It also had a wonderful aura of European-ness about it. Newsstands selling *Figaro* and *Le Monde*. Fruit and veg stalls with queues of commuters buying fresh fruit and bottled water on their way to work – now there's a change from Coke and chocolate bars. Above all there was the language. Not an English voice to be heard – just that marvellous ever-present background of wholly indecipherable French. This was great, and we were still only in the railway station.

We got cash from a cash machine. I was amazed at how easy it was. Select English from a menu and it's just like being at the shops in Birkenhead, except you get French money.

Then we headed for the Champs Elysees. We stopped in at the first café we could find and had breakfast: coffee and croissants, sitting outside in the rain, watching people. Most of the people were also watching us, probably thinking, look at those idiot English tourists sitting outside in the rain. The bill was huge. Evidently you pay for the privilege of being a poseur.

Then we hit the honey traps; we went up the Arc de Triomph; we whizzed up the Eiffel Tower; we took a boat tour along the Seine. You expect to pay through the nose for full-on tourist stuff like this, but in this case, unless I had completely messed up the exchange rate, the prices all seemed quite reasonable. We queued to pay for the Louvre and I hardly moaned about it. In the days before UK museums and galleries were free, even the Louvre seemed reasonable. We saw the Mona Lisa. Now, I don't mind art. I'm not a great lover of art but I can appreciate it. But the Mona Lisa, I have to say, is not up to much when seen in the flesh. It's small, it's behind glass, and on a good day it's about a hundred yards away and behind three hundred bobbing heads. Better to see it in a book, because you don't have to stand on tippy-toes.

The rest of the art in the Louvre you can measure by the cubic mile. It's a big place. There's a lot of art. You can call me a heathen if you like, but after two or three hours of big paintings, medium paintings and small paintings, I was losing interest. There had been a lot of controversy, at the time, about the glass pyramid entrance. Well, I'm sorry, I thought that was the best bit. I liked the smooth water features outside where we queued. I liked the entrance hall. I was impressed by the efficiency of the automatic ticket machine system; but after that I'm afraid it all went a bit downhill for me. I've always suffered a little from museum foot. A day in the mountains is no problem to me, but an hour in a big museum and I'm on my knees. The Louvre has to be the biggest and toughest challenge to sufferers of museum foot in the world. It's the Ironman triathlon of culture. Up and down, in and out of tall, vaulted, endless galleries; better make sure we haven't missed something important, let's try down here, oh god, more bloody paintings. To do the Louvre you have to train. A week in the V&A might work. You need stamina, good feet, and an insatiable love of art.

Now, I have another confession. We had lunch in McDonald's. Yes, I know that France is the capital of good food, and we were in the capital of France. I know that 99 percent of people would roar at the blasphemy of eating McNuggets for lunch. I don't even like McDonald's that much. The thing about French food, though, is this: I'm not that fond of food that looks at you with plaintive eyes. I prefer my fish, for example, to be distinctly rectangular with little evidence of its maritime lineage. I really didn't feel up to any surprises, and my language skills were in no way up to the task. So when we saw the discrete little golden arches tucked away from the discerning public eye down a side street we were unanimous in our relief. The Parisians are, I think, a little embarrassed at allowing something so overtly American onto French soil, so in Paris they hide them down side streets, out of the way. The menu was, more or less, in English. All it needed was a French accent. I got nothing that I'd ordered of course, but it was all recognisable. There was nothing lurking and wriggling in the buns, so lunch, it must be said, was a success.

After lunch we went to La Defense. This was a real eye-opener. It's not really on the main tourist route, but I wanted to see the grand arch, and it was so worth it. It is awesome. The entire area is breathtaking. Huge buildings of steel and glass, like modern sculpture on a massive scale. (Also on a massive scale is the cost of the coffee. Refreshments in La Defense are even more expensive than on the Champs Elysees.)

We finished the day with a bit of shopping then rushed for the last train back to Breval. We'd have preferred the earlier train, because the last train required a change at Mantes La Jolie. This was a shade of added stress that we did not need, but how hard could it be? It's trains, right? We alighted at Mantes La Jolie to find a railway junction the size of Yorkshire. Next to Mantes La Jolie, Crewe Junction looks like a Hornby N gauge. Everywhere you look there are tracks and signals and wires, but no passenger information – or none that we could understand. We thought we might follow people as they alighted, but only a handful did, and they all disappeared out of the station and climbed into Renaults. We were alone and we didn't have a clue. We wondered what it would cost to get a taxi from here, and we guessed it would be a lot. We had to resolve this. I found a lonely little building at the end of the platform. Inside was a man in uniform, working in squalor, buried beneath mounds of charts and graphs. I asked him, in broken French, which platform for the train to Breval. He replied with just one word, then lost himself amongst his charts again. The word sounded like "ash".

"What did he say?" Sarah asked.

"Don't know. Sounded like ash."

"What's ash? Is it a number? A letter? Is it French for 'nob off'?"

"Sounds like nothing I've heard."

I didn't like to ask again. He seemed so busy, and if one single word was beyond our comprehension what chance would we have with a sentence? The one thing I did know was the train schedule, and if we didn't find the right platform soon it would be irrelevant; we'd be facing a very long walk or we'd be sleeping rough until morning.

I looked up and down the platform again. I noticed that we were on platform C. The one next to us was B.

"Look," I said, pointing. "The platforms are not numbered, they're given letters."

"Okay," said Sarah, "so which letter sounds like ash?"

We started a slow trawl through the alphabet. A, B, C... H. Could H be "ash", or "hash"? In English it's "aich" not "haich". I looked at Sarah, she looked at me, and we saw, simultaneously, the lights coming on in each other's eyes.

"It's H," we said together, and, urging the children ahead, we started to run. We were near the steps, so up we went and along an endless bridge that crossed from one side of the colossal junction to the other. We came to H, where a double-decker train was waiting. It hadn't arrived recently, it seemed to have been waiting for a long time. There were people on it looking patient. Again, though, nothing in the way of passenger information to give us a clue so we boarded and I shouted down the carriage.

"Breval?"

A few bored-looking commuters looked up from books and newspapers. One nodded absently then went back to his *Figaro*. We weren't sure. The doors closed and the train pulled out. We were going somewhere. Could be Breval, could be Toulouse. We stared out of the windows with gob-stopper eyes searching for things we'd seen before. Was this the right train? It didn't feel right. If not, where the hell would we end up? How would we get back? We didn't even have a map. Our trusty road map was in the car. Each minute felt like an hour. We passed stations with names we did not know. My geography is okay but I don't know every little village in France. If the train stops do we get off? Which direction would we walk?

The sense of relief, when we pulled into Breval, cannot be put into words. It would be bad enough alone, but when a wife and two children are relying on you to safely steer them through a foreign land the stresses of responsibility can be hard to take.

Our car was still the only one parked outside Breval station. There was a note tucked under the windscreen wiper. It was hand written and in French, of course, and I couldn't read it. So we took it back to the caravan where I settled down with my trusty French dictionary. After an hour of word-by-word effort I sat back to read what it said.

"Sir, you have parked in a blue zone. Only setting down and picking up are allowed in this area. Please do not do this again or you will be fined." Or words to this effect. The note was signed and identified as coming from the Mairie, or Town Hall. Imagine if this town hall official had been as tolerant as our own beloved traffic wardens in Britain. It would have been a long walk back to the campsite, and an even longer walk back to the Mairie the next morning to get the car unclamped.

So ended our fleeting visit to Paris. Next morning we moved on and headed for the Marne Valley, to a site near to the town of Joinville, where we planned to stay another three nights.

Our site was La Forge de Ste Marie in Thonnance les Moulins. We were shown to our pitch, which was on a terrace with a view down to the small lake. It had been a hot sticky drive in the car and we chose, for once, to fly in the face of custom (putting the kettle on) and instead we headed straight for the indoor swimming pool. Glorious. We were the only ones there. We had the whole place to ourselves.

La Forge Ste Marie is a strange site, really. It's not particularly near to anywhere. The countryside is largely agricultural, so there's no walking of any great merit round and about. Yet the site itself is a real joy – one that we would have been happy to stay at for a little longer. The swimming pool was built from a converted outbuilding that had been part of the old forge, and it had character by the bucketful. At the same time it felt modern and was spotlessly clean. When we were staying at the previous site, near Paris, we hadn't felt drawn to use the pool at all, because it was uncovered and always crowded. Here, the pool was ignored by the other campers and for the first time on our travels we realised just how wonderful it was to be able to take a walk from the caravan down to a private swimming pool whenever the mood took us. It's certainly something that had never arisen in the sites we'd stayed at in Britain.

The next day we visited Joinville. We'd passed through Joinville on our way to the site on the previous day and noted that the main tourist attraction was Le Grand Jardin. It's a chateau with a large ornate garden that is well worth a visit if you like gardens. I don't mind gardens, but I do start to flag and trudge a little after I've been circulating for an hour or so. This one certainly had more than an hour's worth of trudging in it, even in the midday heat, but I was told, by my garden-appreciating wife, that this was a particularly fine example, and that I should shut up moaning and look around me and thrill to the wonders of a beautifully restored sixteenth-century renaissance garden. So I duly did as I was told. I crunched up and down the gravel paths in the wake of our little party, nodding and making appreciative botanical noises whenever they seemed required.

Opposite Le Grand Jardin there was a supermarket. When I'd been marched up and down the gravel for long enough to thoroughly break my spirit, Sarah decided that it was time to finish the job with a bit of food shopping. Now, ordinarily this would have met with howls of protest and sobs of despair, but I have to admit, I was curious. For one thing, it isn't immediately obvious, in France, which shops are the supermarkets. In England they're called Tesco, Asda, Morrisons and Sainsbury. They have acres of glass up front so that you can look in and see the shelves full of food. In France there are no familiar names at all, and if you don't know the names you can't even be sure that they are supermarkets. They are square white buildings with trolleys outside. There is rarely any glass, so you could be going into a DIY shop or a tyre warehouse for all you know.

This one was an Intermarché. As luck would have it, it turned out to be a supermarket, and what a fascinating place it was. We spent a happy hour or so wandering around the aisles, looking at the pictures on the cans and packets and bottles, and trying to figure out what might be inside them. We, Sarah and

I, make it harder on ourselves by being partly vegetarian whenever we can, a throw-back from our need to protect ourselves from BSE in the early nineties. (I think we succeeded. Nobody in our family has started walking into walls yet – at least not often in my case.) We were also fascinated by the sweets and chocolate. This was at a time when I was a black belt in chocolate appreciation, and so I just had to try some. In fact, I'm like a magpie in supermarkets at the best of times; "Oooh, look. Shiny stuff. We've never tried this before. Get a few of these, they look good."

Sarah was all boring and sensible:

"There's no point in getting frozen things; we don't even have a fridge.

"Put that pizza away – it's bigger than the oven.

"Get some chocolate if you want, but it won't last, it's over eighty degrees out there."

Then I came across the wine.

I knew wine was cheaper in France. Everyone knows that. I don't really drink much wine and I'm certainly no connoisseur. I prefer red to white, but if blindfolded I think I'd be pushed to tell the two apart. I like the shape of the bottles, though; the shine, the colours and the sensuous curves. I love the sound when you pour: glop, glop, glop. I look for labels that have lots of curly writing and a nice picture of a chateau. I always think you can't go wrong with wine that has a good picture and lots of curly writing on the label. When I shop for wine I shuffle along the shelves mumbling the prices. "£3.99, £3.40, £2.99. Ah, £2.99 – an excellent vintage."

So when I did the same exercise in francs – "12 francs, 11 francs, 10... hang about," a quick bit of mental arithmetic and, "My god, this stuff's less than a quid a bottle!" Suddenly I'm a wine buff. The basket's loaded up. Don't need a fridge for wine. Doesn't need cooking so it doesn't matter how big the oven is. It's cheap, cheap, cheap!

Sarah's eyes told me she was disgusted at me. She doesn't drink, ever. She now believed I'd been seduced by the demon drink. She was expecting to be sharing our caravan with a slobbering drunken beast for the rest of the holiday. Not true. As I said, I don't drink much wine. I don't really like it that much, and until recently I still had the last bottle of cheap Joinville red sitting on top of the kitchen cupboard. That holiday we dragged boxes of the stuff, clinking and jingling, all around Europe with us, displacing other more important things from the caravan, like food. I'll give it this, though, it's certainly a well-travelled little wine.

Here's a funny thing we found about France. There wasn't much fresh milk. If you are lucky you might find the odd plastic bottle tucked away in the corner of one of the fridges, but for the most part the French seemed to prefer UHT, commonly called Long Life in the UK, or, even worse, they go for the hard stuff: rigid white plastic bottles of sterilised milk. I remember "sterrie" from my youth, and I remember it being integral to visits to my grandparents in Bolton. They didn't have a fridge, so they bought long slender glass bottles of sterrie with beer-bottle caps. This is not a fond memory. I can remember it being amongst the worst things about having to visit grandparents, along with the terror of being kissed by old people, and the constant references to my remarkable rate of growth. When you are young your memory (or common sense) seems to let you down. When asked the question, '*Would you like a nice glass of milk*?', you say, 'Yes please.' What is wrong with you? It's only been two weeks since you were last here and suckered by that same innocent question. Your young mind pictures a fridge door being opened and a delicious bottle of cool, fresh milk being poured into a glass, rather like on the chocolate advert: "a glass and a half of full-cream milk in every bar". Incidentally, they used emulsion paint for the adverts. Somehow they had difficulty getting the milk to look milky enough. But I digress. So, you are given a full glass of temptingly delicious-looking milk, and at the first sip of the warm, slightly sour, putrid liquid, all the fortnight-old memories come flooding back. There is no fridge, there is instead a dusty recess beneath the sink where the bottles of sterrie are stored. Now, after the merest sip, there is still a full glass left and you know that you are going to have to drink it all. It's no good screwing up your eyes and constricting your throat, none of this is going to help. You have to drink it and it is going to taste like horse wee. Why, oh why, did you not just ask for water? Then, in the next two or three weeks the offer will be made again. You will forget again, and the whole bitter nightmare will recur.

"Sarah, they seem to only have Long Life. We've already got plenty of that in the caravan."

"What about this?"

Sarah passed me a plastic bottle called Lait. There was a picture of white creamy liquid, not too dissimilar to the velvety, mouth-watering Cadbury's emulsion paint. On the side, in small type, hidden in amongst unintelligible tracts of nutritional and advertising blurb was the word *stériliser*. I missed it.

"Hmm, okay. We'll try it. Maybe they put the fresh milk in hard plastic bottles in France." (So, fool, why wasn't it stored in the fridge?)

Poor schmuck. Forty years later and still getting suckered. I spent the evening devising a system to keep that one lone bottle cool – muslin cloths soaked in water standing in a shallow bowl – all for the pleasure of proper milk on my cornflakes the next morning. I was, of course, destined to destroy those cornflakes with sterrie, and crack open the door to ancient and terrible memories. *My haven't you grown. Give your gran a kiss. Would you like a glass of milk, dear?*

Back to Intermarché. I couldn't get over the bike bits. There was a whole aisle of them. Puncture kits, bike hats, tools... You could even buy bike tyres. In a supermarket, for heaven's sake!

I was also fascinated by the books. Bestselling writers, some of their books strangely familiar, others I'd never seen before. Authors I knew and loved, whose names were above titles that meant nothing to me. Even those I could translate turned out to be titles I'd never before encountered. Surely the likes of Stephen King and John Grisham weren't beavering away at a whole alternative catalogue specially for France. I felt the urge to buy one, something I'd already read, but I couldn't even get beyond most of the titles, so I didn't know which ones I *had* already read.

The best thing of all about supermarket shopping is the checkout. Any linguistically-challenged buffoon can do it. It's just like home. You load up the conveyor, the checkout girl passes it over the barcode reader, she smiles and says:

"Trois-cent-soixante-huit-francs-quarante-et-un, s'il vous plaît." All in one breath.

You just smile as if you know exactly what she just said. You look at the till where it says ff368.41 (if you can be bothered, it's not really necessary because you don't know what it means in real money, anyway) and you hand over the plastic. Easy. You don't have the vaguest inkling as to how much you've spent, and you won't really care until the bill turns up after you get home. In supermarkets you can get by with just three words of French: *bonjour, merci, au revoir*. It's all remarkably stress-free.

Back outside we carried our bags of shopping over to where the car had been sitting for most of the day. It was a hot day. Up to now we'd had more or less British weather, but now it felt great to feel the sun on our backs. We loaded up the boot, then I opened the car door. The wall of heat rocked me back on my heels. The inside was like a pizza oven. All four of us said the same thing:

"Whoa!"

We waited. This kind of thing happens back home (two or three days a year, maybe), and usually things improve once the doors are opened. After ten minutes of patient waiting there was no sign of the inferno abating.

"We need to open the sun roof," Sarah suggested.

"Okay, I'll... ow... ooh... Ooh!"

I couldn't get near it. I couldn't even put my hand on the back of the seat to support me while I leaned in. What we needed, here, was a veteran steel worker, or maybe one of Satan's heating engineers.

The car was cooling. A bit. It was a slow process, but eventually the time came when I could stick my head and arms inside for enough seconds to open the sun roof. We needed a flow of air. To get a flow of air we needed to get inside and drive it.

I leaned in and started the engine, then switched on the fans. The hot air started to circulate in a feeble sort of way, but enough to risk, after five minutes, getting into the car. We'd have to do this with military precision. We each stood by an open door and I counted down.

"Are you ready? Three, two, one..."

We leapt in. I listened for four door clunks, then roared up the road.

"Go, go, go," shouted the children from the back seat.

"Right," shouted Sarah. "Drive on the right!"

I veered across the road, away from the oncoming truck with the flashing lights and wailing horn, and as cool air filled the car we slowed and gave a collective sigh, each of us leaning forward in our seats, still not daring to put any weight on the backrests. We'd learned something. The climate had changed. We had done a remarkable thing. We had driven, mile by mile, so far south that the weather had changed. It gave us a sense of distance; a sense that we had done more than drive to a different country; we had driven to a different part of the globe. We were getting nearer to the Alps.

On our last day at La Forge Ste Marie we drove to Grand.

Why did we choose Grand? In the campsite's reception there was a book with tourist information. We knew nothing about the region, and the minimalist leaflet about Grand seemed to suggest that it was an interesting town with some Roman remains. Importantly, it wasn't too distant. The day after, we'd be facing the longest leg of our journey thus far, so we didn't want to spend too long sitting in the car today, and Grand was only ten miles away.

The route took us through a network of very minor roads in the heart of the Lorraine countryside. There were few road signs, and we began to wonder if we had chosen to visit the wrong place on our only remaining day in the Marne valley.

We came to Grand and our fears appeared to have been realised. Nobody else was in town. Nobody even seemed to live in the town, it was so deserted. It was the kind of town where you might expect to find the odd tumbleweed rolling down the main street. There was a small sign pointing to the Mosaic and another to the Amphitheatre. We stopped at the side of the road near to what appeared to be the amphitheatre entrance. There were two other cars parked. Nobody was moving. We went to investigate and found a sign that suggested it was closed for lunch. This was a little disheartening. What kind of tourist attraction closed for lunch? We walked around the town for twenty minutes while waiting for lunch to end. It appeared that the whole town was also closed for lunch, so there wasn't much to see. We are no longer used to this kind of thing in Britain. Nothing ever closes – for lunch or on Sundays. France seems to have avoided this pressure towards twenty-four hour commercialism, and, although this is inconvenient to our pressured way of thinking, it's also quite civilised and refreshing. Sometimes there is good in being forced to stop and take a breath; to have a little time to reflect and put things into perspective.

We drifted back to the amphitheatre entrance, just in time to see a lady arriving on a bike. She took out some keys and unlocked the door. It seems that lunch in France is not the hurried sandwiches-at-your-desk-and-answer-the-phone-every-two-minutes culture that we are used to. In France they go home for lunch. What a splendid idea.

We went into the amphitheatre visitor centre and paid a paltry sum to see the main attraction. The visitor centre was modern and interesting and had a good scale model, but we didn't hang about, we wanted to see the real thing. We went out through a door and the sight knocked our breath away. We were looking at a full-sized Roman amphitheatre that seemed perfect in every detail. It was incredible. We walked down a slope towards the arena and it began to dawn on us what had happened here, and a little bit of research later confirmed it.

When the amphitheatre was first uncovered the stone came in contact with the elements for the first time in centuries, and it started to erode. A roof was needed. So rather than do the economic thing of covering the amphitheatre up again and closing it to the public, some unnamed genius hit on the idea of creating a roof that was an exact replica of the amphitheatre itself, whose remains could lay protected beneath. They built a roof of wood, of iroko wood, a kind of teak that weathers to a grey colour and looks exactly like stone. It's not just cosmetic, either. It's a functional amphitheatre. You can go up and sit on the terraces and imagine what it was like in Roman times. It is truly a remarkable achievement. I was at a loss as to what to admire the most, the amphitheatre itself or the wonderfully elegant solution that was adopted for its preservation.

Here's the other baffling thing. Why? Why did the Romans build a 17,000-seater stadium all the way out here? It isn't near anything, it isn't on the way anywhere. It's not just a bit of a stadium, either. The amphitheatre at Grand is up there in the top ten biggest amphitheatres in the Roman world. For both the Romans and for modern day tourists, though, Grand seems to be an awfully long way from anywhere and it has to be one of the world's most under-appreciated relics.

It didn't end there. After we'd had our fill of amphitheatres we headed through town in the direction of the mosaic. We hadn't intended to bother with this bit, but it was explained to us that our entry ticket also allowed us entry to the mosaic, so what could it hurt?

What was this mosaic, anyway? The signs and information boards outside were, again, understated to a remarkable degree. I expected a few lumps of damaged tiling that might enthuse the history buffs. The building resembled an oldish church on the outside. On the inside we were in for yet another of those oh-my-god moments.

In the building is a room with cathedral-like lighting and

atmosphere. There is a vast floor – the mosaic. It's like a ballroom (224 square meters of uninterrupted mosaic, I looked it up) and it is surrounded by an elevated gallery that tourists can shuffle around, drooling and gasping in awe.

We shuffled and we drooled and we gasped. The mosaic is not only big, and perfect (like it-was-only-laid-last-week perfect) but it's also really interesting. You can gaze at it for hours. If I sound like I'm getting carried away here, I'll try to put this into some sort of perspective. I am not a history buff, not at all. I do not get wrapped up in the lost wonders of the ancient world. Usually I'm a bit dismissive ("it's just old stuff"), and I'm easily prone to boredom, but we spent over an hour in there, and we could not get enough. If I can get this enraptured, people who actually appreciate history should be forewarned; it could mess up your head. Go to Grand. Go now. It will change you.

But now back to the caravan, for something else was beckoning. Something pointy and white and very, very big. What's that smell? Could it be Alpine air?

THREE ALPS, TWO DREAMS AND AN
ALPINE: 2000

Okay, we got to Europe and so I know how the French do motorway lanes and, yes, I have seen their speed limit signs. All the Europeans, not just the French, are quite ingenious when it comes to designing speed limit signs. It must be lateral thinking. They do this clever thing where they put a number inside a red circle. Okay, it's in kilometres per hour, but that is, after all, the way they measure speed in Europe. But the idea of a number inside a red circle... brilliant. There is no language difficulty with numbers. "50" means fifty in English and cinquante in French, but it's still 50; half a hundred or five lots of ten.

Here was I, thinking that the only sensible way to instruct drivers on the maximum speed limit for a particular stretch of road was a white sign with a black diagonal stripe. Then all you have to do is find a Post Office, buy a copy of the highway code, and read it from cover to cover in order to ascertain what the various permutations, of road-type, street-lighting, number of carriageways, in combination with this simple sign, actually mean, and if you get it wrong you get your photo taken and you have to cough up a great deal of money. Ahh, so that's why we do signs the British way. The fines pay for the hospitals, and we need all the hospitals to look after the people who are injured by speeding cars, who are speeding, not because they are bad people, but because they don't know what a white circle with a black diagonal line means.

Okay, I know I'm going on a bit about this, but I've just looked in the highway code. A white circle with a black stripe means: "National speed limit applies." So now I've looked up the national speed limit. There are four national speed limits depending upon whether you are in: a) built-up areas, b) single carriageways, c) Dual-carriageways, or d) Motorways. What's more, these four speed limit zones are different depending on which of five (or six if you count trailers) different classes of vehicle you are driving. What's more, the 30mph limit applies to all roads in England and Wales (only class C and unclassified roads in Scotland) with street lighting unless signs show otherwise. (So what if the sign to indicate otherwise is a white disc with a black stripe?)

What a marvellous system. What must the Europeans think when they come over here? Do they think: what a fine nation of road-builders, or do they think: what a bunch of nob-heads. Not only must they memorise all of these combinations, they must do it in a quaint and archaic system of measurement called Imperial units, that was defined in the Weights and Measures act of 1824.

—No. 62 from the Moanicles of Michael.

I didn't sleep well that night. None of us did. The moment was upon us. We had worked our way down through France and it had been fascinating and enlightening. We'd seen wonders and we'd tasted, for the first time, a foreign culture. Now, however, it was time for the main event. Our pack, that morning, had an air of ritual about it. It was performed in a kind of reverential silence, each of us deep in our own thoughts, each with our own tasks to fulfil.

I emptied the waste, taking my time, rinsing and cleaning the mud off the wheels of the Wastemaster; I disconnected the electrics and carefully wound the hook-up cable, making sure it didn't tangle. Sarah tidied the inside of the 'van, folding sheets and towels and stowing them neatly. Everything had to be right for today.

At around nine-thirty we hitched the caravan and slowly crunched through the gravel roads of La Forge de Ste Marie. At the site exit we turned west. We headed through glorious, typically French, minor roads, on the one hand enjoying the scenery, but on the other wanting to be racking up the miles. We faced a two-hundred-and-fifty-mile journey and we didn't fancy doing it all at ten miles per hour on farm tracks. Eventually, though, we joined some faster roads, and we drove on towards and through Epinal and into the Vosges mountains. This felt, for all the world, just how we imagined the Alps. There were Swiss cottages everywhere and the mountains were becoming serious. We passed through an area called Les Grands Ballons des Vosges and made a note that this would be a good place to visit in its own right, but not today. Today we were going to the real Alps, and they were beginning to feel close. Nothing would stop the dream now.

I pulled into an Agip petrol station for my last fill-up in France. I was preoccupied with thoughts of snow and needle-sharp peaks. I forgot to do my little mental rehearsal before going into the check-out. For a moment I was flustered.

"Oh, er... five... er,"

un, deux, trois...

"Quatre! No, cinq. Pompe numéro cinq, s'il vous plaît please." I punched my thigh in frustration. I wished I could be more natural about this. Every conversation became a sweaty, panic-stricken effort.

Then I noticed that the girl was taking no notice of my blundering and painful attempts to speak, instead she had removed my credit card from the verifying machine and was examining it closely. She looked up at me and said some French stuff, quite a lot of French stuff, and she waved my card around, and the only words I picked up on were *carte* and *credite*. Then she turned and shouted across to her colleague.

"Joëlle, Joëlle, regarde. Regarde cette carte de crédite. Vite."

I understood some of this. Her friend's name was Joëlle. *Le garde* – wasn't that French for police? I had gone cold. Oh my god! A problem. A problem with my credit card. Why now, of all times?

Joëlle came over and the two of them bent over my credit card and scrutinised it. A rapid and excited dialogue passed between them and I understood nothing. I had taken a full tank of fuel, forty litres, and something was wrong with my credit card. How would I survive in a French prison? What would Sarah and the kids do without me, and without the money to buy fuel or food or pay for hotels... or bail me out? The back of my neck was hot. My legs were cold, and they felt like rubber. I tried to think of some words.

"Je suis désolé," I blurted. (Start with an apology. Always a good idea, even before the police become involved.)"Est-ce une problème avec ma carte de crédite?" I said.

The first girl looked up. "Une problème, monsieur? Non, non monsieur, non. Pas de problème."

Now it was Joëlle who spoke.

"No, sir. There is not problem. My friend wish to show me card. See? Picture on card?" She showed me my credit card. I have an affinity card, the sort with a picture on the front. Mine had a picture of a campsite in Folkstone.

"We know this place. Joëlle and I stay here last summer. It is Folkstone, no? Look, here is where we put our tent, you see?"

Waves of relief washed over me. I smiled the smile of a prisoner reprieved. My legs were still shaking but this was now a shock reaction. The after-effects of a near-miss. I gathered my dignity as best I could.

"Did you have a good holiday in England?" I asked.

"No," she said. "It rained. All the week."

We descended from the Vosges mountains. The road kept on winding, down and down. I told myself that whichever route options we chose for our return, after Switzerland, this would not be one of them. The thought of dragging a caravan up this interminable mountain made me shudder. We must have descended for twenty miles, all downhill.

Once clear of the Vosges the character of the countryside changed. There were more factories and they all had German names. We were nearing the convergence of three countries: France, Germany and Switzerland. The influence of rural France was fast falling behind. I could see that Sarah was getting more and more excited; our transit into Switzerland would be a thrilling moment.

Then I made a mistake. I have said before, I love maps. I love planning itineraries. I had planned a perfectly reasonable route, but then I had dabbled. I wondered why my route differed from that venerable piece of historic software, Microsoft AutoRoute 1999. I should have stayed resolute. There had been nothing wrong with my plan, but somehow I had managed to convince myself that programmers, locked in a basement in Silicon Valley, might have a better understanding of the road network of Western Europe than me and Édouard Michelin. *Hey dudes – let's try it this way for a change. These little white roads are kinda cool, man.*

We rolled in towards Mulhouse on the A36. According to my plan we should have stayed on the A36 into Germany, then followed the A5 – a grand, sweeping motorway/autobahn –

into, through, and out the other end of Basle. Easy.

The programmers, however, said turn right onto the A35, then exit at a place called St Louis. I took their advice. I will one day find it in my heart to forgive them.

We entered a grim and grey council estate that had been forsaken by each of the three nations that merged in this corner of Europe. There were no road signs, no road markings. There was precious little you'd call a road. We got all agitated and started to argue. I blamed Sarah's reading of the Auto (Fantasy) Route listings, she blamed my interpretation of her reading.

I stopped the car and we spread the map out on the bonnet. There was nothing to learn from the map. We had no idea where we were. Sarah said that she would drive and I could demonstrate my superior sense of direction and get us out of this place. She drove. I looked at the map. I looked out of the window. I looked for inspiration. We found our way into an industrial estate. There was nothing like it on the map. I suggested we take a right. It was an inspired idea; we drove into a factory.

If you have never towed a caravan you won't appreciate the horror you feel when you find you've driven into a dead end. It is not so scary, these days, because we get more practice at driving into dead ends, because these days we have satnav. A motorist sans caravan would simply turn around. Easy. Caravanners keep going, hoping there will be a way out. Driving on inevitably makes things worse. Narrow roads get narrower. Our narrow road wound through a giant pharmaceutical company. We pressed on, sucking great lung-fulls of steroids and dioxins and god-knows-what other noxious vapours leaking from the elaborate pipe works. French workers stared at us bemused. What were a family of British holidaymakers doing cruising around their factory with a caravan in tow?

Sarah drove, and cursed, and drove, while the rest of us offered moral support by sitting in the car with mouths open and eyes on stalks but keeping our thoughts to ourselves. She got us out of there. We came to a kind of guardhouse, where two security guards stopped us. This was exciting.

They walked around the car and the caravan in their crisp black uniforms and jack boots. One of them indicated for me to wind down the window.

"Wo du gehend bist?"

Ah, German now. Fantastic. A new language for me to practice.

"Uhh?" I said.

"Ver are you going?"

"Oh, er, Interlaken."

"Die Reisepass?"

His attitude seemed a bit over the top, but I handed over our passports nevertheless. We had just driven out of his factory with a caravan and four bikes strapped to the roof of the car. Did we appear suspicious or just plain odd?

While the one guard scrutinised our passports the other continued on, to circle the car and the caravan, peering at everything, staring in at us. At last they seemed satisfied that we were merely idiots, and a threat only to ourselves. They returned our passports and raised the barrier. As we drove through I couldn't help thinking that it was a pity their security wasn't a bit better on the way *in* to the factory.

As we drove on, we began to notice some things. The streets had become very clean. The road signs seemed different. Then we noticed flags; red flags with big white crosses on them. *We were in Switzerland.* The factory security barrier had, in fact, been the border. We'd entered Switzerland and had completely missed the moment. I was disappointed. Sarah was gutted.

Sarah still drove and there were still no road signs to give us any kind of clue. There was nowhere to stop and switch roles again so we carried on. The fact that we were now across the border was our only clue as to where we were.

"Follow the sun," I said. "It's mid-afternoon so the sun should be vaguely south-west. Follow the sun and we can't go wrong."

"What?" Sarah laughed a scornful sort of laugh. "We're in the third largest city in Switzerland, and the best that Map Boy can give me is '*follow the sun*'?"

We followed the sun. The city became denser and busier. We were surrounded by cars. Big black and grey Mercs and BMWs. Cars with attitude and arrogance. Then there were trams. In Basle nobody yields; not the Mercs, not the Beamers, and especially not the trams. We didn't know the rules of the road. We didn't know the prevailing road etiquette, although on the face of it there wasn't any.

Thinking back, Basle was probably a beautiful city. We didn't appreciate any of it. Basle passed in a turmoil of yelling, veering, braking and horn tooting. Sarah was great. She held the wheel wearing a North Atlantic lone yachtswoman kind of expression: gritted teeth, straight back, going wherever I pointed. At one time we got between two converging trams – car, caravan and everything – and we emerged with mere inches on each side.

We saw a sign for Bern. We saw it late. Sarah went for it anyway, crossing three lanes. Mercs and black-windowed Beamers scattered like chaff.

We were on a slip road joining a motorway. The motorway was full of steel-eyed Swiss businessmen. Nobody would give way to let us out. The slip road was fast disappearing and we had nowhere to go. I wound down my passenger window and hung right out into the traffic. I stared down the man in the navy-blue Mercedes immediately behind and to the left of us. I pointed straight at him. I glared. I gestured that we were pulling out and that he should back off.

"Go. Go!" I shouted to Sarah.

"But I can't see a space."

"Don't worry about it, just pull out."

The blue Merc got my meaning. He lifted off and eased back.

A mile or so later we pulled into a motorway services. Sarah switched off the engine and held her head in her hands. Neither of us spoke. I stared out of the window. The children, I realised, had been silent throughout the whole episode. I think they were in shock. I turned round to speak to them.

"You two okay?"

"Follow the sun?" said Kevin. "I can't believe you said that."

Sarah passed me the car keys.

"Your turn," she said. "But I think we need a cup of tea first."

We continued, turning south onto the A2 then the A1. We were headed towards Bern. Leaving Basle there were a few craggy hills and the road passed through several tunnels, which I must say were seriously scary, because the traffic did not reduce speed at all. There is the ever-present psychological pressure from the other road users to push on at unabated speed whatever the prevailing road conditions, and I was none too happy about it. The craggy hills soon fell behind and we were surprised to find that northern Switzerland is flat. It's flat and boring. There was also a surprising amount of it. The bland scenery dragged on for about sixty miles, made worse by the road signs that said *"Bern 100"*, since we had to go almost as far as Bern before turning south towards the Alps. I was certain that we'd be able to see the Alps by now, but all I could see when I looked south were clouds.

We turned south onto the A6. The clouds were in front of us now, and they were getting nearer. They weren't normal clouds. There was something strange about them.

"Funny looking clouds in front."

"You don't think..."

"No, they're clouds. They're too high for..."

We all realised at the same time.

Yes they were clouds, but they had mountains sticking up out of the top of them. We were looking at the Alps.

I stopped for petrol. This was our first petrol stop in Switzerland, but for once I wasn't worrying about language problems, even though we had switched to German for the first time. I wasn't worrying or concentrating on anything. I couldn't tear my eyes away from the mountains that now loomed up in front of us. The A6 went straight on, perspective narrowing to a point that seemed to spear straight into the towering mass of rock and snow that lay ahead. I mumbled something in poor French to the German-speaking checkout girl. She didn't seem to understand, whether from her lack of French or from mine, I couldn't be sure, but this snapped me back into the real world as I had to quickly switch my head into German-speaking mode. German was an even bigger problem to me than French had been. At least I did French at school. My faltering knowledge of German had been gleaned entirely, over the last three months, from a single Linguaphone pack that I'd borrowed from the library. I could repeat all the tunes and jingles that punctuated the recording with complete familiarity, but the words eluded me, then and now.

"Er, pompe numéro trois, er no, sorry." I went back to fingers

– *eine*, *zwei*... "Drei. Pompe drei, er, bitte." Again I hated myself for my pitiful attempts at being a proper European. Coming back out of the shop, though, my self-recriminations faded. My senses were assaulted, once more, by the majesty of those mountains. We were nearly there.

But we weren't nearly there, not at all. We kept driving and the mountains just kept on getting bigger. I knew the Alps were big, of course I did, but nothing prepared me for anything like this.

We reached the mountains at last, and strangely, some of the grandeur was lost. They were too big. They went up, past the top of the car windows, and were lost to our eyes above the roof of the car.

Our route now took us alongside Lake Thun, which we later learned is pronounced Toon, and here was a new wonder to distract our attention from the mountains. The lake was turquoise. I'm not using turquoise in a metaphorical sense in order to suggest a particularly strong shade of blue; no, the lake really was the most surreal turquoise colour imaginable. I've seen photos of Swiss lakes before, and I've often thought that the colour seemed a bit off – perhaps from dodgy film, or the effects of leaving postcards out in the sun for too long, or even from a bit of fanciful touching up on Photoshop after a long night on the schnapps. Here though, was the evidence. The colour was real. This really was the most amazing colour for a lake. As we came into Interlaken we realised that the colour was not the usual reflective trick of light from the sky that makes the sea look blue on fine days, for the fast-flowing Aare river that passes through the middle of Interlaken was exactly the same colour. It was the colour of the water itself. The colour of melting glaciers. Between the mountains and the lakes, the most overused word in the car that afternoon was,

251

"Wow!"

Our campsite near Interlaken was named the Lazy Rancho. I know, sad isn't it? If you have a campsite that nestles in a valley with ten-thousand-foot mountains towering on either side and that has a clear view, from the caravan window, of the Monche, the Jungfrau and the North Face of the Eiger, you'd want to call it Die Eiger Ansicht or something like that. Lazy Rancho serves up visions of dusty plains, cacti, baked beans and cowboy boots. I was sold by the photograph in the Carefree brochure. Lazy Rancho is not a spectacular site in itself – the pool is like a big bucket, the shop is only okay – but the location is stunning.

Shortly after we arrived the sky clouded over and it began to rain, and the scenery could easily have been Wales. That was okay, though. It allowed us to set up the caravan without distraction. We had quite a small space in which to squeeze everything: the caravan, the awning, Kevin's little pup tent, and of course the car, but once done, and with our first cup of tea in our hands, the rain stopped and the clouds began to lift. They became wispy and clung in thin tendrils to the trees. They began to break up with shafts of sunlight lancing through. Suddenly the peaks appeared, high up in the sky, high above anywhere that rock and snow had any right to appear. We were truly in the Alps. There ahead of us, as advertised, the three peaks of the Monche, the Jungfrau and the Eiger.

We pulled the bikes down from the roof of the car and headed into Interlaken. It was late in the afternoon but we just had to explore. We were only a ten-minute cycle into the town, and our route took us across a bridge over the Aare River; that incredible turquoise again, and now with the time to stop and really take it in. We spied out the supermarkets and the two train stations: Interlaken East and Interlaken West. The east station would be our destination the day after tomorrow. This is where we would catch a train to Grindelwald, up in the mountains. I wanted it tomorrow but there was this thing waiting to spoil it.

We called into a supermarket on our way back to the caravan. This would be even harder than in France because of our profound lack of German. Like in France, though, it was a fascinating experience. It was a Co-op! Is this the same as our Co-op? It didn't look like our Co-op. There were all kinds of strange and exotic things. I was once again on a chocoquest, and Switzerland really is the place to be for the up and coming connoisseur of the brown stuff. There were slabs of Lindt and Milka with the lilac cow on the front, and real Toblerone. (Actually it's all real Toblerone, it's all made here, in Bern, but it seems even better eating it on home turf. Maybe they keep the best stuff for themselves and toss the rest into the export crates, I don't know.) I resisted, on this occasion though, because I had seen a cake with whorls of wonderfully chocolaty squashy layers squeezed into it from every angle.

"We need something for tea, tonight," I said, all nonchalant.

"No, we're okay, I think. I'm doing a veggie stew," said Sarah.

"For afters, I mean."

Sarah gave me one of those looks.

"It's been a long hard drive. All that trouble in Bern. We deserve something, don't you think?"

"What have you seen?" said Sarah.

"Nothing, nothing. Just looking."

"We could buy some fruit."

I tried not to show a pained expression.

"Yes, we could buy fruit," I said. "Wait there, what about this?" I produced the gooey chocolaty thing with a flourish.

"This looks okay. It's different."

"What is it? Can you read what it says?"

"No, I can't read the packet, but it looks like some kind of cake. Looks quite nice, don't you think?"

"Okay, we'll try it. I'd be happier if I knew what was in it, though."

"Oh, it will be fine," I said, stashing the cake-thing into the basket and smacking my lips before there was time for second thoughts.

We bought a few other staples, like milk and bread, and took them to the check-out where we encountered an unexpected hitch. Credit cards are not allowed! Was my German giving me problems here? No, the checkout girl repeated it in clear English. No credit cards allowed. This is Switzerland, the land of banks and Zurich gnomes, and numbered Swiss accounts for international criminals and spies, and you can't buy a loaf of bread, a bottle of milk and gooey-chocolatey-cakey stuff using a credit card. Incredible but true.

I parted company with most of our meagre supply of paper Swiss Francs and we left the shop. We cycled back to the caravan. I held forth for most of the way with a moanicle about Swiss finance, until Sarah told me to give it a rest.

We had Sarah's veggie stew, which went down very well, then I impatiently ripped open the wrapping of the chocolatey-cakey-gooey thing, mouth watering, saliva glands pumping. I took a big slice, put it on my plate, and waited politely, with all the patience of a heroin junkie, while everyone else took a slice. It looked even more appealing on the plate, all squashy and heavy with calories. I lifted it to my mouth, feeling the satisfying weight and substance of it. I took a big bite.

"Urrgh, my god, it's horrible!" I couldn't swallow it. I couldn't keep it in my mouth. I spat it onto my plate. Kevin whooped in delight, Amanda feigned disgusted nausea, but both found it highly entertaining and worthy of copying.

Sarah tried next, but a small, refined bite that she gulped down with an expression that suggested she was swallowing razor blades. She agreed; it was appalling.

This evil thing looked like cake; it looked like it contained chocolate. It tasted like... well, it was indescribable. It wasn't chocolate inside. We prodded it and poked it. We experimented. We came to the conclusion that the "chocolate" was, in fact, squashed raisins. Raisins are okay scattered about in a scone or in Christmas cake or a Christmas pudding even; but these were puréed and concentrated and matured and really, badly, seriously abused.

We dropped the cakey-gooey-raisiny thing into the bin. I felt cheated. All those rows upon rows of wonderful Swiss chocolate bars and I go and choose this... abomination.

"I think I've got some apples," Sarah said.

"Yummy."

Next day was laundry day. Frustrating. I wanted to go up into the Alps. I wanted to feel the crunch of rock beneath my boots, but we had no clothes and no towels and no underwear, and Sarah believed that these were important. As it happened, it rained all day, so confinement to the laundry proved no great loss. Kevin refused to go near the laundry so he announced he was taking off on his bike to do some *real* mountain biking. Oh yes, these were proper mountains. Wet and muddy mountains. The sort of off road he did with us was far too tame. Amanda said she'd go with him, not to mountain bike, but to administer first aid when he fell off. Kevin was scornful of this, but allowed her to tag along. She brought him back five minutes later with his arm gashed and bleeding. They hadn't even got off the camp site. Kevin had, apparently found a small heap of gravel, for maintaining the paths, that he'd used for a warm-up. One run at it had proven to be enough. We patched him up with plasters and TCP and left the two of them reading in the caravan while we set out to do the washing.

One thing about the Alps, about any mountain region, is that it rains a lot. Now, wouldn't you think that a large international campsite, located in a very wet region of the world, would have more than two tumble driers? Plenty washing machines. Plenty opportunity for getting things wet, over and above the stuff coming down from the sky. Inevitably, competition and international rivalry were intense. Everyone wanted a piece of the tumble-dryer action. We staked out our territory and we waited. We waited for hours. British stoicism, however, is no match for German stubbornness. After several hours we conceded defeat and took our washed but soaking-wet laundry back to the caravan. We emptied the awning into the back of the car and threaded washing line in zigzags back and forth across the inside from pole to pole. Then we hung up our laundry and watched it fail to dry.

The rain eased off in the afternoon so we cycled into Interlaken to kill off the other disagreeable (to me) part of the holiday. We did our souvenir and gift shopping. Switzerland is not as expensive as people make out, at least it wasn't then. Petrol is cheaper than at home (it's cheaper everywhere else in the world, too, let's face it) and groceries are more or less comparable. But souvenirs! Five quid for a fake cow bell. Twenty-five quid for a genuine Swiss Army knife that's only good for cutting butter or mashing up the cork in wine bottles. Thank god nobody fancied a cuckoo clock. I tried not to sulk too much as we shopped, because a little voice kept saying, *it's raining, just be glad we're not wasting a sunny day doing this.*

The next day was sunny. We rose early. The awning was full of steam as the towels and T-shirts and knickers gave up their moisture to the hot sun. This day was planned and it was exciting. I had already researched train times and *juniorcarte* passes (these are passes that allow heavily reduced children's fares on the trains). We drove to the station. We should have cycled, it would have been environmentally preferable and I was feeling all ecological and Swiss and at one with the mountains, but time was against us and cars are quicker. At the station, when we parked, we made sure that this particular car park was for train passengers, and we made sure that we were surrounded by plenty of other cars, environmentally-friendly Swiss cars, like beefy BMWs, Mercedes and four-litre Chevrolets. We watched people arrive and we followed them to see what they did. They paid at ticket machines. We paid at a ticket machine. They returned to their cars to display their tickets, we returned to our car with our ticket. No mistakes this time. We bought our train tickets and went onto the platform to wait.

This was different to Paris. This was no commuter train. This was old-world European tourism. It was just one step on from the Victorian grand tour on a donkey. It was wonderful. The trains were all called BOB. At first I worried that this naming convention might signal a serious lack of originality on the part of the Swiss, but BOB is the name of the railway: Berner Oberland Bahn.

Again the platform is not really a platform, it's only a few inches high. This time, though, the trains were small. The BOB trains are narrow gauge so that they can cope with the narrow twisting track that winds through the mountains. They're also rack and pinion trains, having a third rail (the rack) that engages with a cog (the pinion) beneath the train.

I stood on the platform and watched everything that was going on around me. So much atmosphere: the big old clock, the people, the uniformed railway staff. It's the stuff of spy movies and cold war thrillers.

The BOB railway runs on time, and just like in France, if your watch doesn't quite agree with the big platform clock, then change it.

Make no mistake, I am not a train crank. I do not collect numbers and I do not possess, in my wardrobe, an Anorak. But I could feel it. The excitement was all around. As our train drew up to the platform you could pull the pheromones out of the air and bottle them. If I'd have been in possession of a train crank's tatty, elastic-band-bound notebook, I'd have whipped it out and started scribbling down numbers so as not to feel left out. This was train-spotters' nirvana.

We had to get into specific carriages. This was one of those trains that splits and goes separate ways. One part of the train goes to Grindelwald, the other goes to Lauterbrunnen, and you have to make sure you are in the correct part of the train. It was all clearly explained in three languages. No ambiguity. We stopped at Zweilütschinen, and the guards moved through the train shouting instructions, and I chuckled at the number of lump-heads who now realised they were on the wrong half.

"What?" said Sarah.

"Wouldn't you think they'd read the..." I stared at the information board. We were in the wrong half of the train.

I leapt up with a start, shouting instructions to Sarah and the kids. We grabbed our rucksacks and stumbled and tripped along the gravel track bed to get to the Grindelwald carriages. I could see the smirks on all the faces watching us from the train windows. We climbed up into the back carriage of the Grindelwald train, now heaving with confused and displaced tourists. We would never find a seat, now. Fortune smiled on us, though. A family of four leapt from their seats nearby. They were Lauterbrunnen bound, and even slower on the uptake than I was.

The train was soon on its way again. The track began to climb. Craggy cliffs soared to our right. To our left were the lush green pastures of Sarah's dreams, and dotted about were picture-book Swiss cottages, their balconies ablaze with colour from window boxes filled with red geraniums. The excitement on the train was palpable. People stood and pointed and stuck heads out of windows regardless of the explicit warnings against doing just this. Video cameras waved and zoomed. Shutters clicked.

The Eiger soared into view. The North Face. I'd seen it from the campsite, but now it was big. In-your-face big. Daunting. A hush fell on the train at the sight of the mountain. Everyone understood the power and fatalistic attraction that this mountain held. More than fifty people had died on that face over the years.

The train slowed for another steep section so that the rack and pinion could be engaged. The train rattled on, twisting and turning. The Eiger kept disappearing and reappearing through the trees, until at last the track levelled and the train pulled into Grindelwald Station.

The station at Grindelwald is little more than an open area with a canopy and a booking office. It's full of activity because it's a junction where passengers change for Kleine Scheidegg and the Jungfrau. For us that would be later, for today our destination was the Oberer Grindelwaldgletsher.

We left the train and made our way through the town of Grindelwald, bigger and far more bustling than I expected. I had imagined a scattered collection of buildings with no real centre. Grindelwald had shops, banks, restaurants, and more window boxes filled with geraniums. There were signs for footpaths everywhere. Walking takes priority over traffic in the mountains and I noticed the signposting for the footpaths, giving distance in terms of the time it takes to walk. You have, for instance, "Mannlichen: 1 hr 45 mins". Distance is irrelevant. When you are walking you're not really bothered if it is two miles away or seven. What you really want to know is how long it's going to take you, and this very much depends upon how much of it is up-hill. What a sensible way of organising the countryside.

The walk to the Oberer Grindelwaldgletsher Glacier is one of the easier destinations in Grindelwald, but it is none the less spectacular. Alpine meadows, melt-water streams, forests. It's got the lot. The surprise comes at the end, though, when you find the ticket office. Because you have to pay. After walking here, though, you are not about to turn around for the sake of a few Swiss Francs, and it's not all that expensive, not really. What might make you turn back, however, is your first sight of the route. A hulking wall of rock fills your eyes, smooth, vertical and hundreds of feet tall. Then you notice the wooden ladder. You crane your head back and you see a line of tourists, like scurrying ants, some going up, some coming down. As the ladder-full of tourists reaches ever upwards it becomes a thread, a pencil line, with little black moving dots on it, stretching up to heaven. Hmm.

I'm exaggerating. A bit. It's not like an ordinary ladder. It's not quite as steep as a ladder, and it has hand rails. The rungs are wide enough so that they might be termed steps. It could be called a staircase but you would have problems with the Trade Descriptions Act if you tried. Evidently the Swiss do not have a Trade Descriptions Act. Nor do they have a Health and

Safety Executive. Thank heavens for that. The Alps are a wonder not to be missed, and any Health and Safety Executive following the UK model would, by now, have put up fences ten miles south of Bern.

"I hope you're not going to tell me we go up that thing." Sarah was not going to be cooperative on this, I could tell.

"It's only steps," I said. "It's not a problem."

"It goes on forever."

"We'll take it slow. We've come this far."

"What does that sign say?" Sarah pointed to a sign in German. Her German was even worse than mine but the stick-man pictures of people on stretchers and red exclamation marks seemed to get most of the meaning across.

"I think it means there's medical assistance if you need it. For those with weak hearts and stuff."

Sarah gave me one of those looks that showed she didn't believe a word of it and that she knew that I didn't believe my own line either. Then she surprised me by sighing and saying that we'd better get on with it then. I thought I'd have my work cut out with this, but Sarah was as keen to see a real glacier with her own eyes as I was. The children had no such reservations of course. They had already set off like monkeys.

It wasn't as bad as it looked. I had been correct about this. It was not a staircase though. It was especially not like a staircase when it came to passing people. This was, by necessity, a delicate and careful operation, and it involved letting go of one of the hand rails and putting all one's faith in the grip of a single hand. Scary stuff. It had to be done with tedious regularity, too, because a lot of people were coming down, and they seemed even more reluctant to release their grip on the hand rails than we were. Every now and again there was a place where one ladder ended and another began, and here there was usually a bit of a refuge on the rock itself, sometimes with a place to sit; a place where one could pause and recover one's breath. These places were packed with tearful and hysterical tourists. The Samaritans could have set up a regional office here with great success. Never have I seen a place where so much outpouring of emotion was in evidence. The main casualties for us were our calf muscles. It quickly became clear that we were not as fit as we like to think. It was a long way up.

Nearing the top there was a sudden and dramatic change in temperature. We had been dressed in shorts and T-shirts since Joinville. Now, suddenly, it was cold. The hairs on our arms were standing on end. Long before we could see it, we could sense that a lot of ice was nearby. The ladder then gave way to smooth rounded rock whose only features were long parallel scratch marks.

Amanda became very excited at these. Of all the GCSE work at school her favourite had, for a long time, been geography. She had a particularly enthusiastic and motivating geography teacher. I can vouch for this, because he always made such an impression on me at parents' evenings that I felt half inclined to pack-in work and study geography myself. His infectious enthusiasm for his subject had him up there with the Moonies.

In recent weeks Amanda had been studying glaciation, and they had covered such things as striations and erratics. She was full of enthusiasm and knowledge for the subject. She was able to tell us, for instance, that the dizzying wall of rock we had just climbed was a glacial moraine. This was a great comfort to us. Now, when we fell off it, we could be sure of having the correct geological terminology used in our epitaphs.

She pulled me over to a particularly clear series of scratches and demanded that I photograph them. I could see her point.

It's one thing to be shown a sample of rock in a classroom with billion-year-old scratches on it. It's another thing entirely to have climbed a glacier-manufactured precipice and to see marks that evidenced the path of millions of tons of ice during the previous winter. Amanda then ran over to a lone and displaced boulder sitting on the smooth rock. This, she told me, was an erratic, a boulder left behind when the ice receded. I had seen them before, in Wales. This, though, was new. The processes were all around us. We didn't have to be told that it was caused by ice, we could feel it from the way our fingers and toes had begun to go numb.

We carried on up the slope until at last, there it was. The end of the Ober Glacier. There was that colour again. Turquoise. The colour of Lake Thun. The colour of the Aare river. The top of the glacier was rock-covered and dirty. It was not ice at all; it was a layer of detritus shed from the mountain peaks through which the glacier had passed. Lower down, deep within the glacier was a glowing, rich colour that could never be captured on film, because it would look wrong.

The ice was melting quickly and streams of water cascaded down from the face of the glacier to form valleys and ravines that twisted and turned deep in the ice.

From this vantage point our impression of the glacier was that it was not very big. We were only seeing the scrag-end of it, of course, but we expected bigger. We weren't disappointed at all, it was a spectacle and well worth the cost and effort and nerve-jangling fear needed to get here, but... it *was* quite small.

We hovered around for a bit, not wanting to appear too easily satisfied by the geological spectacle, but at the same time feeling some nostalgia for the warmth and security that waited for us in the valley below. What is the protocol? How long is considered correct in these matters? We took a last look then headed down.

The descent was ten times worse than the climb up. Coming up the ladder you face the rock. Your eyes look ahead. You have no reason to look down. In fact it's not that easy to look down. The return trip is so, so different. The ladder, with its hand rails, is similar enough to a staircase to ensure that you descend in staircase fashion, facing away from the rock and looking where you are putting your feet; in other words, looking straight down. In fact the stairs seem to be directly below your feet. There is no comforting angle to speak of, you find yourself perched atop a delicate and rickety tower of woodwork with nothing to distract your gaze other than the ants moving about on the valley floor hundreds of feet below. As if this isn't bad enough, when you come to pass those who are still coming up you realise why others had had such reluctance to let go of one of the rails when you had been the one in the privileged position of being the climber.

Mind you, we were faring better than many. We passed some that were also going down; people who had frozen part of the way, and were taking a few moments (or hours) to try and regain their composure before continuing; people who were hugging the hand rail like a long lost friend. At times it was like an international evangelists' meeting: *Meine Gotte*! Oh god! Ahh, *mon dieu*! We saw tears. We saw hysteria. We heard prayers in many languages and faiths. Yet we prevailed. We got to the bottom. We took to our knees and kissed the very ground. But it was worth it. Scary, yes, but so worth seeing.

We noticed that many of the walkers in the Alps had telescopic walking poles. This was long before they had become commonplace in the mountains and fells of Britain. In fact we began to feel a little left out. Most of the shops in Grindelwald sold them. They seemed expensive, but not prohibitively so, so we treated ourselves. They became part of our regular and indispensable kit during our week in the Alps, and we'd be bang up to date when we took them home and used them on our own hills. Here, we felt like true Alpinists. All we needed to complete the package was an Alp to ascend.

So, day three, we took the train back up to Grindelwald, from where we would attempt our first Alp, the Faulhorn. 8,796 feet. Sounds mighty impressive doesn't it?

Okay, so we did most of it by public transport. Grindelwald itself lies over 3000 feet above sea level, (nearly as high as Snowdon) then there's the cable car to First (pronounced fee-urst) which nibbles away at another 3700 feet, leaving only about 1700 feet of climbing to do on foot. It's not cheating. It's the Swiss way. I read this in a book so I feel no sense of dishonour at all. It wasn't all free lunch of course, the cable car trip was humongously expensive. Then there was the fear factor. Cable cars are frail-looking devices. This one was also quite small, seating just the four of us. The kids and myself were able to get by with a bit of mild apprehension. Sarah, however, never particularly good with heights, began to seriously freak when she saw the little boxes sailing up into the sky on gossamer threads. Getting her into one of those little boxes was a serious challenge. She needed a long and careful session of counselling and persuasion.

The ride up was breathtaking for those of us who kept our eyes open. Grindelwald shrank beneath us. The glacier we had climbed to on our previous day lay on the far side of the valley. In no time at all the river of ice lay beneath us and we could see the full length as it snaked out from between the mountains that flanked it. We realised how narrow and insignificant was the end we had seen compared to the full expanse of the glacier that was now visible from above. Soon even that became insignificant as it, too, began to shrink away beneath us. In no time at all we slowed, the doors opened and we quickly stepped out of the slowed, but still-moving car at the top of the mountain.

The whole ascent had only taken minutes, but as the doors opened the change in air temperature was immediately apparent. It still wasn't cold, and we were now more than twice the height of Snowdon, but it had been oppressively warm below and now the air felt cool and fresh. (Snowdon, you'll notice, was to be our yardstick for our time in the Alps. Stating heights in multiples-of-Snowdon proved to be a convenient measure of what was involved in each excursion.)

Another surprise was that the excellent footpath provision we'd noted in the valley below was still to be found up in the higher mountains. The path was clear and substantial, and there were yellow signposts pointing to all the worthwhile destinations that could be attempted from this new vantage point, and they all gave the distance in minutes. We set off following the route to the Faulhorn. Twenty minutes took us away from the civilisation of the cable lift into a more secluded world of high mountain pastures. A new sound came to our ears. It was a wondrous and melodic sound that evoked images of peace and tranquillity. It was the clonk, clonk of Alpine cowbells. The only other time I had heard this sound was in a Mahler symphony, the third, where Mahler had used them to create just that effect, of peace and other-worldliness. Here they were for real. The sound was magical and we never tired of hearing them.

We rounded a corner and there was a bench with a view straight down into the valley below where the houses were no more than dots. This is where we stopped to eat our sandwiches. I doubt if there is any finer place on earth to eat lunch. The green, lush Alpine pastures, dotted with wild flowers. The restful sound of Alpine cow bells. The white-topped peaks of the tallest mountains in the Berner Oberland. The sweeping, heart-stopping view down to Grindelwald below. A sky of rich, deep blue – so blue, so dense, you could almost grab handfuls of it. We had found paradise. We loitered in paradise for more than an hour. I photographed it. Sarah painted it. Neither of us were able to capture it properly. It was too perfect.

Leaving nothing but breadcrumbs and a determination to return, we pushed on.

During our wet laundry day, soon after our arrival, my attention had been drawn, over and again, to a poster hung on the laundry-room wall. It depicted a high mountain lake with a backdrop of rugged snow-capped peaks. I wasn't sure if it was real, it was so idyllic a location. If such a place existed, surely it could only be reached by some serious and strenuous effort. We rounded a bend on the tarmac (yes, tarmac!) footpath, and there was the lake, and the backdrop, and it was real. The lake was Bachalpsee. It was surrounded by recumbent walkers munching on sandwiches or just staring at the view and drooling. They, also, had found their paradise. Was there no end to this? Could one place really have so many wonders? Well, actually, yes; and there was more to come.

We had to work a bit now, though. Our route took us onto steeper terrain. The tarmac path gave way to gravel. Our new telescopic walking poles moved from being trendy accoutrements to being really useful tools. We now had to put our backs into it. For the first time we were beginning to notice that a bit of effort was far more taxing than it should be. We had walked a lot in the Lakes and in Snowdonia, so we were used to stiff ascents, but this was hard. We were, of course, beginning to feel the effects of altitude. We were pushing up to seven thousand feet, and although it's certainly not an extreme altitude, it was noticeable. We puffed and panted our way up. There were patches of snow around now, sitting in the hollows, for it still felt very warm. Then, rounding a corner, we got our first view of our goal. The clouds parted and there it was: the Faulhorn. Wild. Rugged. Lonely. With a restaurant on top. Now that was a surprise. The path twisted up a final steep climb and we were there. Eight thousand eight hundred feet. Top of the world. We felt proud, even though we'd only climbed the last seventeen hundred feet of it. We walked across the veranda of the restaurant to admire the view on the other side. What a view. Straight down to Interlaken and Lake Brienz below, all turquoise and sparkling in the sun. Then a cloud appeared, below us, and the view was gone. It had only lasted a few seconds but it had been stunning.

The return was a little frantic, because the last cable car down from First was at five-thirty. Now what a tale that would have made if we had missed it. There's no way we could have descended on foot and made the last train back to Interlaken. We got there before the last car. Just. The timings given on the sign posts are accurate, but you cannot hang about. We made it with less than five minutes to spare.

Our excursion the next day involved getting the same train from Interlaken but this time we were to get into the Lauterbrunnen carriages on purpose.

When you pull into the station, at Lauterbrunnen, and leave the train, there is something you notice immediately. There is a waterfall. We have some fine waterfalls in Britain, but nothing... *nothing* like this. The valley walls are vertical and a thousand feet tall, and the water free-falls down from the top, barely even touching the wall. In Britain there would be a vast car park at the bottom, filled for three hundred and sixty-five days each year with cars and coaches, and people would wait in line for hours to pass through the turnstiles. In Switzerland it is largely ignored. It features on a few postcards, but other than that it's just there, one small part of the jaw-sagging beauty that is the Lauterbrunnen valley. There's just so much good stuff here it's difficult to give much priority to the mere achingly stupendous.

We waited in line and climbed aboard a coach. It was called a bus in Switzerland, but it was really a luxury coach, having little in common with the vehicles through which I make my daily living at home. The bus sped us along the valley to the end where the Murren cable car awaited. This particular cable car was a pretty big affair, and we were all hoping that its size would be an encouragement to Sarah, who was going several shades paler with each passing moment. She did well, though. While most of the cheek-by-jowl tourists jostled for position by the windows of the car, Sarah was happy to work her way into the middle, amongst a knot of large, Big-Mac-nurtured Americans who successfully spared her the anguish of seeing out of the window.

We were whisked up into the sky accompanied by a whoop of joy from the Americans. It was incredible how quickly the cable car buildings disappeared below us. In no time at all we were in Murren, but not to stay – not yet – for our destination lay two more cable car stages ahead. We were heading for the Schilthorn. We were pushing for yet another Wood altitude record. The Schilthorn is 9,744 feet.

In Murren there isn't time for second thoughts. You move in

a tide of foot-shuffling tourists, and you are soon aloft on the second leg of the journey.

The third leg is scary. You have time to stand and watch as a little box appears in the sky, swooping down from an impossible pinnacle ahead of and above you. There is plenty time to contemplate your own mortality. The little box grows as it gets nearer. The cable span is so great that for the final third of its journey towards you the cabin is coming up, not down, because its weight has pulled the cable down below your position. You have already paid your Swiss Francs. There is no turning back. The car on this third leg moves fast. As it leaves the station it drops and swoops out over the abyss. Somewhere below you, you realise, is your stomach. The car reaches the bottom of its arc then begins to climb. It's interesting that there is a dial in the cabin to show your progress. It is a barometer. As the car begins to climb towards the summit station the air pressure begins to drop at an alarming rate. There are notices warning of moving too quickly at the top. At almost ten thousand feet, the effects of altitude are noticeable, especially when you are climbing at this breakneck pace.

We arrived at the top. There is a spectacular futuristic building that sits on the summit of the Schilthorn. It is a building that will be familiar to any James Bond fan, for it is the location for the James Lazenby film, On her Majesty's Secret Service. It isn't one of the best Bond films – it could be the worst – but the setting is memorable. If you haven't seen the movie, it doesn't matter, because there is a cinema on the summit that shows the Schilthorn sequences from the film on a continuous loop. There are also posters and other reminders about the building's tight-focus cinematic heritage. A pity, because these things are not necessary. The building and location are spectacular enough in their own right, and don't need the in-your-face marketing from a failed James Bond movie to promote them.

Moving around on top you are soon aware of the need to pace yourself. There is not much air to breathe and if you rush you soon find yourself panting and dizzy. We found that we acclimatised quickly enough, but we thought that it would be a good idea to eat lunch first, because this would give us the opportunity to sit down and teach our lungs to evolve. It was also an opportunity to learn a couple of other interesting facts about going up in fast cable cars:

Fact number one, sealed bags of crisps do not always survive. Mine hadn't. The pressure had caused the bag to burst and the contents had distributed themselves around the inside of my rucksack. Everyone else's was okay, but it was fascinating to see how they blew up like balloons and became almost rigid.

Fact number two, beware of fizzy drinks. Kevin was a little overeager to open a bottle of cola, the contents of which instantly transformed into brown, wet, sticky bubbles, and we all got a bit; our family, and everyone within twenty feet of our picnic.

Kevin was fascinated by these atmospheric effects. Having lost his drink he put the bottle to good use by sealing it again, empty, and labelling it "Alpine Air". On the way back down the plastic bottle was crushed by the sea-level weight of air. Kevin later wrapped tape around the neck to stop anyone breaking the seal and spoiling the effect, and to my knowledge he still keeps the bottle safe. It is one of his most treasured souvenirs from our Alpine adventure.

All of this kind of deviates from what we found up there. What was the view like?

Well, we looked down on all but the last few hundred feet of the Eiger's North Wall. There was not a cloud in the sky, and looking north we could see, across the flat plains of northern Switzerland, the Jura mountains in France. Looking south-west we could see the summit of Mont Blanc, its northern aspect in France, its southern side in Italy. In short, we could see all of Switzerland, north to south, and most of the countries that flank it. The view south was white. Snow, glaciers and craggy, vicious white peaks. I think I've used the word spectacular before, probably more than once. One moment while I consult Roget's Thesaurus... magnificent, sensational, stunning? No, I'm sorry, I've run out of superlatives. I don't have the words for it. The English language doesn't have the words for it.

A flight of steps took us off the space-age construction sitting atop the summit and onto the bare, grey rock of the mountain itself. There was plenty of snow and ice and the footing was not at all sure. The rock sloped downwards in every direction becoming sheer and deadly in just a few feet. The only flat bits of rock were occupied by people who sat eating sandwiches and gaping at the view, fantasising about feats of mountain adventure. There was a sign, exactly like the other signs that were scattered around the Alps giving distances in minutes, on foot, to destinations below. I could not believe that there might be a path somewhere down there, but just as I was doubting, a bobble hat came into view closely followed by a Berghaus-clad walker, all puffing and wheezing. He'd climbed up from the valley. He had all the gear: rope, ice axe, crampons. Yesterday I'd felt proud to ascend the last seventeen hundred feet of the Faulhorn. I was a walker, a rambler, or even, during the odd moments of hands-on scrambling, I might call myself a climber. This was different. Here was an Alpinist, and I was in awe of him. He staggered up the last bit of slope and leaned heavily against a pole, his head obscured by the plumes of steam from his heavy use of the cold, rarefied air. I noticed that the pole against which he leaned was a warning sign. It showed a picture of a stiletto heal and said: "Danger! No High Heels beyond this point!"

Kind of obvious. A little like the warning ticket on flat-pack furniture that says, 'Do not eat!'

We descended to Murren. If anything the wait for the downward cable car was more terrifying than the upward trip. This time we were looking down. This time we could see how far we could fall. Sarah was very quiet. Very white. I knew that under any other circumstances she would not be induced into stepping into that frail gondola that swayed above the abyss, but there was no choice. We couldn't stay up here, and we had seen the footpath down.

She was very brave. She clung to the pole in the centre of the car and stared straight ahead, tendons standing out like steel bands. Smoothly and without fuss, we dropped. The barometer climbed. Something started to creak. It was the empty Coke bottle in Kevin's rucksack being crushed by the irresistible weight of air.

On arrival at Murren, Sarah staggered out of the cable car and dropped into the first seat we could find. It was outside a bar. I ordered beer, soft drinks for the kids and strong tea for Sarah. We took in our surroundings. We were on a veranda looking straight across at the Eiger. Below us, almost vertically, three thousand feet down, was the floor of the Lauterbrunnen valley. We were in a large village and yet there was something strange; something unreal.

No traffic.

Traffic is not allowed in Murren. Bikes and horses, okay, but no engines. Apart from the flapping sun-shade umbrellas, stirred by the gentle breeze, we could hear no sound. We breathed deep draughts of the fresh, clear air. No fumes. No blue colour cast. The drinks arrived, and the beer was the finest, most perfect I have ever tasted. We were in paradise. Again.

Sarah looked more relaxed now. The trip down to the valley floor from here would be less hair-raising. We took a steam train along the top of the cliff for about four or five miles, then we transferred to a funicular railway that took us back down to Lauterbrunnen. All gentle stuff. No fear, and something of a transport enthusiast's dream. I've said before, I am not a train buff, but they were here, standing apart from the ordinary tourists; skinny, pale men dressed in sixties' fashions. They have staring eyes, notebooks and a tendency to spray when they converse.

The day had been perfect, until I realised that I had left my fine new walking pole somewhere; probably on one of the trains or cable cars. I was gutted. I'd only had it a few days but it already held sentimental value. This was the pole that had accompanied me to the summit of my first Alp. Sarah suggested I ring lost property at the Schilthorn cable car company.

Before ringing I had some homework to do.

I reached out my German dictionary and began to compose sentences for every possible question and answer that I might encounter. It's one thing trying to communicate face to face, there are always hand signals when blank faces signify failure. But on the phone...

I was, of course, confident that I would find an English-speaker. The preparations were really just a precaution. The most important phrase I needed was the first – *Sprechen sie*

Englisch? After this, I felt sure, it would be easy enough.

I dived in and dialled the number.

"Ja?"

"Guten Tag. Sprechen sie Englisch?"

"Nein."

Nein? What does she mean, *nein*? *Everyone* speaks English. I just thought this. What I said, for quite a long time, was nothing. Silence. The phone felt like a hot coal in my hand. I was close, not so much to hanging up but to throwing the easy mechanism as far away as I could, and giving it all up as a bad job.

"Okay, er..."

I began to flick through all my bits of paper. I fumbled and panicked and sweated. The ink on my scraps of notes started to run.

"Fundsachen, bitte?" Lost Property, please?

Despite my dubious pronunciation she seemed to understand. She said some stuff, and I kept on saying *ja*, despite not understanding a word, until I heard a click. She had transferred me.

A male voice answered with some fast and utterly incomprehensible speech. I went back to the script.

"Guten Tag. Sprechen sie Englisch?"

"Nein."

I sucked in a good supply of air through my teeth, and flicked through the paperwork again.

"Ich haben verloren mein wander stick." I have lost my walking stick.

Actually I didn't know the German for walking stick so I improvised with *wander*, a word that was used to prefix all the footpath signs, and it seemed logical. For stick I used the English word stick. It turns out the right word is *stock*, but he understood, much to my amazement. I threw in a few random adjectives like blue, and brand-spanking-new, and cost-a-bloody-fortune, you know, stuff like that, that we German linguists are just able to rattle off at will. He put the phone down and I heard boxes being emptied and shelves swept clean as a major search was instigated. My hopes were raised.

I heard the phone being picked up.

"Hallo," I said.

"Nein," he said.

"Nein?"

"Nein."

Bet you thought there was going to be an uplifting and amazing finale to this little story, yes? Well, no. That was that. I had lost my walking stick.

The next day Sarah bought me another one. It was kind of her. I love her for it, but I now have a single walking stick with an aggregate cost of over eighty pounds. In fact, after buying the original sticks for Sarah, Kevin and Amanda it turns out we have spent two hundred quid on walking sticks. Back home, months later, you could pick one up from The Works for a fiver. Now here's the thing, you walk on your feet. You don't need a stick. Maybe it was the altitude that made us do it. Maybe we were suffering from a little oxygen debt.

Or just plain debt.

So I took my new walking stick up the Eiger.

Yes, our last day would be the big one. We were going up the Eiger. Well, not exactly *up* the Eiger. We were getting the train to Kleine Scheidegg, then another up to the Eiger Glacier station, from where we would take the Eiger Trail, a footpath, across the foot of the North Face and on, back down to Grindelwald.

First, we took in the view from the station, high above the Eiger Glacier. Like everywhere else in Switzerland, each view surpasses the previous one, and looking down on the Eiger Glacier is no exception. I drank it in by the eye-full, then with huge reluctance, turned away and placed a boot on the Eiger itself.

We walked for half an hour then stopped and had our sandwiches right at the foot of the North Face, the Nordwand. Now here, it has to be said, I was disappointed. It didn't look so big at all. The North Wall is a shade under six thousand feet straight up. It has killed over fifty climbers and is one of the world's greatest mountain challenges. To me, though, it didn't look like much. Not that I'd want to climb it. I haven't painted the eaves of my house for thirty years because I'm scared to go up the ladder that extra few feet. Rock climbing does not seem the best way to spend a weekend. The Eiger, though. I don't know. Snowdon, I felt, is more impressive.

Then I earwigged a conversation between a mountain guide and a young American lad who had also taken advantage of our picnic site. They were gazing up at the rock.

"There," said the guide. "Do you see? On the White Spider. Three of them."

The American was peering through a pair of binoculars that Patrick Moore would have been proud of. I looked up but could see nobody. It was one of the disappointments. I had hoped to see some intrepid climbers tackling the face.

I rummaged around in my rucksack and found my own binoculars that I'd brought along for this very purpose. I found the White Spider. It's an ice field with radiating legs that looks something like a spider, and became quite well-known amongst mountain people when it was used as the title of a book by Heinrich Harrer, describing his successful climb in

1938.

I swept back and forth across the White Spider. Nobody there, the guide must have been mis... Oh. Three tiny black dots. They were moving. My binoculars have a zoom function that gives 24X magnification. I don't use it much because I can't hold them still enough. I used it now. I rested against a rock. They were still three tiny black dots. They were still moving. Very slowly, but enough for me to fully comprehend just how far up they were. My jaw dropped open. I took the binoculars away from my eyes, rubbed them, blinked a few times, then looked up again. Then I went back to the binoculars.

The thing is, with the Eiger there's nothing on it to give the eye a sense of scale. If you're used to the mountains in Wales, you see a mountain of Welsh proportions. There is no reference point to tell you how much farther away the top is. In fact, the closer you get to the sheer wall, the smaller it appears, because you are looking up it at a tighter angle.

Then you see three black dots, three people, and the whole gob-smacking size of the thing swings into being. It's quite humbling.

We finished our sandwiches in silence.

The Eiger Trail walk is fabulous. Grindelwald lies far below, the only activity discernable was the movement of the little toy railway. Ahead, always, is the imposing sight of the 12000 foot Wetterhorn. Snow-covered; dramatic; forever drawing your gaze so that the walk becomes a series of trips and stumbles from not paying attention to your footing.

We came upon a waterfall. A monster. The air was wet from the spray thrown up. A waterfall far bigger than anything you can find in Britain, and yet by now it is just part of the scenery; another spectacle but one of many. The spray was wonderfully cooling, though, and we lingered. We'd been walking for about three hours and it was hot. This also drew attention to the peculiarities of the region. We were walking in 80 degree sunshine, in shorts and T-shirts, and yet our path took us along the leading edge of glacier ice that was, in places, ten or fifteen feet thick – towering above us. There were the constant sounds of stones and rocks tumbling free from the melting face of the ice, just feet away from the path – yet we had to stand in the cool of the waterfall spray to cope with the heat. Just to the right of us, a couple of hundred yards measured flat on a map, but high on the face of the Eiger, three people were battling against life-threatening cold and dangers beyond comprehension. It was surreal.

The path began to zigzag down away from the ice. It got hotter. We had finished all the drinks that we had brought with us and I was having hallucinatory visions of cold glasses of beer, condensation running down the side. Impossible, of course, in this remote wilderness.

We rounded a clump of trees and there was a pub.

This is the thing about the Swiss. There are no obstacles to common sense. At this point on the Eiger Trail most people are probably regretting that they have not packed enough liquid refreshment. So the Swiss take an old Alpine chalet – miles from anywhere – and convert it into a pub.

We fell into seats on the veranda. We goggled at a view that could never be faithfully transferred to screen, celluloid or canvas. A young girl, in Alpine garb, appeared at our sides and took our orders. We probably paid a premium for the view and the location, but this is the advantage of paying in Swiss Francs; if you don't want to calculate the damage in English money, you don't have to. Our drinks arrived. I took a sip of the finest, most savoured glass of beer I'd ever consumed.

We were in Switzerland. We were high in the Alps. We'd finally done the thing. We were content.

We packed to leave on the next morning, each of us quiet with our own thoughts. We pulled out of the Lazy Rancho and joined the road that runs alongside Lake Thun, then out onto the northern plain. The majestic mountains of the Bernese Oberland receded in our wing-mirrors. There was a gloom in the car. The holiday was not yet over, we had a couple of stopovers in France on the way home, but we realised that each mile, now, took us further up the map. Yes, it is nonsense, but it felt uphill all the way.

We came to a road junction – I don't remember where exactly. The road sign offered two choices. Our route was north, but I couldn't tear my eyes away from the alternative.

"Sarah, do you see that?"

"Hmm?"

"The road sign. See what it says?"

Sarah looked at it. Then she looked at me.

"You've got that look," she said.

I shrugged and turned the car north.

As we drove on I glanced over at Sarah. She seemed lost in thought. She had that look, too. She was thinking about the road sign, I could tell. A road sign with just one name.

Milan.

Thank you for reading Travelling in a Box. I hope you enjoyed the journey as much as I enjoyed taking you along. Perhaps we can do it again sometime, because, you know, things just seem to keep on happening: We've scattered exhaust pipes all over Belgium. We've been Carless in Chaumont. Then there was that first ever trip in one of those big silver boxes in the sky.

Oh and yes, Milan. Did we ever get to Milan?

You might like to sign up for my newsletter. No spam, I promise, but you'll receive details of forthcoming books and special offers, not only sofa travel but also science fiction, which after all, is what I do these days. Just drop your email into the box on my website, **www.mjkewood.com** (No, not a typo, that's Mike with a j, my Science Fiction persona. Long story, involving politicians, historians and basketball stars.)

Thank you.

Mike Wood

Printed in Great Britain
by Amazon